Urban
Development
in
South-Central
Ontario

H$3.95

66R 2104
Sept 1976

Urban Development in South-Central Ontario

Jacob Spelt

The Carleton Library No. 57

McClelland and Stewart Limited

0-7710-9757-3

The Canadian Publishers
McClelland and Stewart Limited
25 Hollinger Road, Toronto

Urban Development in South-Central Ontario
was first published in 1955 by Koninklyke
Van Gorcum and Company, Assen, Netherlands;
one of the series Social Geographic Studies
under the direction of Prof. dr. A.C. de Vooys,
University of Utrecht.

Printed and bound in Canada

Contents

Preface and bibliographical note to the Carleton Library edition, xi

1. **Introduction,** 1
   Approach to the subject, 1
   The Region, 4

2. **The Era of Early Settlements, 1780-1820,** 12
   The French and Indian Period, 12
   British Settlement Until 1791, 17
   The Simcoe Decade, 22
   Growth of Settlement Until 1820, 30
   Town Growth Before 1820, 45
   Summary, 53

3. **The Northward Expansion,** 55
   Immigration and Population Growth, 55
   The Spread of Settlement Between 1820 and 1850, 58
   The Transportation Network, 64
   Agriculture, 69
   Lumber Industry, 72
   Manufacturing, 73
   Trade and Finance, 79
   Urban Centres in 1851, 88
   The First 70 years of Urban Growth, 100

4. **The Building of the Railways,** 101
   Settlement in the Ottawa-Huron Tract, 101
   The Population Pattern in 1881, 106
   The Economic Structure in 1881, 108
   Transportational Changes, 109
   Agriculture, 118
   The Lumber Industry, 121
   Other Primary Industries, 123
   Manufacturing, 123
   Trade and Finance 1850 to 1881, 130
   Urban Development 1851 to 1881, 139

5. **The Rise of Modern Manufacturing,** 150
   Distribution of Population in 1911, 150
   The Economic Structure, 151
   Agriculture, 151
   Lumber Industry, 155
   Transportation, 158
   Trade and Finance, 164
   Manufacturing, 166

Urban Development 1881 to 1911, 176
Conclusion, 186

6. **Urban Predominance, 1911-1951,** 187
Extent of Urbanization in 1951, 187
Density of Population, 188
The Changing Occupational Structure, 191
Agriculture, 192
Other Primary Industries, 197
Manufacturing as a Factor in Urban Growth, 198
Transportation, 211
Trade, 219
The Urban Pattern in 1951, 227
A Century and a Half of Urban Growth, 239
Conclusion, 244

Maps, 247 to 271

Note on the Author, 273
Bibliography, 275
Index of Place Names, 293

Urban
Development
in
South-Central
Ontario

Preface and Bibliographical Note to the Carleton Library Edition.

I

South-Central Ontario – that part of Ontario which is situated to the north of Lake Ontario – forms part of a rapidly developing industrial and urban belt between Quebec City and Windsor. South-Central Ontario itself is largely dominated by Metropolitan Toronto, a conurbation with more than one million inhabitants in 1951. This part of Canada rose from a practically uninhabited area in 1780 to a region with a highly urbanized economy in the middle of the 20th century. During this 170–year period, the region passed through an urban development which in Europe took many centuries to be completed. In Europe the beginnings are shrouded in obscurity, whereas in Southern Ontario there are many sources recording the first rise of the towns and villages. Many persons are still living whose grandfathers and fathers took an active part in the clearing of the land.

This study is focussed on an analysis of the growth of cities and towns in this region, which gradually fell under the influence of one rapidly growing large centre. The approach is an historical one. The book is divided into five parts, each covering a period in the history of South-Central Ontario. Each part begins with a survey of the population density and pattern of settlement in the region. Next the various industries are discussed, such as agriculture, lumbering, manufacturing, etc., in order to explain the population densities and patterns. This in turn serves as a framework for the treatment of the urban centres and the process of urbanization. An attempt is made to grade the cities and towns as service centres, after which they are compared as to their growth and decline.

I wish to express my gratitude to my wife Gerda, to whom the first edition was dedicated. Her encouragement and support contributed in no small way to the completion of the study during our early years of "pioneering" in Canada.

II

This study of the process of urbanization in South-Central Ontario first appeared in 1955, in the series *Sociaal Geogra-*

fische Studies under the editorship of Prof. A.C. de Vooys of the University of Utrecht.* This reprinting again makes available a book which has been out of print for many years. Except for copy-editing directed to the correction of minor errors, and the addition of a few clarifying sentences, the text is essentially the same as that of the first edition.

Judging from the steady demand for it, the book seems to have carved for itself a niche as it is. Therefore it was decided to leave the text as it originally was, especially the final chapter, which provides an interpretation as seen in the early 1950's. Some aspects of the chapter, such as the question of industrial decentralization have not stood the test of time. Others, in particular the impact of the St. Lawrence Seaway, the call for regional planning, the urging for the preservation of open space, and the suggestions to direct some of the growth of Toronto to other centres (e.g. Barrie), have become at present more relevant than ever.

When the book was published, it was, with D.W. Kirk's Ph.D. thesis from Northwestern University, the first attempt to make a comparative study of urban development in Ontario. Since then, the problem of urbanization has rapidly gained interest, and a substantial number of studies have appeared. For the most part these deal with Metropolitan Toronto and to a lesser extent with the rest of South-Central Ontario. Specifically related to certain aspects of this study are Hans Carol's "Development Regions in Southern Ontario Based on City-Centred Regions" (*Ontario Geography*, No. 4, 1969. London, Ontario) and John U. Marshall's *The Location of Service Towns* (Toronto, 1969). Carol used the central functions of cities and towns as a basic criterion to delineate planning regions. The essay includes a number of maps showing functional regions of different orders and their relation to road traffic flows. Marshall's book includes a treatment of the urban system centred on Barrie.

A most valuable source for the study of Ontario is W.G. Dean and G.J. Matthews, the *Economic Atlas Of Ontario* (Toronto, 1969). This internationally known volume comprises an excellent selection of maps dealing with all aspects of the economic geography of the province, including urban centres and urbanization. Cities and towns can be compared readily as to specific characteristics and factors in their development. In

---

* The series is published by Van Gorcum & Comp. N.V. Assen, the Netherlands.

this context, mention also must be made of D. Michael Ray's study, *Market Potential and Economic Shadow. A Quantitative Analysis of Industrial Location in Southern Ontario* (University of Chicago, Department of Geography, Research Paper No. 101, 1965). Its point of view and conclusions should be balanced with N.C. Field and D.P. Kerr, *Geographical Aspects of Industrial Growth in the Metropolitan Toronto Region* (Regional Development Branch, Department of Treasury and Economics, Government of Ontario, 1968).

For a more recent treatment of the geography of Southern Ontario by the author, the reader is referred to his chapter on the region in *Canada, A Geographical Interpretation*, edited by John Warkentin, Canadian Association of Geographers (Toronto, 1968). It partly replaces and supplements some of the discussion in the final chapter of this book, taking into consideration developments since the early 1950's. A second edition of the *Physiography of Southern Ontario* by L.J. Chapman and D.F. Putnam appeared in 1966 (Toronto).

The Metropolitan Toronto and Region Transportation Study (MTARTS), created by the Ontario Government in 1962, laid the groundwork for the formulation of the Government's concept for the future development of the Toronto area. This was published in 1970 and entitled *Government of Ontario, Design for Development. The Toronto-Centred Region* (Toronto, 1970). In this publication, the Government envisages a linear conurbation along the shore of Lake Ontario between Hamilton and Bowmanville, some 80 miles long and 5 to 15 miles wide. This proposed urban belt will consist of two rows of centres, separated by a transportation-parkway corridor, incorporating also powerlines, pipelines, water and sewage lines. Eventually the lakeshore ribbon would have a population of some five or six million people. In the commuter shed to the north of the linear city, urban growth would be restricted, except for the historic northward extension along Yonge Street. Centres farther away, such as Midland and Barrie, would be treated as towns to be expanded and encouraged to grow. Thus it is expected that by the year 2000 the region would be able to accommodate some 8 million people compared with a population of 3.6 million in 1966. The important point is not whether the population forecast is realistic (most likely it will not be), but that development be encouraged to proceed in such a manner that if the forecast of population were to become a reality, the region would still be a pleasant place to live and work.

The beauty and charm of the Southern Ontario landscape

were placed in focus by Verschoyle Benson Blake and Ralph
Greenhill, *Rural Ontario* (Toronto, 1969); and Marion Macrae
and Anthony Adamson, *The Ancestral Roof: Domestic Archi-
tecture of Upper Canada* (Toronto, 1963). These two volumes
have greatly contributed to a revival of interest in the cultural
heritage embodied in the Ontario landscape. Eric Arthur made
a similar contribution for Toronto with his *Toronto, No Mean
City* (Toronto, 1964). It called attention to buildings of cultural
and historical value, and as the other two, has contributed
substantially to the creation of attempts to restore and preserve
at least some of them.

Donald Kerr and Jacob Spelt, *The Changing Face of Toronto* (Ottawa) first published in 1965 and several times reprinted, deals with the historical and contemporary development of the metropolis. Its writing was partly a response to the
suggestion made by D.C. Masters in a review of this book
(*Canadian Historical Review*, Vol. XXXVII, 1956, pp. 85, 86).
The Changing Face of Toronto has been rewritten and will be
published in a new and expanded form in 1972.

In recent years Toronto has been the object of intensive
research by a wide variety of scholars. Only a few can be
mentioned here. First of all there are those of a predominantly
historical nature, like Edith Firth's *The Town of York 1793–
1815: A Collection of Documents of Early Toronto* and her
subsequent volume, *The Town of York 1815–1841: A Further
Collection of Documents of Early Toronto.** The developments
in the Toronto area before 1793 regained attention with the
second edition of *Toronto during the French Regime* by P.J.
Robinson (Toronto, 1965). The first edition was in 1933 and
the author has added appendices dealing with his research on
the topic since then. The part played by an interesting but
nearly forgotten personality during the early years of Toronto
is discussed by John Andre in *William Berczy, Co-Founder of
Toronto* (published by the author, Toronto, 1967). An abridged
version of the well-known *Toronto of Old* by Henry Scadding
was edited by F.H. Armstrong (Toronto, 1966). The editor has
made the book stronger and of greater interest with the addition
of supplementary and explanatory footnotes.

Several studies on Toronto have resulted from doctoral
theses in geography at the University of Chicago. Toronto in
the second half of the 19th century has been examined by P.G.

---

* These volumes appear as Vol. V (1962) and Vol. VIII (1966)
respectively in the Ontario Series of the Champlain Society.

Goheen in *Victorian Toronto 1850–1900. Pattern and Process of Growth* (University of Chicago, Department of Geography, Research Paper No. 127, Chicago, 1970). In the same series, but dealing with more contemporary aspects are James W. Simmons, *Toronto's Changing Retail Complex: A Study of Growth and Blight* (No 104, 1966); Larry S. Bourne, *Redevelopment of the Central City* (No 112, 1967); and Robert A. Murdie, *Factorial Ecology of Metropolitan Toronto, 1951–1961* (No 116, 1969).

The development of local government in the Toronto area has received world-wide attention. It is a process which has contributed a great deal to the evolution of local government not only in other parts of Ontario, but also in Canada in general. A thorough treatment is found in Harold Kaplan, *Urban Political Systems: A Functional Analysis of Metro Toronto* (New York, 1967). The present form of metropolitan government is largely based on H. Carl Goldenberg, *Report of the Royal Commission on Metropolitan Toronto* (Toronto, 1965).

Since the first edition of this book, many publications dealing with areas and places in South-Central Ontario outside Toronto have become available. In part, this is due to the greatly increased flow of publications at the time of Canada's centennial, when a large number of counties and places produced local histories to commemorate the occasion. They generally have been written by persons with a long-standing interest in local history, very rarely by trained scholars. As such they tend to be collections of fragments of information and of limited value from a scholarly point of view. However, like their counterparts in the past, they do contain photos, maps, sketches and a certain amount of factual data which may be of value. For the purposes of this bibliographic survey only a few will be mentioned.

Pioneering in North York, by Patricia W. Hart (Toronto, 1968) contains a wealth of information, including easy-to-read location maps of early settlers, good sketches and clear photos. *Muskoka and Haliburton, 1615–1875*, a collection of documents by Florence B. Murray (The Champlain Society, Toronto, 1965) is a thorough study with good sections on settlement and notes on the villages and colonization roads, lumbering and agriculture. It has a very good bibliography. Finally, as part of this genre, the re-issue in facsimile form of some of the county atlases should be mentioned. These atlases were originally published between 1875 and 1881. Their maps and drawings can be very instructive, although they also vary a great deal in quality. One of the best is the *Illustrated Historical Atlas of the County of York* (Toronto, 1969).

Our knowledge of early urbanization in South-Central Ontario has gained substantially with the publication of *Kingston before the War of 1812*, by R.A. Preston (The Champlain Society, Ontario Series III, Toronto, 1959). It deals with Kingston as an early commercial emporium, which had a headstart on Toronto, but was outdistanced after all. R. Legget, *The Rideau Waterway* (University of Toronto Press, Toronto, 1955) provides much detail about the canal.

Several important scholarly books about Southern Ontario or Ontario as a whole contain material and discussions which are of direct relevance to the topics discussed in this volume. The old question of land and land policies is treated in *The Clergy Reserves of Upper Canada: A Canadian Mortmain*, by A. Wilson (Toronto, 1969) and by Lillian F. Gates in *Land Policies in Upper Canada* (Toronto, 1968). Also G.M. Craig, *Upper Canada: The Formative Years* (Toronto, 1963) is among others concerned with this topic. The role of the Family Compact, and economic growth are other relevant topics in this book. *The Union of the Canadas: The Growth of Canadian Institutions, 1841–1857* by J.M.S. Careless (Toronto, 1967) deals with the period when Toronto begins to gain complete dominance in Southern Ontario and when important economic developments occur, including the building of the first railways.

G.M. Craig, *Early Travellers in Upper Canada* (Toronto, 1955) provides an evaluation of the observations made by early travellers and has excerpts from their accounts. G.P. de T. Glazebrook, *Life in Ontario: A Social History* (Toronto, 1968) is an excellent book with valuable chapters on town, farm, and urban life in the 19th century.

Numerous articles have appeared in journals, both scholarly and of a more popular nature. A good bibliography appears regularly in the *Canadian Historical Review*. The most relevant journals, not necessarily in order of significance, are the following: *The Canadian Geographer*, *Ontario History*, *Historic Kingston*, the *Canadian Geographical Journal*, and the *York Pioneer*.*

* Of particular interest are J.W. Simmons' "Urban Geography in Canada" in *The Canadian Geographer*, vol. XI, 4, 1967, and R. Colebrook Harris' "Historical Geography in Canada" in the same issue. See the respective bibliographies, ff. 351–6, and ff. 245–50.

This survey of the literature which appeared since the publication of the book in 1955 is far from complete, but it should enable the reader to find a key for further reading. The region is a most fascinating area for study. It faces problems which at present are more challenging than ever before, but we still have the possibility of finding satisfactory solutions. As a Western society, Southern Ontario enjoys the best of two worlds: it not only has a high standard of living, but unlike other countries with similar standards, it still has the opportunity to turn its wide open spaces, its expanses of water and air into carefully nurtured and treasured resources for its people.

Jacob Spelt
Toronto, 1971

1. Introduction

Approach to the Subject

Ontario is the most populous province of Canada. In 1951, it had 4,597,542 inhabitants in a total area of 412,582 square miles of which 88.1 per cent is land. The population is not at all uniformly distributed; 88 per cent of the inhabitants live in that part of the province which is south of the Nipissing lowland, or on 14 per cent of the land surface of the province (21).* The urban population is mainly concentrated to the south of a line from Sarnia to Ottawa. In this belt, Toronto is by far the most important urban agglomeration. The city had, in 1951, 675,754 inhabitants. But, this does not provide a true picture, as the city is surrounded by a belt of large and small suburbs. The metropolitan city which includes the 13 southern municipalities of the County of York had, in the same year, a population of 1,117,470 persons. The next largest metropolitan centre was Ottawa, with 281,908 inhabitants in 1951, followed by metropolitan Hamilton (259,685) and metropolitan Windsor (157,672). As a centre of population, metropolitan Toronto towers far above the other large cities in the province. Did the phenomenal growth of Toronto occur to the detriment of other urban centres? This study is an attempt to trace the rise of cities and towns in an area in which one centre grew disproportionately. To what extent did the expansion of the large city affect the growth of the other centres? Therefore, the area to be studied was limited to the districts in which the Toronto influence may assume to be most powerful.

Delimitation of the region

In order to determine the boundaries of the area in which the Toronto influence is dominant, the circulation of daily newspapers was used.[1]

---

[1] The author acknowledges the helpful services of *Canadian Advertising* which supplied the necessary data.

* For explanation of the reference system see footnote on the first page of the bibliography (p. 273).

North-American newspapers seem to be a fair indicator of urban patterns and influences, especially of the larger centres (349; 350). The survey of daily evening papers was done on a county basis and depicts the situation as it existed in the spring of 1951 (fig. 2). It appears that in a large part of Ontario, the Toronto papers attract a larger number of readers than any other paper. The Toronto newspaper area is limited to the west by a belt of counties in which the papers of smaller centres have a larger circulation than the Toronto papers. A group of eight counties in South-western Ontario comprises the London newspaper area in which the Toronto dailies have a smaller circulation than those of London; in four of the eight counties the volume of circulation of Toronto papers is third in size. It may be noted that the Hamilton newspaper area comprises only two counties.

Nine counties in Eastern Ontario constitute the Ottawa newspaper area in three of which the circulation of Montreal dailies is larger than that of the Toronto papers. In Northern Ontario, the Toronto papers compete with the North Bay, Sudbury and other dailies. The districts of Rainy River and Kenora belong to the Winnipeg newspaper area; here, the Winnipeg daily evening papers have a larger circulation than those of Toronto.

Within the Toronto newspaper area proper, the city of Peterborough has its own area in which its paper competes successfully with those of Toronto.

On the basis of this distribution pattern, the boundaries for the area of study were determined. For historical reasons Guelph has been included in the west and Kingston in the east. In order to facilitate the use of statistics, township and county boundaries were followed. The area thus determined extends from the shore of Lake Ontario to Georgian Bay and the northern boundaries of the district of Muskoka and the counties Haliburton, Hastings, Lennox and Addington, and Frontenac. The western boundary runs parallel with the Niagara Escarpment along township and county lines, approximately 15 or 20 miles farther west. The eastern boundary of Frontenac County constitutes also the eastern boundary of the study area. The area so defined may be called South-Central Ontario. It covers an area of 18,255 square miles and had, in 1951, a population of 1,920,446. The outstanding feature of its human geography is the presence of one large urban centre and a considerable number of much smaller cities and towns. Metropolitan Toronto contained in 1951 more than 58 per cent of the entire population of the region. The cities which followed next in size were Oshawa (41,545), Peterborough (38,272) and Kingston (33,459).

South-Central Ontario rose from a practically uninhabited area in 1780 to a region with a highly urbanized economy in the middle of the 20th century. For several decades, it remained deeply rural and largely self-sufficient. It was not until the 1850's, that settlement reached the border of the Canadian Shield. The second half of the 19th century saw the building of most of the railways, while at the end of that century modern manufacturing began to gain in importance. After the first world war, but more particularly after the second, this became the essential factor in urban growth. According to the occupational census of 1951, only about 7 per cent of the gainfully occupied population in South-Central Ontario was employed in agriculture.

Method

In order to determine the factors which have influenced the growth of these urban centres, an historic approach to the subject is necessary. The growth and expansion of any urban centre is largely influenced by the assets and liabilities it has accumulated in the past. Only a study of historic events can explain why Toronto began to overshadow Kingston, although the latter was originally more important; or why Oshawa became a centre for the automobile industry.

Urban settlement is defined as non-rural settlement and is the areal expression of non-rural activities (341). The rise of those non-rural activities is a *sine qua non* for the birth and growth of urban settlement in general. Agriculture has to break through its phase of self-sufficiency before it can provide the basis and market for urban services. It is with this in view that the economic activities will be analyzed in order to ascertain to what extent they constituted factors in urban settlement.

The study is divided into five parts, each covering a period in the history of South-Central Ontario. Each part begins with a survey of the population density in the region. Next, the various industries, agriculture, lumbering, manufacturing, transportation, etc. are discussed, and finally the urban settlement itself is dealt with. A special attempt is made to grade the centres as central places on the basis of a number of key services, after which the towns are compared as to their growth and decline.

The Region

Situation

South-Central Ontario occupies a strategic position with respect to the upper and lower Great Lakes. It is flanked to the south by the arterial St. Lawrence and lower lakes transportation route, and it lies athwart the isthmus between the easternmost extension of the upper lakes – Georgian Bay – and Lake Ontario. The region's location with respect to those wide stretches of water has influenced profoundly its geographic development. A number of river and lake systems, separated by low and narrow divides, made the crossing of the isthmus relatively easy for the first travellers. From the headwaters of the Humber, the Trent and other rivers, it is only a short portage into the Nottawasaga and Lake Simcoe systems, leading to the Georgian Bay.

Landforms

The surface features of South-Central Ontario result from an ancient cuesta and vale topography which has been thoroughly remoulded by a continental ice-cap.[1] Glaciation features dominate the present-day landforms. The only outstanding structural phenomenon is the Niagara Escarpment (fig. 3). In South-Central Ontario, this scarp runs from the head of Lake Ontario in a general northern direction to Georgian Bay, where, near Collingwood, it swings to the northwest. The brow of this limestone cuesta is about 430 feet above Lake Ontario near Dundas and, near Collingwood, it has a local relief of about 850 feet. In other words, it rises from 700 feet above sea level in the south to about 1,625 feet near Georgian Bay. Here and there, the cuesta has been notched by pre-glacial streams. Those gaps have attracted the roads and railways seeking to surmount this structural barrier. The most important of those breaks is the Dundas gap which is thought to be the remnant of a pre-glacial stream flowing from the Lake Ontario basin into that of Lake Erie. Later, the gap was largely filled with glacial debris. Nowadays, it carries some of the main road and rail communications to and from Southwestern Ontario.

---

[1] This section is largely based on Chapman and Putnam, *The Physiography of Southern Ontario* (104).

The other cuestas in South-Central Ontario are of much smaller importance. The edge of the Black River limestone forms a low cuesta overlooking the border of the Canadian Shield. It is seldom more than 50 feet high; in a few places it rises to 75 feet. To the north of Lindsay and Peterborough, a low scarp of the Trenton limestone can be traced.

The dominant features of the landforms of South-Central Ontario, however, are the result of glaciation. At the time of the Wisconsin glaciation, the region was covered by two individual ice lobes of which one occupied the Georgian Bay basin and the other that of Lake Ontario. As a result of this dualism, the landforms of South-Central Ontario show a considerable amount of symmetry in their major outlines. The central axis of this symmetrical system is the morainic ridge extending from Orangeville, where it buries the Niagara Escarpment, in a general eastern direction to the Trent River, a distance of 100 miles. Built up between the two major ice lobes, this interlobate moraine consists of a boulder-clay core, covered with sands and gravel. In places it is about 800 feet deep. The surface is hilly with a knob-and-basin topography and rises in general more than 1000 feet above sea level, or over 750 feet above Lake Ontario. The Oak Ridges, as this moraine is called, has a few saddles which have attracted important transportation routes. In particular, the one to the north of Port Hope has been of far-reaching consequences for the growth of that town and the settlement of the Peterborough area. At its western end, the interlobate moraine is linked with the recessional moraines of the Georgian Bay and Ontario ice lobes. Those recessional moraines form part of a more extensive moraine system in Southwestern Ontario. These are till moraines, while the Oak Ridges is mainly a kame moraine. Finally, another recessional moraine, the Dummer Moraine, covers partly the Canadian Shield, in the counties of Peterborough and Hastings. This is also a till moraine, but its ridges are quite low. Its topography, however, is extremely rough and the soils are stony and dry.

The Oak Ridges is flanked by extensive till plains in which are numerous drumlins, especially to the north of the ridge. Between Rice Lake and the Kawartha's lies the Peterborough drumlin field where these oval hills are so crowded that they leave litle intervening space. The lower parts are generally poorly drained and swampy. Another drumlin field is found near Guelph, and extends westward from the brow of the Niagara Escarpment to beyond Guelph Township. In this area, drumlins are less crowded and in the wider lowlands are many broad sandy and gravel terraces left by meltwater streams. Elsewhere, the drumlins give way to flutings as is the case on the till plain in Scarborough Township, to the east of Toronto and on the Dundalk till plain, to the northwest of Orangeville. On this latter plain, the gently undulating surface is over large areas covered with a layer of silt which is thought to be wind-blown material (104). The topography of the till plains varies in general from rolling to gently undulating. The best soils are found on the well-drained higher parts, while the lower parts often suffer from excessive water. Extensive swamps are found on the Dundalk till plain, especially in the townships of Luther and Melanchton.

Sometimes, the meltwater from the withdrawing glacier could not find an outlet and was temporarily ponded; then the till plains were buried under deposits of stratified silt and clays often varved. One of these is the Peel Plain, a clay plain to the south of the interlobate moraine. It extends from the Niagara cuesta in a northeastern and eastern direction as far as the York and Ontario county line. Others are situated to the north of this moraine. The topography of the clay plains in general reflects the underlying till plain and is gently undulating, but it also may be entirely flat. On the two western clay plains, north of the Oak Ridges, many of the larger drumlins were not com-pletely buried by lacustrine deposits, while the Peel Plain is more a bevelled till plain.

Far more extensive were the till areas flooded by lakes Al-gonquin and Iroquois, the predecessors of Lake Huron and Lake Ontario respectively. Those large water bodies prevailed over considerable periods of time and created well-marked beaches and shore lines. The Lake Iroquois plain is a relatively narrow belt of sandy deposits hugging the Lake Ontario shore. In the counties of Ontario and Durham it is in places more than seven miles wide. A narrow belt of sand plains runs parallel to the old shore line and in those counties, the major part of the Iroquois lake plain consists of clay plains. Near the head of the Bay of Quinte the lacustrine deposits extend farther inland, forming the so-called Trenton Embayment of Lake Iroquois. In this embayment, drumlinized sand and clay plains prevail. A similar mosaic of sand and clay plains and also bevelled till plains is found in the area at one time inundated by Lake Al-gonquin. It comprises the basins of Lake Simcoe and the Notta-wasaga River. However, no drumlins occur. Parts of the original till plain remained islands in the glacial lake and in places, their surface rises 200 feet above the adjoining lake plains. Elsewhere, the lacustrine deposits are shallow and the surface of the underlying till continues to be the controlling factor in the topography. Penetang Peninsula was submerged in Lake Algonquin, but the original rolling topography, though covered with a boulder pavement, sands and silts, has been preserved.

Not all of South-Central Ontario, however, is buried under this thick mantle of glacial deposits which varies in depth from 75 to 100 feet (104). Wide areas have only a very shallow overburden or none at all. Limestone plains with a thin regolith are found on the Niagara Cuesta, north of Dundas, in Prince Edward County, on the Napanee Plain to the north and northeast of the latter county, and on the Carden Plain to the northeast of Lake Simcoe. The latter plain was submerged in Lake Algonquin. More than half of Prince Edward County has shallow and dry soils. Most of the overburden on those limestones plains was stripped off by the advancing glaciers.

The scouring and denuding action of the ice was most pronounced on the pre-cambrian Canadian Shield. This rock-knob upland in general has very little soil cover. Over wide areas, the bare ice-scoured bedrock appears at the surface. Later, the area of exposed bedrock was considerably enlarged through soil erosion resulting from an injudicious clearing of the forests. Occasionally, pockets of good arable land are found, as around Bracebridge, while better soils also occur along the streams. The rock-knob surface extends in a southeastern direction and reaches the St. Lawrence River as the so-called Frontenac Axis. In the river itself it forms the Thousand Islands. In Frontenac and more so in Leeds County the depressions between the rock-knobs were filled with deposits laid down in the Champlain Sea, a marine transgression after the withdrawal of the ice from the St. Lawrence lowland. The rock-knobs themselves were washed bare by the sea.

Drainage pattern

The pleistocene glaciation also profoundly affected the drainage pattern which was entirely disrupted and deranged. The preglacial streams drained in general in a southwestern direction, as is still evident from the alignment of lakes and valleys. The Kawartha lakes near the edge of the Canadian Shield are a system of drowned and interconnected preglacial valleys. They belong to the drainage system of the Trent River which flows through a preglacial valley into Rice Lake, another flooded valley. For a short distance, after leaving Rice Lake, the river continues to follow this preglacial valley and then takes a tortuous and zigzag course to the Bay of Quinte. The interlobate moraine was thrown across preglacial valleys and created Rice Lake and Lake Scugog. The latter drains into the Kawarthas through a tributary with an extremely low gradient. In general, the rivers originating in the Oak Ridges and flowing northward have a low gradient and flow sluggishly through marshland. Extensive marshes are situated along the Schomberg and Holland Rivers which empty jointly into Cook Bay, the southern extremity of Lake Simcoe. Also the course of the Trent River between Peterborough and Rice Lake has a low gradient and marshes along its banks. Lake Simcoe drains via the Severn River into Georgian Bay. Besides the Trent River, the Moira and Napanee Rivers also empty into the Bay of Quinte. The Napanee is another stream which for a considerable distance follows a preglacial channel. The Cataraqui River empties into Lake Ontario near Kingston. The rivers draining into Lake Ontario between the head of the Lake and the Bay of Quinte are not very long; they often have eroded deep valleys. Those of the Credit and the Humber to the west of Toronto are from 75 to 100 feet deep. At the site of Toronto itself, the Don is the most important stream, while farther east of the city the Rouge empties into the Lake.

Thus was the effect of continental glaciation in South-Central Ontario. It placed in sharp contrast to each other the agriculturally sterile area of the Shield and the fertile soils of the southern part of the region. Those latter soils, together with its situation and climate, constitute the most important geographical assets of the region. The mineral resources are of no significance.

Climate

South-Central Ontario is situated in the zone of westerly winds and cyclonic storms; Toronto is at 43.38 N. latitude. Several of the principal tracks of cyclones in North America converge upon the lower lakes and the St. Lawrence lowland making the weather very varied and changeable. Its climate is humid continental with short summers. (Köppen classified it as Dfb). The average length of the frost-free period varies from 147 and 154 days near Lake Ontario to about 126 days farther inland, between this lake and Georgian Bay. The period is again somewhat longer in the Lake Simcoe basin, while it shortens rapidly with increasing elevation in Haliburton. In Algonquin Park it is about 84 days. The average January temperature declines from 24° F at the head of Lake Ontario to 11° F in northern Haliburton. The average July temperatures vary from 70° to 66° F between the same districts.

The mean annual precipitation ranges from 30 to 34 inches in South-Central Ontario, and has a fairly uniform distribution throughout the year. A considerable amount of this precipitation is in the form of snow, which varies from 60 to 100 inches per year in different parts of the region. The number of rainy days is from 100 per year in Prince Edward County to 150 days in the highlands of Haliburton and near Barrie. Occasionally, the region suffers from droughts. These are particularly frequent in Prince Edward County which has the additional disadvantage of shallow soils.

Research based on Thornthwaite's work has shown that South-Central Ontario has an average annual water deficiency from 2 to 6 inches and a computed water surplus which varies from about 8 to 20 inches. The seasonal variation in effective moisture varies from "little" in most of the region to "moderate summer deficiency" in the Prince Edward County area (359).

Natural Vegetation

South-Central Ontario was originally covered with a dense forest, and it constitutes a part of the Great Lakes-St. Lawrence Forest Region (105). The deciduous forests which dominate in Southwestern Ontario jut northeastward along Lake Ontario and reach the Toronto area. This deciduous forest association consists primarily of beech and sugar maple, together with basswood, red maple and (northern) red, white and bur oak. In addition, a wide variety of more southern species occur and find their northern limit in this association. Only a very few coniferous species are represented.

Northward, the forest changes into the Huron-Ontario association, the northern boundary of which approximately follows the edge of the Canadian Shield. It covers also the Frontenac Axis area. This association is still predominantly broadleaved, but there are fewer species. About three-quarters of the forest consists of sugar maple and beech (105). Other species in this forest are basswood, white elm, yellow birch, white ash, red maple and red oak. On the lighter soils are found stands of white and red pine, which originally were quite extensive.

The Shield in South-Central Ontario is covered with the Algonquin-Laurentides association. Here, the white pine is thought to have been wide spread, but the greater part of it has been removed by large scale lumbering and fire. Red pine was also important. The association is generally speaking a mixed forest. The most important species are sugar maple, yellow birch, hemlock, and white pine.

The natural vegetation of South-Central Ontario was not an unbroken forest. On the drier sandy soils, in the southern part of the region, natural parklands were found, the so-called "oak plains." They were most extensive to the south and southeast of Rice Lake and consisted of grass lands interspersed with clumps of trees and shrubs. As a whole, the forest cover on sandy soils tended to be lighter and the trees farther apart.

The natural vegetation was a valuable guide for the prospective settler as to the fertility of the land. The settlers preferred the thickly forested lands over the more open parklands, while the various species were indicative of the agricultural values of the soil. On the other hand, there are only a few instances where climate is recorded as a factor to be considered when settling in Southern Ontario. Dunlop praised the Huron Tract among others because snow was in sufficient quantity to afford good winter roads, and to prevent frost from penetrating into the ground. He said that when it melted, spring began and cattle and horse pastures in the woods were ready fully three weeks sooner than in the same parallel of latitude on the shores of Lake Ontario (116). Penetang Peninsula was considered a poor district for the settlement of pensioned soldiers because of the severity of the winter (129, II/55).

Soils

The soils of South-Central Ontario are divided into two major soil zones: the Brown Podsolic Soil Zone and the Grey-Brown Podsolic Soils (104; 21). The area with Brown Podsolic Soils is more or less coincident with the Canadian Shield and the Algonquin-Laurentides forest association, although some of these soils are found as far south as the latitude of Barrie and Rice Lake. The Brown Podsolic Soils are a transition between the true Podsols farther north and the Gray-Brown Podsolic Soils to the south. They differ from the Podsols in that they

have a very shallow A_2 horizon, which may be missing altogether. Those soils are in general not very valuable agriculturally. The Grey Brown soils on the other hand are of moderate
fertility. They coincide with the Huron-Ontario and Niagara
forest associations.

As a result of the great variety in landforms and drainage
conditions in South-Central Ontario, several different soil types
occur and the fertility varies considerably. The soils of the
morainic hills consist of sandy loam, sand and gravelly sand.
Much of the Oak Ridges Moraine is hilly, sandy and subject to
blowing. Large parts should never have been cleared. The soils
on the gentler hillsides and the outwash aprons are more valuable. The soils of the Dummer Moraine are very stony and dry.
Droughtiness is also a serious handicap of the soils on the limestone plains. The better soils are found on the till plains and
lake plains. The soils on the till are good for general farming
including both fieldcrops and pasture (21). However, farming
in the intensely drumlinized areas faces the problems of steep
slopes, stoniness and poorly drained, swampy hollows. The loam
on the till plain in the counties of York, Ontario and Durham
is an excellent soil. The clay loams to the west of Toronto
having developed on shaly tills are acid and not so productive
and harder to cultivate. The Schomberg and Peel lake plains
possess some very good clay loams. Favourable soils are also
found on the Lake Iroquois plain. The Lake Simcoe basin
contains extensive areas of bog and wet sand and farming in
this basin is generally poorer than on the lake plains of the
Nottawasaga basin. However, some bog areas, notably the Holland Marsh, have become rich producers of vegetables, and
with increased population density other such areas may follow.

South-Central Ontario is a glaciated and originally densely
forested region with a rather favourable climate and relatively
good soils. The region does not possess important mineral resources, but on the other hand, is well situated as far as transportation is concerned. In the following chapter, the beginnings
of white settlement will be discussed.

2. The Era of Early Settlements, 1780-1820

The French and Indian Period

In South-Central Ontario, no direct link exists between the settlement pattern of the French and Indians on one hand, and that of the British on the other. However, certain elements of importance for the future human geography of the region can be recognized during that early period. These elements influenced the thinking and concepts of those persons who played an important part in the settlement of the area during the succeeding British period. Most important from this point of view was the system of routes during the French and Indian periods, and especially the relative importance of the overland routes between Lake Ontario and Georgian Bay.

The French Forts

During this early period, South-Central Ontario was situated between two great French trade routes, one to the north and one to the south. The northern route followed the Ottawa River and the Lake Nipissing passage to Georgian Bay. It was by this route that the French reached the Upper Lakes for the first time. They travelled southward through Georgian Bay to Lake Ontario which they reached in 1615. The Iroquois, allies of the Dutch and British, barred the St. Lawrence River and not until 1657 could the French break through (254/11). This, then, became their southern route: along the St. Lawrence River, Lake Ontario, Lake Erie to the Mississippi Lowland and the Upper Lakes. The latter route was of the greatest significance for South-Central Ontario, as it led to the establishment of French forts at strategic points along its course. This southern route linked Montreal with lands as far as the Mississippi Delta, and forts were built to protect it against British interference and Iroquois attacks, and also to prevent the diversion of the fur trade to British trading posts south of the St. Lawrence River and Lake Ontario. In 1673, the French erected Fort Cataraqui, later Frontenac, on the site of present-day Kingston. This was a strategic location at the entrance to Lake Ontario, at the mouth of the Cataraqui River, which afforded excellent shelter for the French ships. Shortly after, the district was granted as a seignory to the discoverer La Salle, but this did not lead to any settlement. The Iroquois attacked it fiercely and, in 1689, it was even abandoned for a short time. It remained, however, an important French trading post and stronghold till it was captured and destroyed by the British in 1758. The British, possessing the entire eastern part of the continent, did not require a military base on Lake Ontario, and it was not until the American Independence had become a fact, that the British built a stronghold at Kingston, in 1783 (118, I/471). For about 25 years, the site had remained unoccupied.

The fort at Kingston was the only major French stronghold in South-Central Ontario. However, some of the other forts and settlements along the Lower Lakes route may be mentioned, as the time of building illustrates the relative importance of the Toronto site. Shortly after the erection of the fort at Kingston in 1673, the French built a fort on the Niagara River. But soon, they had to abandon the site under pressure of Iroquois attacks. The fort was rebuilt in 1721 and remained until its surrender to the British in 1759, an important base for the French. A tremendous volume of trade passed here. Montreal merchants estimated, in 1787, that two-fifths of the western trade in point of value came via the Great Lakes, the remaining three-fifths being transported over the older Ottawa route (23, IV/542). In 1763, a waggon road was built between Lake Erie and Lake Ontario. The third fort was established in 1701 on the site of present-day Detroit. This stronghold, Fort Pontchartrain, became a strategic trading centre and a supply base for food. Nearby, a French rural settlement sprang up which still exists today (166).

Many years later, in 1720, and 42 years after the erection of the first fort at Niagara, the French erected their first post on the overland route between Georgian Bay and Lake Ontario. This was Fort Rouillé and was located a little over two miles east of the mouth of the Humber River. It was destroyed in 1730, but rebuilt in 1750, after which it remained in French possession until it was destroyed by them in 1759 in order to prevent it from falling in the hands of the English (254). After this, except for the presence of a few Indians, the site remained unoccupied until the arrival of Governor Simcoe in 1793 (146). Rouillé was the last fort in Southern Ontario to be built by the French. It was erected in order to collect the furs from between Lake Ontario and Georgian Bay at an old trading centre near

the fort and to prevent the Indians from forwarding the furs to
the British at Oswego, at the south-east corner of Lake Ontario.

Indian routes

South-Central Ontario was traversed by a number of Indian
routes – overland trails and water routes – which were also
followed by the French, because they used the same means of
transportation as the Indians. The most easterly one was the
route which followed the Bay of Quinte and the Trent and
Kawartha Lakes system to Georgian Bay. This route was followed by a group of Hurons which led Champlain from Georgian Bay to Lake Ontario in 1615. In the second half of the
18th century, however, it was used very infrequently (207).
Farther to the west was a route which led from present-day
Port Hope to Rice Lake and the Kawartha system. About 1778,
a trading post was established at its southern terminus. Similarly, other streams were followed upstream from Lake Ontario
in order to reach Lake Simcoe and Georgian Bay (207/374-
377).

The Toronto route

The route controlled by Fort Rouillé was the most important
one. It followed the Humber River upstream to the west branch
of the Holland River which empties into the southern bay of
Lake Simcoe and then continued by portages from this lake to
Georgian Bay. In 1615, Etienne Brulé, an aide of Champlain,
followed this route accompanied by Huron Indians and was the
first white man to reach the site of Toronto. In that period, also
the Dutch and English traders knew from the Iroquois about
the area north of Lake Ontario. Jansson showed on his map of
1636 the hills north of Toronto (254/13). Robinson gives a
reproduction of a map of the Frenchman Joliet (251). This
map, dating from 1674, is the earliest map of Toronto Carrying
Place – a dotted line runs from the mouth of the Humber to
Lake Simcoe, which is connected with Georgian Bay via the
Severn River.

The control over the fur trade of the Toronto Carrying
Place, and in general over the fur trade north of Lake Ontario,
led to a severe struggle between the Dutch and English on one
side and the French on the other. The actual fighting was done

by the Indian allies of the two opposing groups. The Iroquois, sedentary hunters, lived south of Lake Ontario and were armed by the Dutch and English. They made repeated raids into the territory north of the lake, which belonged to the Hurons, sedentary agriculturists and allies of the French. On these raids the Iroquois often followed the Toronto Passage. The outcome of the warfare was the complete extermination of the Hurons by the Iroquois, in 1649. On all maps after 1658 Southern Ontario is shown as hunting grounds for the Iroquois (166/49).

The route via Toronto was often used by travellers (254), but it never carried very much trade beyond that which came from the area between Georgian Bay and Lake Ontario. Compared with the volume of trade which went via Niagara and the Ottawa route, the amount which came down the Toronto route must have been rather unimportant. The French erected Fort Rouillé at its terminus at a relatively late date, and they maintained it only for about 19 years. After 1759, there was no trading post at all at the site. In 1767, an official urged the establishment of such a post, and in 1770, Jean Baptiste Rouseau – St. John – received a license to trade at the mouth of the Humber River. It is doubtful whether during the last decades of the 18th century any trade at all came down from Georgian Bay via the Toronto route. When Simcoe visited the Georgian Bay in 1793, he met a French trader, Cowan, who made a yearly trip to Michilimackinac – situated in the strait between Lake Michigan and Lake Huron – to receive his supplies and to forward his furs to Montreal. He did not ship those by the Toronto Passage or the Trent system (213, I/21). The trade of the Toronto route was one of local significance. This may also be concluded from a passage in one of Simcoe's letters. He wrote ". . . persons who have been used to the trade between Montreal and the Lake Huron by the Ottawa River, having recently passed to this communication, express their satisfaction at its discovery and are surprised that it has not been hitherto made use of." (195, III/178).

Indian settlements and trails

During the Indian and French period, important changes took place in the landscape, especially when the Hurons occupied the area. But those changes had very little influence upon the later human geography of the region. The Hurons lived in a

densely populated area on the till plains and lake deposits between Lake Simcoe and Georgian Bay. When Champlain visited
it, in 1615, the major part of the land had been cleared, and
was farmed by the Indians. Schott estimates that the population
at that time must have reached a density similar to the present-
day rural population, the small towns included (166/46). A
large number of villages dotted the countryside and winding
trails led from one to the other. However, all this disappeared
completely after the annihilation of the Hurons by the Iroquois.
During the 150 years which elapsed between this event and the
arrival of the first European settlers, the natural vegetation
returned entirely, and the new settlers had to start clearing the
land all over again.

Also the Jesuit missions which had been established among
the Hurons did not leave any trace in the present-day settlement. Even in the case of Mount St. Louis, where a modern
settlement carries the name of a former mission, no connection
exists between it and the ancient mission, as the latter was about
ten miles farther north (213, I/7).

The Indian trails were the only element which was preserved
by the succeeding tribes. They continued to use them and kept
them open till the beginning of settlement by white men (213,
I/5). Those trails were also used by the European settlers before the opening up of the survey roads. Later, they were
abandoned. In a few cases, however, their influence is still
noticeable, as they were incorporated in the new road network.
Consequently, they interrupt the regular grid pattern on our
modern maps. These Indian trails wound through the woods
from one navigable water course to another, because the Indians followed waterways wherever possible. Well travelled
trails were often from six inches to one foot deep (207/373).
Lizars compares them with buffalo traces, and mentions that the
Iroquois trail across New York was known among the Jesuits
as the "Beaten Road" (221/16).

Elsewhere in South-Central Ontario, a few Indian villages
and a small number of individual French traders was the only
population living in the area when British colonization started
in 1783.

Thus, there was an almost complete break between the
settlement pattern of the French and Indian period and that of
the British era. Only a few Indian trails broke the monotony of
the regularly laid out road pattern, and no Indian settlement
formed a basis for modern villages or towns. During this period,
however, attention was called to certain transportation routes

and strategic sites, particularly Kingston and the Toronto Carrying Place. They were the threads woven into the new fabric of white settlement.

British Settlement Until 1791

Beginning and spread of Loyalist settlement

Many inhabitants of the revolting British colonies in North America could not accept the measures and political theories of the rebels who had become the leaders (13/10). They constituted the Loyalist element in the population. Many of these Loyalists belonged to the more influential groups in the colonies; economically, socially and culturally, they belonged to the upper classes of the population. But, also, many of the lower classes found themselves, for one reason or another, on the Loyalist side of the struggle. The Loyalists were the more conservative members of the population; they deplored the British policies and mistakes, but were nevertheless convinced of the desirability of continuing to live under British rule.

Early in the war, an exodus of these unfortunate people had already started and they tried to find refuge elsewhere. Many Loyalists went to the Bermudas, to Florida and to England. A large number came northward, to what later became Canada. The migration started in 1775 and 1776 with people from the Mohawk Valley.

The Loyalists followed several routes to Canada. The majority went by sea to the Maritime regions of Canada – Nova Scotia and present-day New Brunswick. Another large group went up the Hudson Valley and down the Richelieu and camped, during the winter of 1783-84, near Sorel. In the following spring the group came to Ontario. Others came to assembly points along the boundary, such as Oswego and Niagara. South-Central Ontario, therefore, was not directly on the routes followed by the Loyalists.

About 5,000 Loyalists went to the virgin country along the St. Lawrence River, upstream from the most western French settlements, while a few hundreds settled on the Niagara frontier and on the St. Clair River. This influx of Loyalists was the beginning of British settlement in Ontario.

For the further development of South-Central Ontario, the settlement of Loyalists along the St. Lawrence was of the greatest significance; it was the overflow from this district which initiated the settlement on the north shore of Lake Ontario.

The St. Lawrence shore had been selected as the site for the new settlements for various reasons. The area was adjacent to the districts already occupied by the French, and close to the market of Montreal. For the time being, the British did not give up various posts such as Oswegatchie (Ogdensburg), Oswego, and farther westward, Niagara and Detroit. The government, therefore, hoped that the new settlements would find a market for their products in the garrisons maintained at these posts, Also, the fur trade was expected to provide a market for farm products of the Loyalists. However, considerations from a military point of view seem to have been more important. General Haldimand was specifically instructed to develop settlement in such a way that the new frontier would be protected against invasions from the new state to the south. The General's attention was called to the present Eastern Townships of Quebec. But he wanted to reserve this district for settlement by loyal French Canadians and proposed instead the granting of land on the other side of the river extending to Cataraqui (Kingston) and the Bay of Quinte (136). Haldimand offered the Loyalists a wide choice of places in which they could settle, but nearly all of these locations had a frontier position.

Settlement in South-Central Ontario began with the surveying of ten townships in 1783, in the following order: Kingston, Ernestown, Fredericksburg, Adolphustown, Sophiasburg, Ameliasburg, Marysburg, Sidney, Thurlow, and Richmond (fig. 1 and 4). Initially the townships were simply known by number. Tyendenaga became an Indian Reserve to be settled by Loyalist Indian refugees (186). This beginning of settlement in South-Central Ontario was the result of the natural growth of a prong jutting out from the last French settlement on the river. Military planning also played a part, but it was not contrary to the trends of the natural development. Settlement was bound to move gradually upstream along the St. Lawrence and then westward following the north shore of the lake. A similar condition existed in the Niagara Peninsula where settlement moved westward along the shores of Lake Erie and Lake Ontario.

Settlement did not increase much before 1791. The Loyalist farms were scattered along the Upper St. Lawrence, the Bay of Quinte, Niagara River, and the Detroit River. The first two districts contained most of the settlers in Upper Canada during that period. The land granted to Loyalists in Upper Canada before 1787 is estimated to have been about 3.2 million acres (30/60). Along the Bay of Quinte and in the Kingston area, settlement was limited to the first few concessions of the town-

ships, and in particular along the upper part of the Bay, settlement was still very thin, as it was considered too remote
(186/165). Everywhere, the settlers located close to the lake
and the bay, because the only means of transportation was by
water. The estimates for the population of the area between the
Ottawa and Detroit Rivers in 1791 vary from 20,000 (30) to
between 25,000 and 30,000 (39, XIII).

Procuring a new livelihood

The settlers received a considerable amount of governmental
assistance, although not as much as the eastern and other groups
(175/102). The government had purchased the land from the
Indians and gave it in free grants to the newcomers. The size
of the grants to the Loyalists varied according to the military
rank of the recipient. In 1789, it was decided that children of
the Loyalists would also receive grants. Each child would be
entitled to 200 acres, free from all expense, upon arriving at the
age of 21 years, or at marriage in the case of girls who married
before they were 21 (118, I). For this purpose, a list of Loyalists
was prepared and they were allowed to call themselves United
Empire Loyalists. However, government assistance went further
than the granting of free land. It included free rations, farming
implements and tools, seed, clothes, and many other articles and
facilities. The government erected a gristmill on the Cataraqui
River, about five miles upstream from Kingston and small
portable gristmills were distributed among the settlers (175).
In 1787, another mill was built at the site of Napanee, which
until 1796 was the only mill west of the one on the Cataraqui
River (212/41). Finally, the policy of the government to settle
the Loyalists as much as possible according to the corps in
which they had served during the war simplified the problems
of clearing the land and starting life anew. Protestant and
Roman Catholic members of the same corps were settled
separately (175/99). This greatly strengthened the defense of
the new boundary, but it also led to more co-operation and a
better communal spirit among the pioneers.

A large number of the Bay of Quinte Loyalists were of
German and Dutch extraction (163; 175). Persons of English
speech and descent may even have been a minority among the
settlers on the St. Lawrence and the Bay (13/117). When a
new judicial organization was set up in 1788, the four districts
were given German names – Lunenburg, Mecklenburg, Nassau,

and Hesse – out of consideration for the large German element (163). These settlers of European origin were skilled farmers and this, undoubtedly, is one reason for the later agricultural productivity of the Bay of Quinte sector.

The task of clearing the land, nevertheless, was tremendous and many hardships were suffered; 1788 was a particularly hard year and is known as the "Hungry Year." In the previous autumn crops had failed causing a terrible famine. The old sources contain many descriptions of the frightful conditions during the following spring. Some of the settlers actually died of starvation. But, when a few years later, in 1792, Mrs. Simcoe passed through the district, she was full of praise for the well-kept farms of the German and Dutch settlers and the high quality of the wheat (175/106, 107).

First urban settlements and settlement schemes

The Loyalist settlements on the Bay of Quinte were predominantly rural. Actually, those elements among the population which could have contributed to the rise of an urban way of life were relatively small in numbers. It has been mentioned earlier that the Loyalists in general belonged to the upper classes of society. However, the majority of the group which came to Sorel and then to the Bay of Quinte district was, according to Wallace, of humble origin: Major Van Alstine seems to have been a blacksmith before he came to Canada (175/111). Only a few of the half-pay officers settled above Montreal before 1791. Many of the Loyalists were illiterate. Consequently, the number of potential leaders in manufacturing, commerce and finance must have been relatively small.

Kingston was the only urban nucleus of importance. Its small garrison had been instrumental in attracting settlement to this area. The Loyalists had been directed to its surroundings in the expectation that the garrison would provide a ready market for the farm produce. At the same time the military strength of the base would be reinforced. It was indeed true that the demands of the garrison benefited agriculture. From 1786 on, the government paid more for farm produce than was necessary in order to increase the economic strength of the farmers. The demand of the garrison stimulated pork-packing, and caused the early establishment of breweries and distilleries (292/23).

By 1791, Kingston was not more than a hamlet whose most

important street was the quay along the bank of the river. However, despite its smallness, it was the district's capital. Here, settlers arrived from the United States, and its port handled the small import trade.

This insignificant urban growth formed a sharp contrast with the ambitious plans of the government. In each township a town site had been selected and in each of those a town was laid out in accordance with a prescribed plan. The plan consisted of town lots of one acre, town parks of 24 acres, and squares and streets of stated dimensions. Sites for future public buildings and defence works were reserved. Each town plot was one square mile. The corners of the townships were reserved for the Crown. Inland townships were ten miles square, with the town site in the centre. Townships upon navigable water, measured twelve miles deep and nine miles along the waterfront, on which the town site was located. This short waterfront served to create a fair distribution of facilities for water transportation (163/26). However, settlement grew only on very few of these projected sites and in 1794 the government abandoned the idea of a town site in each township.

In later years, private settlers often laid out town sites with space reserved for broad avenues, schools, churches, etc. (even universities). These "towns" were advertised as places which were bound to grow and lots in them were offered for sale. The number of these "paper towns" is considerable; Simcoe County had eleven of such settlements, none of which ever materialized. In that county the practice continued until in the 1850's (213, I/299). Romulus in Beverly township to the west of Dundas, was another paper town. Its founder advertised it in Canadian and American papers as the future site of a great city and defined it as lying on the great highway between the Atlantic and Pacific Oceans! He made attractive promises to the settlers, and even went so far as to build a gristmill and a sawmill. The village, however, never grew (87).

During this early period, Upper Canada formed a part of the province of Quebec. However, the Loyalists missed many privileges they had enjoyed south of the border, and they desired more influence in the government than was possible under the Quebec administration. Quebec was organized on a feudal system of seignorial grants, while the Loyalists held their land free and in common socage. These and other differences caused the establishment of Upper Canada as a distinct province in 1791, an event which led to considerable change in the trends and planning of settlement in the new province.

The Simcoe Decade

The relations between England and the new republic to the South had not developed very favourably after the treaty of 1783. The treatment of the Loyalists by the United States and the maintenance of British troops in a number of posts on the American side of the new frontier led to considerable controversy. Much mutual suspicion existed and the situation was tense. The possibility of a new war in North America had to be reckoned with, and, for this reason, a military man was chosen to be first lieutenant-governor of the new province of Upper Canada.

Simcoe's plans

Simcoe was a veteran officer of the American Revolution and a convinced imperialist. When he arrived in the early summer of 1792, his plans were focussed on two main aims – to bolster the defense of the province, and to develop the resources of the territory in order to make it financially self-supporting. To a considerable extent, the second aspect was a condition for the success of the first. The economic development included the expansion of settlement, the development of agriculture and trade, and the promotion of urban settlement – all to be stimulated by the building of roads.

The outstanding characteristic of the Simcoe decade is that planning became more positive. The results of the natural development were not awaited any longer and Simcoe deliberately guided the trends, particularly of settlement, in directions which were in accordance with preconceived plans. These plans for settlement and road building profoundly influenced the further geographic development of the province. Simcoe himself returned to England in September 1796, but he remained lieutenant-governor and was expected to return and resume his governorship. During his absence, his place was taken by Russell who, as many others in the province, constantly sought advice from Simcoe and attempted to carry out his plans (195, IV; 194, II/138). During the three years, Simcoe was also keenly interested in the welfare of the colony.

From the beginning, Simcoe realized or knew that the British posts on American territory – Oswego, Niagara, Miamis, Detroit, and Michilimackinac – at some time in the near future would have to be relinquished. Accordingly, a new line of defense was needed, not only to protect the young province against a possible attack from the United States, but also to guard the fur trade route through the lakes.

His plan was to settle retired soldiers near the lakes and on all the frontiers towards the United States (125). Simcoe was not prepared to wait for the natural growth of the Bay of Quinte and Niagara settlements to enclose gradually the Canadian side of Lake Ontario. It would have taken perhaps several decades before the two prongs would have met somewhere along its north shore. Instead, Simcoe guided settlement in an entirely different direction by making Toronto the new capital of the province. By doing this, and through the building of roads, he left his imprint upon the geography of the province as did no other person in its entire history.

The founding of Toronto

At the time of Simcoe's arrival, the seat of the government was at Newark (Niagara on the Lake). This, however, was too close to the American boundary, and it was decided to withdraw the capital to a more inland location. Simcoe had selected the site of London for this purpose, but the governor-general ordered him to take the site of Toronto. The defense of the colony was the first objective, and this being naval made the settlement of Toronto more urgent as the chief base of the province (195, II/185). Simcoe, on the other hand, had planned the Toronto site to be the chief commercial and industrial centre of the province only, and always expected to be able to move the political capital to London. Kingston was the largest urban centre in Upper Canada at that time and it would remain so till the later twenties. However, it was not considered suitable for the capital, because it was said to be difficult to defend (195, II/160). Toronto, on the other hand, had the best harbour on the lake and was at a safe distance from the border. These were the only concrete assets of the site, though it was also supposed to have a tremendous transportation and commercial potential, on account of its location at the beginning of the shortest overland route between Lake Ontario and Georgian Bay. Simcoe hoped to materialize this potential, for, as he saw it, it would provide a short and safe transportation route to replace the one via Niagara and Detroit, which was so much longer and dangerously exposed to American interference. There was very little, however, to warrant these optimistic expectations. The Toronto passage-way had been used by travellers, but it had never carried much trade (p. 14). Nevertheless, human ideas and concepts constitute powerful factors in the growth of the geography of an area, and this has been true for South-Central Ontario.

The Toronto site was away from the main transportation route on the lake, which went from Kingston along the south shore to Niagara, and as far as communications were concerned, the site was in a dead corner of the lake.

The traders of Montreal never had been very much interested in the Toronto passage. After 1783, several persons, expecting that the route via Detroit would be obstructed, looked for an alternative passage and petitioned for land grants in the Toronto area. Foremost among them was De Rocheblave, the last British governor of Illinois. He received a land grant on the Toronto site, in 1788, and also petitioned for a monopoly to carry goods between Lake Ontario and Lake Simcoe along a road to be constructed for that purpose (325/40). In that year also, a number of other persons received grants, and a town site was laid out. However, no settlement took place. The division of the old province of Quebec into two parts was pending, and the traders of Montreal were not interested in a route which would not be under their control. A few years later, De Rocheblave called Simcoe's attention to the passage-way and pointed out its alleged importance. Simcoe accepted his viewpoint and resumed the project in 1793; he always kept a very keen interest in it. The original grantees, however, were ignored (253).

Simcoe was convinced that a large volume of trade would start to move along the Toronto passage route, and that this would result in a rapid growth of York, as Toronto was then called. York would thus gain a momentum of its own, and it would develop irrespective of the extent of settlement on the north shore of Lake Ontario (195, II/110).

When Bouchette surveyed Toronto harbour for Simcoe in 1793, he described the site as a dense and trackless forest lining the margin of the lake. Two Mississauga families lived on the shore of the bay, and were the only human beings for many miles around (110, I/89). The site itself consisted of the gradual sloping Iroquois lake plain, traversed by the Don River and a small creek. Here and there, the ground was marshy and not suitable for the erection of buildings. In this untamed wilderness, a small fort was erected, and a garrison stationed in it. Mill sites were not available. In 1794, a sawmill was erected on the Humber, about four miles from the fort. At about the same time, sawmills and gristmills were built on the Don River, some three miles away. The most important asset of the site was the harbour, although it seemed that the entrance was not without difficulties (118, I/89). The plan for the future town was approved in July, 1794. A person occupying a lot in the new town was required to build a house on it within three years (163/51).

During the first years, the garrison of 200 men represented the most important element in the population. In addition there were the officials of the provincial administration and soon landed proprietors, retired officers, merchants, and others. In May, 1797, Parliament met for the first time in the new capital.

The first rural settlers arrived in the summer of 1794. They did not locate near the fort, but on Yonge Street, about thirteen miles farther to the north, where, on one of the branches of the Don River, a mill site was available (146). In the fall of that same year, the first German settlers of the Berczy group arrived (p. 27). On the outskirts of the small settlement, some of the higher government officials owned large estates where they farmed and experimented with the cultivation of native and British fruits and vegetables (207/113). Many an official had left Newark reluctantly. In order to compensate them for their losses, and to encourage the settlement of York, government officials obtained also a farm lot just outside the new town. This retarded the agricultural development of the immediate environment of York considerably, as many did not clear the land, keeping it for speculative purposes.

Roads

The building of roads constituted an integral part of Simcoe's overall plan for the development of the province. The country, however, was still, almost over its entire width and length, an uninhabited wilderness. This made road building extremely difficult.

In different ways Simcoe tried to solve the problems. Firstly, his settlement policy aimed at an early opening of the main roads. In order to attract more settlers, he laid out lots of 200 acres on each side of the future road, and only bona fide settlers were allowed to occupy those lots. Thus, in 1798, settlers on Yonge Street were required to erect a dwelling of at least 16 by 20 feet, and to reside in it within one year from the granting of the permission to settle. In this same year five acres of land had to be cleared and fenced, and the road in front of the lot had to be open for half its width (163/56). In general, much care was exercised in judging the applications for grants on these roads, and an attempt was made to prevent land speculations. Simcoe also formed a military corps, the Queen's Rangers, not so much for the defense of the country as for the clearing of land and the building of roads, bridges, and other public works. They stood under supervision of experts familiar with these non-military projects. The corps opened and constructed Yonge Street. A few years later, the Rangers were disbanded as it was too difficult to enlist recruits, and the English government considered the institution too expensive.

In the early nineties a road had been opened between Montreal and Kingston. Settlement in Upper Canada had commenced here, and the rapids of the river made a road desirable. This early road-building attempted to supplement the water routes, and for the time being, the north shore of the lake was not flanked by a road. First, Yonge and Dundas Streets were built.

Yonge Street, the great link between York and Lake Simcoe, was opened between 1794 and 1796. The road was built for military and commercial reasons. However, for several years the street remained full of stumps, pools of water, and other obstructions (207/514). The expected traffic did not develop. A section of the road of about three miles just outside York was opened again in 1802. This was done on request of the inhabitants of the town, so that the farmers might come into York more easily to market their products (207/96). The traffic apparently was only of a local nature. Although it was constructed to serve the interests of the fur trade, the North West Company did not support or take part in the building of the road. The road was used for military purposes in the War of 1812.

In 1793, the Rangers began the construction of Dundas Street, a road from the head of the lake to London; it was a military road well away from the frontier and safe against attacks.

The next road to be built followed the shore of the lake between York and Kingston and was parallel to the water route. Occasionally it followed an ancient Indian trail, particularly between Kingston and Trenton. The road was completed around the turn of the century.

Plans were also made for a road from Kingston to the Rideau Forks, in order to establish less vulnerable communications with Montreal. The possibility of building the Rideau Canal was also considered.

Expansion of settlement

Simcoe was not only an energetic road builder; he also wanted to settle effectively certain strategic areas in the province and his immigration policy was developed accordingly. He was a staunch imperialist, but he preferred settlers from the United States, and through his agents in that country he made very attractive offers in order to promote their immigration (13/ 162). The successful settlements on the Bay of Quinte demonstrated how valuable immigrants with a pioneer background were, and this perhaps explains Simcoe's policy. Only immigrants from the United States had this pioneer background which enabled them to face the herculean task of land clearing (187/96). On the other hand, they were the only immigrants available, as the wars in Europe prevented immigration from the British Isles for the time being. Thus many Americans came to Upper Canada and Simcoe did not frown upon the fact that they were by no means all distressed Loyalists, but were attracted by the land grants which could easily be obtained. This caused considerable resentment among the older Loyalists, who sometimes recognized persons who had fought against them in the Revolutionary War (187/95). In 1812, perhaps about 20,000 of the 70,000 inhabitants of Upper Canada were of Loyalist stock (13/159).

In South-Central Ontario special attention was paid to a rapid settlement of the Yonge Street zone between York and Lake Simcoe. Here, group settlement played an important part. About ninety families arrived, in 1794, under leadership of William Berczy, an Austrian nobleman (133). These immigrants from Germany were artisans, unfamiliar with pioneer farming, but Simcoe could use their services. They were directed to Markham Township where they helped in the opening of Yonge Street. Simcoe also planned to use them in the erection of public buildings in the new capital. It was also expected that they would play an important part in the building of mills. Their main settlement was at Unionville where they erected mills on the Rouge River. The settlers, however, were in very difficult circumstances, partly because being artisans they were not familiar with the difficulties they encountered. They needed

more assistance than could be given, and when hopes and expectations were not fulfilled they moved away and took up other
occupations. The mills were important in the further development of the district.

Of a similar nature, and to a certain extent for similar
reasons, was the fate of a group of French Loyalists which
settled in the Oak Ridges zone of York County, in the townships of Uxbridge, Gwillimbury and in a part of Whitchurch.
The leader of the group was Count de Puisaye. In total, there
were only about forty persons, although a much larger number
had been expected. They settled on Yonge Street, at a point
where the government believed there was a route for Indian
attacks on York (194). De Puisaye was not pleased with the
location and bought a farm at Niagara. These French settlers
were even less suited to their task than the Berczy settlers.
Several of them were noblemen, and not used to a life of hard
manual labour and privation (132). Moreover, the Interlobate
Moraine was not suitable for farming, and although the government gave farm implements, seed, grain, and other necessities,
the settlement failed. Gradually they moved to other localities
and took up other professions. At present, there is no trace left
of this French settlement.

In his settlement projects, Simcoe paid special attention to
the founding of towns (195, II/284). He believed the best way
to found a town was to select a site with natural advantages,
such as a confluence of rivers, a harbour, the beginning or end
of a portage, and then to station troops in its vicinity. This
created a market for farm products which would attract settlers
to the district, as had been demonstrated so successfully by the
harbour of Kingston and its garrison. Thus he planned towns
at the sites of Newmarket, Barrie, Penetanguishene, and on the
isthmus between Prince Edward County and the mainland. For
a short time, Newmarket became an important centre for the
fur trade of the Lake Simcoe area. Simcoe attached much importance to Penetanguishene, a projected naval base at the other
end of the Toronto passage. He visualized at that point a sub-
stitute for Michilimackinac, and a market which would compete
with Detroit; Yonge Street would then draw the trade to York.

Simcoe's superiors, however, did not share his view and
garrisons were not established at the points he suggested. Actually, settlement at Penetanguishene did not commence until
1818, when a garrison was stationed there. Unlike Simcoe, the
Governor-General, Dorchester, believed that if settlers were

placed in the most suitable districts, towns would soon begin to develop.

As far as South-Central Ontario is concerned, York is the only example of a successful settlement which had been established according to Simcoe's theories. Here, a small garrison and a number of government officials provided a market for farm produce and encouraged agricultural settlement. It is quite probable that Kingston served as an example for Simcoe.

Thus, during the final decade of the 18th century, the settlement pattern in South-Central Ontario underwent fundamental changes. Fig. 4 shows the extent of settlement in South-Central Ontario by 1799. However, it must be remembered that not all the land within the area designated as being settled by that year was actually occupied. Rather the map shows approximately how far the pioneers had moved into the forest to take possession of land. Settlement still hugged the waterfront, but roads made other parts of the region accessible, especially north of Toronto.

In 1799, the Bay of Quinte district was slightly larger and more fully occupied; settlement was still mainly limited to the front townships. Kingston was the most important centre with 100 houses and a population of about 450. In Prince Edward County settlement was largely peripheral. The link between the Bay of Quinte settlement and the York district was very weak indeed. The road had been opened almost over its entire length by 1799 but was still practically impassable (p. 37). Only a small number of families lived in this area and there were no mills between Belleville and the Don.

The area west of the York district was still an Indian Reserve, through which a road had been cut. A ferry and an inn were maintained at the mouth of the Credit River. Farther west, settlement had commenced at the head of the lake, at the terminus of the Dundas road from the west, and was linked with the Niagara settlements.

The virtually isolated York district itself was still sparsely populated. There, settlement extended farther inland as it was mostly concentrated on Yonge Street. This road was lined on both sides by a fairly regular row of small clearings. The crown and clergy reserves had been moved away from the street and this made continuous settlement possible. The farms on Yonge Street and the German settlements in Markham were considered to be valuable and productive (194, II/173). Immediately outside York, however, the first three miles of Yonge Street were practically unsettled, the land being in possession of officials in the new capital. The absentee owners had not fulfilled their settlement duties and Yonge Street there was impassable. A trail, a short distance away from the street, led into York. In 1799, the population of York was about 300.

This, then, was the settlement pattern of 1799. Definite trends for the further development of the region had been set and the concepts on which these trends were based would prove to be some of the most powerful factors in the development of the human geography of the region.

Growth of Settlement Until 1820

During the first twenty years of the 19th century, most of South-Central Ontario was purchased from the Indians (fig. 5). In 1806, a link was established between the York district and the advancing Niagara settlements through the acquisition of a narrow strip of land on the lakeshore. About ten years later, in 1815, a block of land between Lake Simcoe and Georgian Bay was bought. The needs of transport and strategy led to the purchase of these Indian lands (p. 32, 47). Not until the end of the second decade, in 1818 and 1819, were large blocks added, in order to have land available for the rapidly increasing number of immigrants. Thus, before 1820, practically all of South-Central Ontario was legally a British possession.

Immigration was not very important during these twenty years, and at the end of this period the total population for Upper Canada may be estimated to have been approximately 125,000, of which about one third lived in South-Central Ontario. This amounted to an increase of about 100,000 since the birth of the province in 1791.

Until the War of 1812 between Britain and the United States, the immigrants came mainly from the latter country. Up to 1815, probably about 5,000 immigrants from the British Isles came to the Canadas and the Maritimes (149). As tension between the two countries mounted, the influx of American immigrants gradually ceased. There were no longer any "Loyalists" available, and the authorities turned to the British Isles as a source for immigrants. The war, on the other hand, had brought Upper Canada to the attention of the people of Britain.

Returning officers and men told tales of the unexploited wealth of this unknown province. At the same time, peace was restored in Europe, and there were many displaced and unemployed persons, especially disbanded soldiers, but also many weavers, tailors, shoemakers, shipwrights, and so on. Changes in agriculture left many villagers without farmland. For Britain, emigration was a necessity and attempts were made to divert the emigrants to Canada, because the Home Government wished to strengthen the defense of this colony. Many people, however, were doubtful whether Canada could be defended if war broke out again with the United States. This is one of the reasons why the British Government did not launch a programme of large-scale emigration to Canada (149). British immigration, therefore, developed slowly, but in the following three decades it gradually gained tremendous proportions. In the years 1816-1819 inclusive, 29,250 immigrants arrived from Britain.

New districts occupied

The settled areas of 1799 gradually expanded as the population grew (fig. 4). Just outside the borders of South-Central Ontario important settlements took place and had their impact upon the region. In the east, in Lanark County, the government made plans for the Rideau Canal between Kingston and the Ottawa River. Parts of this project consisted of the settlement of disbanded soldiers and loyal settlers along the route of the projected canal. The reason for this settlement scheme (and new canal) was a military one. At the same time it expanded the hinterland of Kingston. In 1816, a group of 250 Scots immigrants settled in the neighborhood of the present town of Perth, about fifty miles north-northeast of Kingston. Soon the settlement prospered, as the location was good and the government supplied the settlers with rations, clothing and implements. In the following years, other settlers from Scotland and Ulster joined these pioneers, and in 1820 the total population in the various townships of this settlement was estimated at 12,000 (163/115).

In the west, South-Central Ontario received an overflow from the Middle Grand area, while many immigrants came through the Niagara Peninsula and settled in the western townships of the region. This development contributed to the rapid filling in of the till and clay plains between the York district and the head of the lake and Middle Grand settlements.

Within South-Central Ontario itself, the oldest settlement, the Bay of Quinte district, did not expand very much in area. By 1820, settlements were moving into the inhospitable, ice-scoured Shield which seals off this district in the second row of townships. The development in the Bay of Quinte area took more the form of an increased density of population. Here, the largest clearings and the best farms were to be found. This in itself made it attractive, and since, for many immigrants it was the first district they reached, they tended to settle there. The many bays and inlets made it the most accessible part of South-Central Ontario and this, together with its being the oldest settled district, undoubtedly contributed to the increase in population density.

Also farther west, the accessibility by water played a decisive part. By 1820, a new prong jutting inland between Port Hope and the Kawartha Lakes had come into existence. From the lake shore to Rice Lake the distance is about 10 miles, while from Rice Lake on, the Otonabee River can be followed upstream. The Otonabee River is the axis of this prong and from it settlement expanded eastward and westward. Settlement began in this area about 1818, but until 1825 only a few persons located in these inland townships. It had been estimated that, in 1825, no more than 500 persons lived north of Rice Lake (23, XVII/84).

In contrast with the growth of the Otonabee and Quinte districts, the expansion of the York district was largely the result of road building. Soon after 1800, a group of Mennonite Palatins settled in Markham and surrounding townships. They were good farmers and in most cases they bought land from previous owners (133). Quakers, mainly of British stock, settled to the north in Whitchurch. The Yonge Street settlements reached Cook Bay, and land was taken in following the shore of Lake Simcoe; by 1820, settlement had advanced as far as the southeast corner of that lake. On the other side of the lake, in Simcoe County, there was practically no settlement until the end of the Anglo-American war in 1815, when the first settlers, a group of dissatisfied Selkirk settlers from Manitoba, located in the southeast corner of the county. Of more importance, however, was the opening up of the northern townships of the county between Lake Simcoe and Georgian Bay. During the last months of the Anglo-American war, a nine-mile portage road was constructed from the present site of Barrie in a western direction, to a tributary of the Nottawasaga River. This was done for military reasons, in order to establish a shorter communication between York and the Upper Lakes. At about the same time, a road was cleared between the head of Kempenfelt Bay and Penetanguishene Harbour. But the road remained practically unused until 1818. In that year, a permanent military post was established at Penetanguishene, and the government successfully induced settlement along the road. Lots of 200 acres were granted to all who would start with the settlement duties within one month of receiving the location ticket: erect a house, clear ten acres of land adjacent to the road and also half of the road itself (163/132). At once, settlement began at both ends of the road, and by 1820, about half of the total length of the road was lined with small clearings. Those settlements were a northern extension of the Yonge Street settlements, Lake Simcoe forming the link between the two roads. Here also, road-building was the primary cause for the rise of settlement. As had been expected originally, the founding of York contributed considerably to a speedy settlement of the area between the Quinte and Niagara districts (187/54).

The present-day counties of Peel and Halton remained virtually unsettled till 1806. Originally, Simcoe had planned here an Indian reserve and a supply area for naval stores (195, III/59). Later on, it was feared that the Indians would ally themselves with the Americans, and, in 1806, a strip from five to eight miles wide was acquired along the lake (fig. 5). A road had been opened several years before and, being hemmed in between the rapidly expanding York and Niagara districts, the strip soon received a large number of settlers. Many years later, in 1818, the remainder of the two counties was purchased, and the settlements of the Niagara-Middle Grand district and the York area began to merge. Once the heavy forest had been cleared, the Peel clay plain proved to be fertile wheatland. The growing market of the young capital was not far distant, and settlers aided by an early building of roads inland, moved in rapidly. Many of them came from the poorer sandy soils in the old strip along the lake, others from the United States and Britain. By 1820, almost all of the two counties had been penetrated by settlers, who were wresting minute pieces of farmland from the unbroken forest.

To the east of the Yonge Street townships, an extensive area around Lake Scugog had not been entered by settlers by 1820. The western and southern portions of this block had been purchased much earlier than the counties of Peel and Halton, but actual settlement was much slower. It was not flanked by rapidly expanding districts as those two counties, because Yonge Street and Lake Simcoe drew the settlers northward. Also in the east, the trend of settlement was to the north, channelled as it was by Rice Lake and the Otonabee River. To the south, this Lake Scugog district was bounded by a ribbon of very sparsely settled land on the shores of Lake Ontario. Furthermore, besides lacking population pressure from the south, Lake Scugog was almost twice as far inland as Rice Lake. It also should be noted that the Interlobate Moraine in this area is 300 feet higher and much more difficult to cross than in the Rice Lake district. Isolation, therefore, was the main factor which delayed occupation of the townships around Lake Scugog.

Another unoccupied portion existed in 1820, between the Quinte district and Rice Lake. Simcoe had made extensive grants in these townships, and large blocks were in hands of absentees who prevented settlement. The townships contained also wide stretches of open oak plains against which settlers had a prejudice.

Such was the extent of settlement by 1820. Accessibility, either by water or by land, had been the main determinant for the general pattern as it had developed by that year. However, in order to assess fully the substratum on which town growth commenced, it will be necessary to consider the economic, social and cultural development of the area which was being opened up by 1820. Thus, it will be possible to evaluate the amount of urbanization which occurred during the first thirty years of the province's existence.

Population density

The areas shown as being penetrated by settlers about 1820 (fig. 4) were not at all densely populated. On the contrary, one of the most outstanding characteristics was the sparseness of population. For 1820, the total population of South-Central Ontario may be estimated at 40,000, of which more than 50 per cent lived in the Quinte or Eastern district of the region. This was the oldest sector and the most accessible one. It had become intensively occupied, as there was no room for areal expansion because of the proximity of the sterile Canadian Shield. The other districts had grown much more in area, especially after 1818, when in a short time wide areas were penetrated by settlers. The first settlers took up land on the Otonabee in 1818, when new settlers also moved into the northern parts of Halton and Peel Counties. In those districts settlements were few and far apart. In 1820, there was no mill north of Port Hope, and settlers farther north had to carry their grain 25 to 30 miles in order to have it milled. At that time, no store existed on the road between York and Port Hope, a distance of 60 miles (163/125).

Reserves and large grants

This scarcity of population was partly due to flaws in the system of disposal of public land. According to the Constitutional Act of 1791, one-seventh of a township had to be set aside for clergy reserves, in order to promote the cause of the Protestant (Anglican) Church. In addition, another one-seventh was retained as a crown reserve, to cover the expenses of government. These reserves were not laid out in one block, but distributed regularly over the entire township in lots of 200 acres. Thus, the reserved lands would be of the same quality as the land granted to individuals, and as the surrounding land improved, the reserved lots would rapidly increase in value and yield considerable returns.

Originally, it had been Simcoe's policy to limit land grants to a maximum of 200 acres. But there were many exceptions, and with the years, those exceptions increased through favouritism. Loyalists were eligible for grants for themselves and for each of their children. For a large family, this could amount to a considerable total. Often, daughters, already having a farm through marriage, did not need the land and it fell into the hands of speculators. This also happened with most of the land granted to disbanded soldiers who made poor settlers and soon sold their rights. Special grants were made to magistrates and other professional classes. Chief Justice Powell received 3,000 acres, three town lots in Newark and a farm lot in York. His wife, a Loyalist, received 1,200 acres, and each of his seven children a similar grant, making a total of more than 12,800 acres (163/63).

These grants also were scattered. Robert Gourlay received an offer of 1,000 acres, "the lots lying asunder," which was said to be in his favour, as the land would become valuable through the efforts of other settlers (118, II/561).

In addition, thousands of acres were acquired by persons making use of loopholes in the settlement regulations. Thus it was possible for groups to obtain grants under sponsorship of an influential person or leader. But actual settlement was often evaded, and gradually the associates became mere signatures who received a small recompensation, while the leader collected all the shares. The system was discontinued in 1799. The outcome of these land policies was that large parts of townships were not available for actual settlement, but were held by absentees for speculative purposes.

Prior to 1804, an aggregate of 4,500,000 acres had been granted in Upper Canada, most of it to Loyalists and their children. From 1804 to 1824, inclusive, a total of 3,500,000 acres was disposed of: 1,472,200 acres to military persons, Loyalists and their children, 1,231,000 acres to immigrants and other settlers, 228,000 acres in the form of surveyors' compensations, and 107,800 acres in large special grants (163/153). In other words, more than 50 per cent was granted to privileged groups and the remainder to the common settler.

In many ways, these unsettled lands impaired the work of the serious farmer; Gourlay received complaints about this from many townships. Uninterrupted settlement rendered the drainage of the land less difficult and made the erection of fences much easier. It facilitated co-operation among the farmers. Also, the uncleared lots harboured birds, reptiles and other animals which damaged the crops. But most serious was the effect upon the road network. One of the settlement duties always consisted of clearing half of the road allowance in front of the lot. This, however, often was not carried out by the absentee owners and consequently the roads were not cleared all the way through. Simcoe realized this and in townships along strategic roads, he moved the reserves to the back concessions. After Simcoe had left, however, this system does not seem to have been adhered to, and the ungranted lots fell into the hands of privileged persons. Among others, this was true for the road to Kingston, along which the actual settlers remained in small groups, cut off from each other, and unable to complete the important road (118, II/310). In 1800, goods could not be brought into York, because Yonge Street was impassable during the greater part of the year. The Government received a request to compel landowners to clear the road in front of their lots (163/91).

Thus, the system of disposal of public lands prevented the development of large areas with a fairly uniform population distribution, and it contributed to the isolation in which many settlers lived. This isolation was aggravated by the lack of passable roads, partly due to a deficiency in the fulfillment of settlement duties.

Transportation

During this period, overland transportation was almost non-existent. The winter was the best time for travelling; then, sleighs were used, and a thick layer of snow gave the rough roads a smooth surface, making travelling pleasant. The farmers preferred to transport their goods in winter; during the summer half year travelling was an ordeal, and was avoided as much as possible. A round about waterway was preferred to a direct road connection. Long after Yonge Street had been opened, the settlers in Markham township went to York by way of the Rouge River rather than via Yonge Street (207/389). The best method of travelling in the summer months was on foot or horseback.

When settlers penetrated a district, they often followed Indian trails, which were subtly adjusted to the topography. If settlement predated the survey, or when the clearing of the survey roads was slow, those trails were incorporated in the road network. However, this was exception rather than rule, and the new road network was not a new expression of the Indian trail system. The new roads were built very slowly. Often, it is difficult to determine when exactly a road was opened, because it often was "opened" several times. This "opening" could consist of a simple blazing of the road – a little bark was chopped from trees standing nearest to the line and perhaps some trees and boughs were cut, so one might ride on horseback. In general, however, it meant the cutting of the trees on the right of way. In some cases, the stumps were left standing, while in others they were removed and the road was ploughed.

In general, the new road network was not in accordance with the topography, and often ran against the grain of the country. This seriously handicapped road construction and travelling. Numerous hills, swamps, marshes and other obstacles had to be surmounted, and increased needlessly the expenses for road construction.

In 1800, the road to Kingston had been opened and declared passable, but soon it fell into disrepair. Actually, overland transportation between Kingston and York was not feasible until 1816, when a new road was opened, which in parts followed the old one. However, even then, it was used only in winter sleighing time (118). To the west of Toronto, the first bridge over the Credit River was not built till 1820 (211). Similar to the Kingston Road, Dundas Street remained in poor condition. Francis Hall writing about his travels in 1816-17 said: "It took us three hours to accomplish the five miles of road betwixt the head of the lake (Ontario) and the main road, called Dundas Street" (207/517).

Mail service and stage connection developed very slowly. Niagara had a post office from 1789, but it did not obtain a regular courier service until 1804. It was not until the summer of 1810 that a regular fortnightly courier service was inaugurated between Montreal and Kingston; the service was maintained throughout the year. In the following year, it was extended to York and Niagara (23, IV/735).

Stage services began to operate a few years later. In 1808, a stage ran regularly between Montreal and Kingston; seven years later, it became a bi-weekly service, and by 1819 it ran also during the summer. The stage connection between Kingston and York was established in the winter of 1816-17, and during the next years it functioned only during that season of the year. About the same time, stages ran to the head of the lake. The first stages on Yonge Street appeared much later.

The service between Montreal and Kingston was by 1820 the best stage connection of Upper Canada. But it was expensive, and many travellers went by boat or on foot. It took about ten or twelve days to go by boat from Lachine to Kingston. On such a trip the passengers suffered many inconveniences and hardships; they slept on shore at night, either at a house, if there happened to be one near, or under a tree. Where rapids occurred they had to land and walk (10/142).

On the whole, land transportation remained backward. Gourlay compared transportation in Canada with that south of Lake Ontario in the United States. That area had been settled eight or ten years after Upper Canada, and had excellent roads. "For a hundred miles west of Utica, the great road is so good, that stage coaches can run with equal speed and safety as in England. In Canada I know not of a single road so made, as to be proof against a wet season" (118, II/359). But the roads Gourlay had in mind were a link between competing ports on the Atlantic Seaboard on one hand, and western country rapidly being opened up on the other. In Canada, however, the St. Lawrence system was a busy traffic artery, and seemed to make the need for capital roads less urgent.

During the first twenty years of the 19th century, water transportation underwent fundamental changes. From 1800 on, the flat-bottomed and sharp-ended batteau on the St. Lawrence was succeeded by the Durham boat. This Ohio vessel was much larger and more efficient. Instead of the batteau's 20 barrels, it could carry 100 barrels and needed a crew of only six or seven men (10/138). On the lake, the batteaux were soon replaced by schooners, and it was not long before the first steamer appeared on Lake Ontario.

In 1819, a steamer plied once a week between Kingston and York. Another steamer travelled twice a week between Kingston and the head of the Bay of Quinte. About this time, the first schooner was built also on Lake Simcoe; it was not until 1831, however, that the first steamer was launched on that lake.

During the early part of the 19th century, the transportation network and means of communication in general remained rather poorly developed. Travelling was expensive, and was accompanied by many hardships and inconveniences. This condition was largely the result of a low population density. It could not help but have a detrimental effect upon the economic growth of the region; it crippled the movement of persons and goods.

Economic Activities

Isolation was one of the main obstacles to be overcome, both for the settlers and the government. During this early period it affected deeply the economic, social and cultural development of Upper Canada, and therefore also urban growth. Isolation fashioned, in particular, agriculture, trade and manufacturing. In this connection, however, it was not only internal isolation which played an important part, but also isolation with regards to the world outside Upper Canada, especially Montreal. The rapids of the Lower St. Lawrence represented a stout barrier between Lake Ontario and the ocean; the communication system with Montreal remained cumbersome and costly. The inhabitants of Kingston pointed this out to Gourlay. "At present every article we want from the sea-ports is brought to us at great expense, time and risk; the same may be said of any article we have to export" (118, I/479). In the early years of the century, the original cost of imported goods rose by 40 per cent because of charges for packing, carterage, river freight, commission, insurance and other expenses at London and Montreal. To this had to be added ocean freight, transport from Montreal to Kingston, etc. (283).

Agriculture

The over-all plan of settlement was the result of military and strategic consideration. Yet the individual settler was careful in the selection of his location. He scanned the natural vegetation as to the nature and fertility of the soil underneath; he wished to settle close to navigable water or a road, near a mill, and in or near an already growing district. As much as possible, government officials tried to satisfy those wishes.

Social factors were also given consideration. Lower cites the case of Scottish settlers in the Eastern District of Upper Canada. The fact that they would settle near Scottish immigrants who had preceded them was of greater significance than their location on the frontier for military reasons (149). The government considered it most important that settlement would be effective and successful. Social factors also had played a part in the settlement of the Loyalists.

Clearing the forest was a tremendous task, and previous experience was almost a vital condition for success. American settlers, therefore, were better than Europeans, who often suffered a great deal.

If he were near enough to a market, the settler could dispose of his first product, potash, obtained from the ashes of the hardwood trees. This was the sole use to which trees could be put; 10 acres of good timber yielded at least five barrels of potash, each barrel containing 500 lbs (172, I/169). Larger pine trees could be floated down the streams and sold. Oak staves, square timber, planks and boards were also shipped. Up till 1820, however, export of lumber from points in South-Central Ontario remained insignificant. After the clearing, the pioneer obtained a crop of wheat. The next three or four years the land had to be in pasture, as weeds would choke the grain and the trees would sprout again. Cattle kept down the sprouts and the stumps gradually decayed. Then the land could be ploughed, and uninterrupted wheat cropping started. After 1800, wheat became the staple industry of Upper Canada. Near Kingston and York, where civilian and military demand provided a market, the farmers produced beef and pork, peas, oats, and potatoes. For settlers farther inland, transportation in most instances was difficult and costly, and some began livestock raising, because cattle could be driven to market (292/30-32). The lack of a market constituted a serious problem for many farmers, and forced them into self-sufficient farming in which they tried to supply their own needs as much as possible.

The farms remained small in this early period. It was impossible to obtain hired help, as it was very easy for a person to become a landowner himself. The amount of land which could be cleared and worked profitably depended on the skill of the farmer and the size of his family. There was no money to pay for imported and therefore expensive goods, and the farmer was entirely dependent upon his own ingenuity, and the products from land and forest. He made his own clothes, leather, furniture, tools, soap, candles, and many other necessities for his daily life. Yet, there were regional variations within South-Central Ontario.

By 1820, the Bay of Quinte district had the largest agricultural production and was much better developed than the other sections. A great number of the Loyalists were farmers from New York; they had a tradition of several generations of frontier expansion behind them, and they possessed a wealth of experience from which to draw. It enabled them to wrest a livelihood from the untamed wilderness they found on their arrival (292). These German and Dutch settlers were not only experienced in pioneer farming, they also had a deep-seated, inherited love for the land. These are the factors which perhaps explain why, for decades to come the Bay of Quinte district repeatedly is mentioned as the most flourishing farming area of Upper Canada above the mouth of the Ottawa River (195, II/160; 110, I/80). This development occurred in spite of the mediocrity of the land. The soils on the limestone plains between Kingston and the head of the Bay are shallow, only a few inches deep, and more than half of the soils of Prince Edward County consist of less than 30 inches of unconsolidated material over the bedrock (104/231). Nevertheless, soon a farming economy prosperous for that time was built up. Within ten years, an exportable surplus of wheat was produced and trade could expand. By 1805, it had even a reputation for the quality of its wheat (292/28). Yet, even in this district, farming remained to a large extent more or less self-sufficient.

South-Central Ontario was a region of small farms and self-sufficient farming. Isolation, which was the result of the low densities of population and the poor transportation facilities, not only within the province itself, but also with the world outside, necessitated that type of farm economy.

Trade

Under such conditions of farming and transportation, trade developed very slowly. Furthermore, the shipment of grain down the St. Lawrence and across the ocean was expensive, and the British wheat market was unreliable as the Corn Laws repeatedly changed its absorptive capacity. On the other hand, the wheat production in Canada fluctuated considerably on account of dry summers and the Hessian fly, as in the years 1794-1797 and 1810.

Until the War of 1812, the American settlements south of Lake Ontario lagged behind those in Canada. A trade in local commodities developed between the two countries, but it remained small, at least until the War of 1812. After the restoration of the peace, trade began to increase.

In 1801 Upper Canada, from Kingston westward, exported to Montreal 13,963 barrels of fine and superfine flour, 322 barrels of middlings and 350 bushels of wheat (292/27). This amount gradually increased, and from 1817-1820 large shipments of wheat and flour were sent down the St. Lawrence. Then, however, the wheat prices in Britain fell below the minimum set by the Corn Laws, and Upper Canada wheat and flour were excluded (292/39).

For Canada as a whole, fur remained an important product, but this was not true for South-Central Ontario. As early as 1794, Simcoe observed that the merchants of Kingston did not concentrate any more on this article, because they looked "forward to the produce of their country as the true source of their wealth" (195, III/228). More important was the export of lumber and staves down the St. Lawrence which could easily be done in the form of rafts; rafts were also used for the shipment of flour. However, the lumber trade did not gain real momentum in the region until after 1820, when the brisk lumber industry of the Ottawa Valley and Eastern Ontario spread westward.

Most of the commerce in Upper Canada was carried on by a system of barter. The merchants were wholesale and retail dealers at the same time. They accepted from the farmer wheat, potash, flour, lumber, hides, butter, cheese, pork, furs, etc. Herrington gives an interesting account of the business of such a country merchant (212). He was a general merchant, and dealt in every article his customers could reasonably expect him to have in stock. In addition to a remarkable variety of goods, he had horses and oxen which were hired out, while sometimes he also dealt in livestock. He had a cobbler and a seamstress working for him.

The currency of those days was flour, pork and potash. The merchant paid the farmer with goods from his store. He also was the banker and clearing house for the district, and a person with a credit balance with a store could pay his own creditors with orders on that store. The position of the merchant was a powerful one, as he determined the value of the products he received from the settlers and the prices of goods with which he paid them. Those conditions did not promote trade; the farmers were extremely reluctant to make purchases and tried to avoid them.

Currency remained very scarce, particularly until the War of 1812. Only the garrisons paid in cash. During the war, however, a considerable amount of currency entered the country in the form of British payments for goods and services provided by the population. There was also much illegal trade between Canada and the United States. After the war, Canada remained for a few years an attractive market for American products. The Yankee pedlar was a serious competitor for the country merchant. With his waggon, which was virtually a mobile store, he trekked from clearing to clearing, selling dry goods, light tinware, etc. He took cash for payment or light, portable products, such as furs and hides (23, IV/563).

Thus, unfavorable trade conditions prolonged the period of self-sufficient farming. There was no large accumulation of capital and wealth, although Kingston had a few prominent merchants. It was not until the end of the period that banks were established in the larger towns.

Manufacturing

Manufacturing before 1820 represented only a very minor development. Almost all forces were against industrial growth. The trade had not built up any surplus of capital, while foreign capital was not interested. The population was poor, largely self-sufficient, and offered no market. As is true for all of Southern Ontario, the region was poor in mineral resources, while agricultural productivity was still low. The result was that during this early period, manufacturing remained an integral part of the self-sufficient farming economy. The small establishments processed or improved the raw material provided by the customer, and kept part of the worked material in lieu of payment. The first provincial parliament settled in 1792 the rate of tolls for gristmills at "not more than 1/12 for grinding and bolting." The sawmills took in general one half of the boards sawn (290).

The grist and sawmills were erected at suitable water power sites which abounded in South-Central Ontario. In particular, the gristmills were of vital importance to the settlers. Numerous are the accounts of pioneers walking long distances carrying a sack of grain to have it gristed at a mill. The distribution of these mills was closely linked with the general distribution of population. Gourlay reported 27 gristmills and 131 sawmills in 1817 for the Midland district – the future counties of Hastings, Lennox and Addington, Frontenac and Prince Edward. However, the number was probably higher, as his report was incomplete. The total number of mills in the rest of South-Central Ontario was smaller than in the Midland district. In general, there were more sawmills than gristmills, the ratio being perhaps three to two at the time of Gourlay's survey. The sawmills were cheaper to construct, and were erected first. In connection with the gristmills, distilleries were established in many districts, and they were almost as numerous as the saw and gristmills. As early as 1801, 51 licensed distilleries were reported in Upper Canada, but most likely there were many more (290). They used the poorer grades of grain as well as the surplus of the better grades from the gristmill. In addition, there were many carding machines and fulling mills. They also formed an integral part of the self-sufficient farming economy. Carding could be done at home, but when possible, it was sent to a machine. Spinning and dyeing were done again at home, and although weavers soon established themselves, many farmers kept handlooms in their homes. After weaving, the cloth was sent to the fulling mill for finishing.

Each of these manufacturing establishments gave employment to only one or two persons. One exception was shipbuilding at Kingston and York. In the Midland district shipbuilding was the most important industry next to milling (290). Kingston had a number of carpenters and shipwrights for the building and repair of warships. York also built warships and commercial vessels, but was not as important in this field as Kingston. On the other hand, York being the seat of government soon attracted small craftsmen like a watchmaker, a cutler and gunsmith (290).

The service industries showed the same characteristics as early manufacturing. The farmer prepared his own supply of leather, but shoes and boots were made by a cobbler who went from house to house. He lodged with the family for a few days till the work was done and received payment in kind. The itinerant tailor, the clockmaker, the pedlar did the same. Even the schoolteacher was "boarded around." The blacksmith came later, as there was a dearth of iron. The farmer made his own ploughs and harrows, buying at considerable expense the iron for the plough.

Such was the economic development in this early period. Although produce was sold for cash, there was a tendency to be self-sufficient, particularly in the townships away from the waterfront. The Bay of Quinte district was the oldest settled area and the one most accessible. Economically, it was most advanced in all aspects, although its soils were not as fertile as elsewhere in South-Central Ontario. Internal and external isolation and sparseness of population distribution largely were responsible for this limited development. The demand for urban services was very small because of the self-sufficiency of the population and scarcity of money. As much as possible, these services were performed within the framework of the farm economy. The only exceptions were the larger merchants, the shipbuilders, the administrators and a few professionals and craftsmen. Indeed, the conditions for a demand for centralized services, a non-rural way of life, an urban development were not encouraging before 1820.

Town Growth Before 1820

By 1820, urban settlement in South-Central Ontario was not very impressive. Although the region had received white settlers for almost forty years, there were only two centres which had become important – Kingston and York. Kingston had in 1820 a population of about 2,300, and was the largest urban centre of Upper Canada at that time; York had about 1,250. There were several other settlements, but they were not more than hamlets. According to an account written in 1824, and quoted by Canniff, there were two or three very small villages between Kingston and York, the largest of which was Belleville, containing 150 inhabitants (134/501).

Attempts to establish towns and to promote their development had not been lacking. In particular Simcoe had been very much interested in these things. Among the various urban points he had planned, only York struck root and developed as a counterpart of Kingston. Both towns, however, developed within a different regional framework, and were exposed to entirely different influences.

Kingston

Kingston had originated as a government-planned garrison town, but soon trade and transportation became the most important factors in the further expansion of the town. Simcoe, Russell, Bouchette, Gourlay and others, all described the importance of commerce for this centre. The merchants of Kingston, like Cartwright, were the largest and most influential of Upper Canada. The lieutenant-governor solicited their advice (187; 23, IV/557). The first banks in Upper Canada were established in Kingston and the initiative and capital for these came largely from the local merchants.

The conditions for the early commercial development of Kingston were favourable. For the Bay of Quinte district, it was the only important market and the best harbour. There were no competitors. The promising settlement of Ernestown (Bath) had been checked in its growth. The first steamer on Lake Ontario was built here and, in 1811, its citizens established an academy which was a rival of the school at Cornwall. The War of 1812, however, ruined the town and it never recovered entirely. Originally Bath was on the main road from Kingston to York, but gradually in later years the main flow of traffic went via Napanee, by-passing Bath (fig. 4).

In 1820, no other settlement was larger than a hamlet. The hinterland of Kingston was not fertile, but still it was among the best developed in the province at that time. Gourlay already went so far as to say: "Kingston is subject to one local disadvantage, the want for a populous back country" (118, I/128). Yet, of much greater significance was the location of Kingston with regards to the flow of traffic on the St. Lawrence and Lower Lakes system.

American settlements in the areas tributary to Lake Ontario, and especially to Lake Erie, could be supplied with goods much more cheaply by way of the St. Lawrence than overland through the Mohawk Gate (23, IV). Accordingly, an extensive British trade developed with the American West. Until 1801 British goods were admitted duty free in the western districts of the United States. But, also after duties had been imposed, the trade remained virtually a British monopoly till the opening of the

Erie Canal in 1825. A survey in 1797 revealed that this trade amounted to half a million dollars (23, IV/552). This trade continued to increase considerably in value and volume. For comparison, it may be stated that according to estimates of contemporary merchants the value of exports from Upper Canada for 1801 amounted to $420,000 (23, IV/557).

Kingston took an active part in this British trade. The goods were shipped upstream in batteaux and Durham boats and at Kingston they were transferred to lake vessels which took them across the lake to Queenston. Similarly, goods coming from the lakes were transferred to river crafts. Kingston had "many spacious warehouses" for goods waiting further shipment. As early as 1796, the importance of his traffic for Kingston was emphasized and it was considered to be one of the main factors in the growth of the town (194, I/147). In 1815, Bouchette called Kingston the main entrepôt between Montreal and all the settlements along the lake westward. "From the commencement of spring until the latter end of autumn; great activity prevails; vessels of from eighty to nearly two hundred tons, employed in navigating the lake, are continually receiving and discharging, their cargoes, as well as the batteaux used in the river" (111/599). On the other hand, it is surprising to note that the inhabitants of Kingston complained to Gourlay about the poor navigability of the St. Lawrence (118, I/479). They must have expected that a loss in trans-shipment business would be compensated by a general increase in volume of trade.

York, trade along the Toronto Passage

In contrast with Kingston, trade and commerce were of minor importance in the growth of York. Its hinterland was much more recently settled and much less developed, although it contained a few prosperous townships. The harbour was better than that of Kingston, but it did not have any traffic beyond the volume required for the town and its hinterland. A traveller, quoted by Scadding, characterized the trade of the town in 1823 as "very trifling" (198/85). York was off the main flow of trade across the lake, which was the lifeblood for Kingston. Actually, till the opening of the Kingston Road, the town was considerably handicapped by its isolated location. Lieutenant-Governor Russell repeatedly emphasized the need for better communications (194). In the beginning, not even government vessels would regularly call at the port. At times of heavy ice conditions or foul weather, York was virtually cut off from the outside world, particularly in winter, when this isolation could last for months. Russell tried to convince the government of the dire need for the construction of roads in various directions.

Simcoe and many after him cherished high hopes about the development of trade along the Toronto passage. Yet, there was no ground for those confident expectations, and the actual development which took place demonstrated this clearly. In 1802, an elaborate plan was prepared for a large proposed town at the site where Yonge Street struck the east branch of the Holland River (252). Nothing was done, however, and another survey and report were submitted in 1811. The town never came into existence, and around 1820, a small hamlet developed a mile to the south of the original town site. This was the beginning of Holland Landing. The extensive town plans had been drawn up, because so much was expected from trade development.

During the last years before the War of 1812, the Americans began to interfere with the fur trade at Detroit. The trading concern involved, the North-West Company, became more interested in the route via York, and contributed financially towards the improvement of Yonge Street and the surveying of the road between Kempenfelt Bay and Penetang harbour. There is, however, no evidence that any freight moved over this route (252; 111/609). After the war, the North-West Company was considerably weakened, as the Americans expelled the fur traders from their national territory, and the flow of traffic over Yonge Street remained insignificant.

This is also evident from the transportational and settlement developments in the districts between Georgian Bay and Lake Simcoe. As early as 1785, a block of land had been bought between Lake Couchiching and the Bay. A few years later, Simcoe selected the site of Penetanguishene, and the harbour and adjoining land were officially acquired in 1798. Yet, the land needed for the road from this harbour to Kempenfelt Bay was not purchased until 1815 (252) (fig. 5). The road between Penetanguishene and Barrie was not opened until 1818, and in the same year settlement began to expand along it. This slow development does not indicate an important flow of trade through this area. The Montreal merchants continued to prefer the Detroit and Ottawa routes; the trade had become entrenched in and accustomed to these waterways.

It was not till 1828, that the first stage services were inaugurated between York and Holland Landing, eleven years after stages began to link York with Kingston and with the head of the lake. How much traffic actually existed by 1820 may be gathered from a traveller's account as given by Hunter: "At the present time (1819) there are no houses nor stores on the north side of Simcoe at the portage, which makes it very troublesome, and also much of the goods transported are liable to be injured by weather. Since the steamboat has commenced to sail on Lake Erie, the cheapest and most expeditious mode of sending down the furs from the interior is by that route, although it is four hundred miles longer than by Simcoe. There is nothing but one schooner upon the Lake (Lake Simcoe), which is sufficient for all the trade at present" (213, I/29).

This same traveller, however, expressed perhaps a general feeling that time, when he mentioned the portage striking westward from Kempenfelt Bay and said: "It is very probable that at no very distant period this will become the most frequented of all the routes to the North West" (213). The old concepts were still strong and the idea of an eventual big flow of traffic continued to influence government and business alike. However, as far as Toronto before 1820 is concerned, there was no northern trade which contributed to its growth.

The main factor in the expansion of this town was the same as that which had led to its founding – the administrative function. York had been selected as the capital for the upper province, and during this early period the town was fashioned to fulfil that function. Roads were constructed to connect it with all parts of the province. A resolution passed by the Executive Council in 1799 pointed out that this was of primary importance to the young capital: ". . . the measures of the Executive Government and acts of the Legislature, which it is of the greatest importance to the subjects to be fully apprised of, are hardly ever known beyond the immediate neighbourhood of the Capital, while the approach to the Superior Court of Justice is equally difficult, and involves the parties in great and unnecessary delay and expence" (194, III/12). Thus York was set as a hub within the framework of the whole province.

The administrative function was also evident in the landscape of the small settlement. The public buildings were prominent. For their construction, a brickworks had been established at an early date (194, II/38). This gave the town an unusual number of brick structures, and the presence of a better building material may have attracted wealthier citizens. But the fact that it was also the capital attracted many immigrants here and encouraged them to stay in or near the town.

Its citizens formed quite a contrast with those of Kingston. In York there were the government officials, the wealthy land-owners, and other well-to-do persons, retired army officers, and so on. Their presence attracted various craftsmen and shops, such as a watchmaker, a cutler and gunsmith, a printing office, and others. It is interesting to note that the assessment for 1820 listed 148 houses and 21 pleasure carriages (249, II/993). This was a high number of carriages considering the number of houses, and the fact that travelling by road at that time was by no means a pleasure.

Much more than Kingston, York grew independently of its local hinterland. Russell described this in a letter to Simcoe in 1797: "The increase of this town bears no proportion to that of the population around it. The head may consequently grow too big for the body, and scarcity and dearness of provisions be the inevitable consequence to the great distress of the officers of Government whose incomes are certainly unequal to their un-avoidable expence" (194, II/282).

On the other hand, its being the capital did not bring a brisk and uninterrupted expansion. Actually the town increased rather slowly when compared with Kingston. Under Simcoe's regime, it was common knowledge that the Lieutenant-Governor still had his eyes fixed on London and the Thames as the future site for the capital (195, II/88-89). In 1797, rumors about a possible removal of the seat of government caused considerable alarm among the authorities in York (194, I/139). This restrained the investment of capital in the new town, as it made the future insecure and uncertain. And even as late as 1815, the question of the suitability of York as the capital of the province was re-opened (229, I/136). But the problems involved in a removal of the capital were too big. The York land grants of the government officials would depreciate very much, and other grants would be justified to recompensate them.

During the War of 1812, Kingston enjoyed much prosperity, as it was the main naval base with a considerable amount of shipbuilding and repair; the armed forces maintained a big demand for agricultural produce. York, however, was taken by the Americans, who set fire to the parliament buildings, and the town in general drew much less benefit from the war. Kingston was the more prosperous of the two, and not only the economic capital but also the cultural centre for Upper Canada (11/96). In the years 1816 and 1817, a course of fifteen botany lectures was given. In the winter there was a drawing school, a singing school for young ladies, and public lectures on mineralogy, chemistry and geology.

Foundations for future metropolitan expansion

Soon after 1815, York was ready for the struggle with its rival, and it began to lay the foundation for its future economic strength. The issue was the establishment of banks in Upper Canada (286; 23, IV). In 1817, a group of Kingston merchants petitioned the government for the inauguration of a regular banking system, and asked for a charter for the Bank of Upper Canada. Not all merchants in Kingston, however, were in favour of this, and they invited the Bank of Montreal, established in 1817, to open a branch in Kingston. Later on, in 1818, another Montreal bank, the Bank of Canada, also established a branch in the town. The Lieutenant-Governor reserved his decision concerning the charter for the Bank of Upper Canada, and referred the matter to the British Government. In the meantime, the Bank of Upper Canada began to operate as a private bank in 1819, with its head office in Kingston. This gave Kingston three banks, while York had none. But the capital was ready to act.

The government of the province was in hands of a clique of privileged persons, generally known as the "Family Compact." They personally were vitally interested in the growth and expansion of the capital.

In 1817, York interests had petitioned for a bank charter, and this decision also had been referred to the home government. Then, after much delay, in 1821 the charter for a Bank of Upper Canada had been assented to and was returned to York. However, in 1819, the names of York merchants had been substituted for the original Kingston list, and the head office had been moved to York. The Kingston merchants had received another charter for a Bank of Kingston, but this bank never came into existence. Meanwhile, the private Bank of Upper Canada failed in 1822.

But the chartered Bank of Upper Canada also faced serious problems, which reveal the weak economic position of Toronto at that time. It had difficulty in obtaining the required capital, even after the act had been amended to solve this problem. Originally, £20,000 in cash deposits had to be paid in before the bank could open for business; but when this sum could not be raised, it was reduced to £10,000. It was rumored at the time that the Bank received an unauthorized advance of specie from the military chest (286).

The Bank was entirely a government affair. The government appointed four of the fifteen directors, but several others were also members of the Family Compact, and in 1823 the government held 25 per cent of the stock. The Family Compact, feathering its own nest, had established York's financial hegemony over the province, although the town itself did not yet have the economic strength to warrant such a position.

During this early period, York, through the Family Compact also laid the foundation for its educational supremacy. In 1812, the government invited Strachan, an able Scottish clergyman who had gained fame as a teacher and who had been teaching in Eastern Ontario for more than ten years, to come to York in order to organize a system for higher education in the province. Soon, Strachan became a member of the government, and it was his energy which led to the founding of the University of Toronto, and his inflexibility which fashioned it into a system of federated colleges.

Other centres

Outside Kingston and York, there were, before 1820, no other important urban centres in South-Central Ontario. Many mills had already been erected, but people had settled around only a few. In general, first the more easily built and cheaper sawmill appeared, and soon a gristmill was added. In time, a store, a distillery, a carriage shop, a church, and others would be established. Belleville was perhaps the only one of the smaller settlements which possessed so many establishments by 1820.

In their distribution these hamlets reflect the importance of transport facilities. One of them, Burlington, had no mill site, but developed as a point of entry for immigrants. For this purpose wharves had been built by 1800, and at the end of the period steamers plying between the important ports on the lake called here (11/106).

Besides the administrative function, and trade and transportation, there were no other factors which induced concentrated settlement. Manufacturing at that time was a service within a local framework. The mill site was a point often visited, and as such it was an attractive location for other service establishments.

Essentially, the mills were not different from the carriage

repair shop, the bakery, the distillery, brewery, or the watch-makers shop. They all employed only a few persons, and oc-curred wherever population had become sufficient to provide a market for those services. Their establishment was a result of growth of population rather than the cause. The most acces-sible, and therefore the most frequented sites, were the ones which attracted the service industries. The chief exception was the shipbuilding industry which, particularly in Kingston and York, served a much larger territory, and contributed to the numerical growth of those towns. In general, however, the self-sufficient economy had no great need for centrally located services, and urban settlement therefore remained of minor importance.

The urban landscape

The appearance of the towns before 1820 was very dismal. Scadding quoted Talbot who gave a gloomy description of them in 1825: "The streets of York are regularly laid out, intersect-ing each other at right angles. Only one of them, however, is yet completely built; and in wet weather the unfinished streets are if possible muddier and dirtier than those of Kingston. The situation of the town is very unhealthy, for it stands on a piece of low marshy land" (198/93). Another contemporary writer was equally uncomplimentary to Kingston: "The buildings are of such an inferior description as scarcely to be worthy of notice" (186/433).

Summary

There was no continuous development between the French and Indian settlements on one hand and the British settlements on the other. Only a few Indian trails were incorporated in the new road network. Yet, during the pre-Anglo-Saxon period the value of certain strategic points and routes became apparent, and this knowledge was inherited by the British.

Simcoe, anxious to make the colony easily defensible and economically self-supporting, expected much from trade de-velopment along the Toronto passage. These expectations in-fluenced his plans for road-building and the founding of towns. He radically changed the natural expansion of settlement by establishing the capital at York, and planning it as a major centre. This accelerated tremendously the expansion of settlement on the north shore of Lake Ontario. At the end of the period, the centre of gravity began to shift from the Bay of Quinte to the Toronto area.

Toronto was started on the road towards metropolitan predominance not by its economic strength, but by the deliberate actions of a self-interested governmental clique. The expected trade over the Toronto passage never came, as is evident from the condition of Yonge Street over many years, and the meager urban growth at the northern end of the route.

By the end of the period, the settlements of the Toronto and Lakehead districts had begun to merge. Farther east, a new prong jutting inland in the Rice Lake area came into existence, while the Lake Scugog area was by-passed for the time being. The settlements in the Bay of Quinte district approached the Canadian Shield, and constituted the most prosperous part of the region and of the whole province.

The low density of population, in part due to the faulty system of land grants, retarded the building of good roads. This in turn kept the population in separate isolated groups.

Also the communication with Montreal and the ocean was difficult. On account of those circumstances, trade developed only slowly and the economy of the region was largely one of self-sufficient farming.

The need for urban services remained small, and in general a non-rural way of life could not be established outside the two towns of Kingston and York; other agglomerated settlements had, by 1820, hardly passed beyond the hamlet stage.

3. The Northward Expansion, 1820-1850

Immigration and Population Growth

In contrast with the first period, the immigrants who came during the next thirty years came largely from the British Isles, especially from Ireland. The twenties saw much poverty in Britain, and the famines in Ireland forced thousands to leave their homeland. Soon emigration to Canada swelled to a surging tide. Passage across the Atlantic was easy to obtain, as the timber ships on their return voyage to North America preferred passengers to ballast (8). Gradually the influx of immigrants gained momentum. In 1827, 12,648 immigrants arrived at Quebec. Thereafter, the number increased rapidly and, in 1832, 51,746 immigrants landed at that port. From 1834 to 1840, the rate of immigration slowed down as a result of the cholera epidemic and the unsettled economic and political conditions in Canada. But in the forties increasingly large numbers arrived again. The total for 1847 was around 90,000.

However, many immigrants landing at Quebec did not settle in Canada, but went on to the United States. This was particularly true of the more enterprising settlers with money and skill, because capital could be employed much more effectively in that country. The United States was more prosperous and land there was cheaper. Also the political upheavals in the decade from 1827 to 1837 induced many immigrants to cross the boundary. According to a contemporary observer in Montreal during those years, the proportion of immigrants bound for the United States was estimated at 60 per cent (23, IV/579). It was during these years that the heavy drain of population to the United States began which ever since has profoundly influenced population growth in Canada. If the trends of the late twenties had continued, Canada, according to Bouchette, would have had a population of about 16,000,000 by 1881. Yet in that year the actual number of people in the country totalled only 4,324,810 (23, IV/587). The adjoining American Midwest was largely settled by people coming either from or through Canada.

Upper Canada nevertheless showed, in spite of these losses, a considerable increase in population. The immigration into the province for the year 1833 alone was estimated at around 20,000 (10/114-115). There were 157,923 inhabitants in 1825; by 1834, this had more than doubled to reach 321,145. In 1841, the province had 455,688 inhabitants. During the next decade, the population again doubled, and the census of 1851 reported a total of 952,004 persons in Ontario.

Land policies

Beneficent changes occurred in the government's land policy. In the early twenties it was generally realized that the system of free land grants had been a failure. Consequently, after 1826, a sales system was instituted by which land was sold to prospective settlers by public auctions (163). The settler could buy the land on reasonable terms, but still had to perform certain duties. Roads and bridges were to be constructed and maintained out of the returns from land sales and taxes. Members of the armed forces and loyalists remained eligible for free grants.

After 1820, with a gradually diminishing friction between Britain and the United States, military considerations played only a minor part in the settlement policy of the government. Individual settlers enjoyed complete freedom in selecting their location, and often they made considerable reconnaisance before they made a decision (154).

Reserves and vacant lands

The reserves continued to handicap the development of the province. Attempts to sell the clergy reserves failed, mainly through opposition of the Family Compact. Together with the whole system of disposal of public lands, the reserves were considered to be at the root of all problems in Upper Canada (23, IV/581-582). The Family Compact had dealt with the public lands much to their own advantage, and the resentment against the government land policy contributed largely to the rebellion of 1837.

The vacant or wild lands constituted a large part of the total area of Southern Ontario. About half of the clergy reserves alone – one million acres – lay in South-Central Ontario. It was not until 1854, that the clergy reserves were secularized. Lord Durham, who was sent out by the Home Government to investigate the cause for the unrest in Canada, reported that half of the 16 million acres of surveyed lands in Upper Canada had been granted to privileged groups and persons or in the form of rewards for public services: to loyalists, members of the armed forces, magistrates, barristers, land surveyors and other public officials, clergymen and the Church of England, and many others. A very small portion (Durham estimated it to be less than one-tenth) of the land thus granted had been occupied by settlers, and still much less had been cleared and cultivated (3). A tax on wild lands, which had been levied as early as 1819 in order to force their improvement, at first was not very effective, as there were many ways of evading it (10/78-79). However, by 1850, a stricter tax policy had led to the desired results. In that year the average size of the farms was 100 acres (in 1825 still 750 acres) (166/150).

The Canada Company

Unlike the clergy reserves, the crown lands were disposed of effectively through the Canada Company. This company was incorporated by royal charter in 1826, and purchased the crown reserves from the government. These reserves were scattered in almost every township throughout the province, but they included also a few large blocks of land in the unsurveyed part. These blocks comprised among others a tremendous triangle of 22 townships to the west of Kitchener and also included Guelph Township. The land had been sold to the company instead of half of the clergy reserves, as originally planned, but which had been rejected by the church authorities. The company built roads and made some clearings on the lots and then sold the land to settlers on favourable payment conditions. The Canada Company was financially very successful and contributed greatly to a rapid settlement of a large part of Southern Ontario (10/89).

In general, the atmosphere and policies which fostered settlement between 1820 and 1830 differed considerably from those of the preceding period. Yet, the trends established in that early period largely continued to influence the expansion of settlement.

The Spread of Settlement Between 1820 and 1850

Importance of roads and markets

Accessibility played a dominant part in the geographic and economic development of South-Central Ontario during the first forty years of its history. After 1820, the handicap of isolation was partially overcome, but it continued to influence the spread of settlement.

The settlers were entirely free as to where they decided to locate, but their choice was largely determined by the degree to which the country had been opened up and the proximity of a town for the marketing of produce and as a source of supplies. In 1832, Picken described Ops, the township in which Lindsay is situated, as one of the finest as far as soil is concerned and said that many settlements had started. But he feared that from the want of roads and mills, the conditions of settlement would be seldom performed (124/162, 163). Otonabee had excellent soils, yet it had few settlers. This was "mainly attributed to its distance from, and difficulty of access to market" (124/157). Hall (119) mentions a settler in Douro who was about to give up, when Peterborough suddenly gained in importance through the Robinson immigration (p. 60). The settler could face all the tremendous difficuties and hardships in the backwoods, but the absence of a small settlement in which he could obtain provisions made him despondent. Bad roads and distance from a village or town were considered two of the greatest inconveniences (171/123).

Distance from a town determined the value of farmland more than anything else. Strickland bought land within a mile from Peterborough. Although it was still wild land, he had to pay a high price, because the prospect of a town nearby had improved the marketing possibilities (172, I/91). Giving advice to the new immigrant in the 1840's, Smith said "Let him on no account whatever, no matter what the price, or the apparent advantages held out to him may be, be induced to purchase land at a distance from good roads and a good market; as nothing tends so much to keep back the settler, and frequently to dishearten him . . . Land in Canada is valued, not according to its quality, but entirely according to its locality and other circumstances" (130/254, 255).

It is not surprising, therefore, that accessibility and proximity to markets were the most important factors which influenced the expanding settlement pattern, especially between

1820 and 1840. Until the early forties, the oldest settled parts of the region continued to receive most of the immigrants.

Morehouse constructed dot maps to show the distribution of immigrants for the years 1841 and 1849 (159). Two areas exhibit a considerable concentration of newcomers in 1841 – the Yonge Street area, bounded by the line Dundas, Cook Bay, Bowmanville and the Bay of Quinte district. In that year, these two districts showed the largest concentrations of all of Southern Ontario. By 1849, the distribution pattern had changed. In that year, the Yonge Street area still had a large concentration of immigrants, but the Quinte section received almost none. Instead, there was a large concentration between Bowmanville and Trenton.

The districts on the Bay of Quinte and Yonge Street were the oldest settled parts of the region; there, the best communication system and the best available markets and supply centres were to be found, and consequently those sections became the most densely populated areas, and economically the furthest developed districts.

.The Quinte District

The actual expansion of settlement in South-Central Ontario during these thirty years exhibited a great deal of diversity. In the east, the Quinte district continued the trend set before 1820; here, increase in numbers led above all to a greater density of population and not so much to an areal expansion. By 1830 at least eight townships had a density of 25 or more persons per square mile, in contrast with the Yonge Street district where only three or four townships had such a density. In general, the densities of the Quinte district were at that time much higher than those near Toronto.

To the northeast of this district the Scotch Lanark settlement continued to expand and this widened the hinterland of Kingston. Farther to the west, in Hastings County, the building of a road to the iron deposits near Marmora and Madoc resulted in a slightly larger population in these townships (fig. 7). In general, however, the population density decreased rapidly as one approached the Shield.

In 1830, this Quinte district was still the most populous and most improved of the province (110, I/75). The area continued to receive a large number of immigrants, but as early as 1833 it was noticed that there was a relative decline in comparison with the numbers that went farther west (10/113).

The Otonabee Area

By 1850, the pioneers of the Rice Lake-Otonabee district also had reached the Canadian Shield. Before 1825, settlement remained relatively unimportant in the townships north of Rice Lake (p. 32). This changed when, in the autumn of 1825, more than 2,000 Irish settlers under Peter Robinson arrived at Cobourg. They built a road to Rice Lake, and went by boat across that lake and up the Otonabee River, where at the head of navigation headquarters and storehouses were established on the site of present-day Peterborough. The settlers took up land on the intensely drumlinized till plains of Emily, Ennismore, Smith, Douro, Asphodel, and Otonabee Townships.

The new immigrants were given food, cattle, tools, seeds, and other supplies. The government erected mills at Peterborough which became the main supply and administrative centre for the townships between Rice Lake and the Kawartha's.

The settlement of the Irish immigrants was very successful. Later, many others came; they all went first to Peterborough and from there selected their location. The immigration to, and settlement of, the surrounding districts remained the most important factors in the growth of Peterborough until 1840, when gradually the lumber industry became more significant. In the early thirties a substantial bridge was built across the river. This increased the town's importance as a regional centre.

To the north, the Kawartha Lakes attracted many settlers as it was generally expected that these lakes would develop into a great waterway suitable for the movement of goods in large quantities and have strategic value (154/11; 10/154-155).

As early as 1822, the government had located a number of settlers on the portage which struck from Peterborough northwestward to Chemung Lake (124/159). To the east, the Otonabee area gradually merged with the Quinte district. Settlement southeast and east of Rice Lake was rather slow, because almost till the end of the period, the settlers continued to shun the open oak plains (113). Furthermore, in those townships large blocks of land were held by absentees. These conditions account for the low density of population in this district, and seriously limited growth of the energetic town of Cobourg.

The Scugog Area

The Scugog area, centring on the lake and river of the same name, had remained unaffected by settlement in the years before 1820. Prior to 1830 there was practically no settlement in Darlington and Clarke except near the shore of Lake Ontario (258/33; fig. 4). In general, the settlement of the till plain in this area was the result of a pincer movement; the range of townships north of Lake Scugog was occupied by settlers coming from both the east and west. The settlers from the east came from Port Hope and Cobourg, either by a trail north-northwest through Cavan past Rice Lake and Peterborough or by the Kawartha Lakes. The western settlers came either from Newmarket overland through Brock Township or across Lake Simcoe and through Beaverton. Newmarket and Beaverton were the original supply centres. Newmarket eventually lost this function to other centres farther east. Lindsay started relatively late and did not gain much importance until the early forties.

Unlike the Otonabee area around Peterborough, the Scugog district was settled from the periphery. Consequently, Lindsay never played such a leading part in the settlement of its future umland as did Peterborough.

The island in Lake Scugog and the two townships east of the lake did not receive settlers until the late thirties and early forties, when a plank road made movement easier from Lake Ontario to Lake Scugog over the difficult morainic terrain, and when the clearing of the pine stands on the Interlobate Moraine approached these townships from the east.

The late settlement of this district and the morainic ridge account for the steep gradient in population density south of Lake Scugog on map 6. The opening up of the Scugog area was of vital importance to the ports of Whitby, Oshawa and Bowmanville.

The Yonge Street section

In contrast to the Quinte area, the Yonge Street section expanded considerably in area, particularly to the north and northwest. By 1850, the lower townships of this section had reached the greatest population densities in the region. Between 1823 and 1833, the Midland administrative division, which mainly consisted of the Bay of Quinte area, had a population increase of 53 per cent, but the Home district, the administrative division which included the Yonge Street area, increased by 187 per cent. Until the late thirties, the population increase in this district took more the form of a territorial expansion than of an increase in population density. As late as 1830, the population densities of the Yonge Street townships were still compartively low, but during the last decade of this period conditions changed rapidly. The population increased to the extent that by 1850 a broad belt with densities of more than 60 persons per square mile fringed Lake Ontario. In this district was the capital of the province, and many immigrants arrived here and decided to settle nearby. About 21,000 persons came to Upper Canada in 1833, and it was estimated that one-third of them landed at York and another one-third at the ports at the head of the lake (163/165).

In the forties, large numbers also came to the Yonge Street area (159). Here the best roads were to be found. The first and second row of townships along Lake Ontario had gravelled or macadamized roads linking them with the lake and Toronto. In contrast to this, settlement of the more inland townships was often retarded on account of lack of accessibility.

To the north, settlement gradually enveloped Lake Simcoe, because water transportation stimulated the opening up of the shore townships. By 1850 the lake was virtually surrounded by a zone in which population densities were ten or more persons per square mile.

The Penetanguishene road had attracted settlement to the northwest, but the population in the Georgian Bay townships remained small owing to the lack of good roads (130/81).

By 1850, there were, in addition to the old service centre of Newmarket, three supply bases in the Lake Simcoe area: Bradford, Barrie, and Beaverton. Bradford, situated on the deeper west branch of the Holland River, replaced Holland Landing and become the point of transfer between the traffic on Yonge Street and Lake Simcoe. On the west side of the lake, Barrie became the main base for supplies, the county town for the new county of Simcoe in 1843, and soon the main centre for the district. Beaverton, on the east shore of the lake, was a small supply base and gateway to the northern part of the Scugog district. Its growth, however, was handicapped by a poor harbour. Its functions as gateway and centre of supply were shared with Cannington, which was at the end of the overland route from Yonge Street. This, perhaps, contributed to the fact that on the east shore of Lake Simcoe no town developed comparable to either Barrie or Orillia. To a small degree Orillia at the northern end played a similar role at that time to the three supply bases in the Lake Simcoe area.

There were, before 1850, no settlements of any importance on the shores of Georgian Bay. In the thirties the Hurontario Road had been surveyed and laid out from Port Credit in a northwestern direction to Georgian Bay. The road attracted settlers, so that by 1850 the township at its northern terminus had a more dense population than the other townships on the Bay. However, the development of Simcoe County in general remained slow, because as late as 1854 more than half the land of the county was still in the hands of speculators (292/64).

Guelph

Quite in contrast with the slow growth of Simcoe County was the use made of the unsettled lands in the western part of Southern Ontario. The Canada Company established its headquarters in the Township of Guelph, and in 1827, it founded a small settlement of the same name at the confluence of two streams, near an excellent waterpower site and at the head of navigation. The beginning of Guelph is analogous to that of Peterborough; it grew as a small capital for the Canada Company and was strategically located between the large Huron Tract and the capital of the province. It was from this point that the settlement of the Huron Tract was directed. In 1832 Guelph already had 700 to 800 inhabitants, and a road had been built from it to the head of Lake Ontario. The rapid settlement of Guelph Township and the growth of the small town encouraged expansion in the interior townships to the east of Guelph, and thus contributed to the growth of the future hinterland of Toronto.

Such was the expansion of settlement before 1850. By that year settlers had penetrated South-Central Ontario as far as the Canadian Shield, although population densities in the northern fringe of townships were still low. Accessibility continued to be the main factor influencing the expansion of the pre-1820 settlement districts, and it largely determined the trend of the isopleths on the population maps for 1830 and 1851. Accessibility in turn was closely linked with the basic pattern of the distribution of land and water. This was particularly true for the Yonge Street area, where Toronto and Yonge Street had been established on the most important portage route between the Upper and Lower Lakes. It also played a dominant part in the early development of the Otonabee district.

The Transportation Network

Between 1820 and 1850, the transportation system of the province underwent considerable changes and many improvements were effected, yet by and large it remained inadequate. Its influence upon, and control over the expansion of settlement has already been discussed. However, the effect of the transport system upon the general economic and urban development of the region is so great that a more detailed discussion of it is warranted.

Road conditions and travelling

The conditions of the roads varied considerably, but in general they were poor, and for several months each year most of them were impassable. Road building in Ontario was difficult. The climate was severe and the frost penetrated deeply into the soil, causing much damage. The forests had to be cleared and many swamps had to be traversed, and the population was small and widely scattered. In the early forties, the forest still dominated the landscape. Even in the older settlements, the edge of the forest was usually a few hundred yards from the road (292/63). There was little capital, and funds were not available for road construction. Essentially, the problem was a typical Canadian one: the finding of the resources for the construction of roads in a sparsely populated area.

The best roads before 1850 were the graveled, macadam, and plank roads. The road between Kingston and Napanee was one of the earliest macadam roads; it was completed in 1839. Yonge Street had also been macadamized as far as Lake Simcoe. This type of roadbed was the most satisfactory, although it was said that in many places the traffic was not heavy enough to consolidate thoroughly the materials used in its construction (322).

The first plank road was built about 1836 from Toronto eastward, and soon they became quite common. This type consisted of a graded and drained roadbed covered with three inch planks laid upon scantlings. The planks rested on the soil and heaved easily in frost. These roads did not last very long and soon needed repair.

Very notorious were the corduroy roads, as may be gathered from the following description by a civil engineer: "In too many places in Canada the roads are carried over broad swamps and wide gullies, on round logs of wood, or rather trees, averaging a foot in diameter, each laid close by one another's side, and no attempt made to fill up the spaces between them. These turnpikes are fancied to resemble that famous King's cloth called corduroy, hence their name. When Dante wrote his celebrated poem the 'Inferno,' the critics blamed his muse for not selecting a proper highway to Pandemonium; but had she been aware of the nature of the corduroy species, there is no doubt but that would have been chosen, as certainly none can be more decidedly infernal!" (122, II/110). The common or graded roads were most numerous. They did not have an artificial roadbed, but were drained and had bridges across waterways; some of them ran far into the interior to places like Peterborough, Lindsay, and Owen Sound.

In general, the road conditions remained very poor until the forties. Widely travelled persons like Hall and Shireff had never encountered such poor roads as in Canada. Shireff found, in 1835, the Kingston Road east of York "worse than any yet travelled on"; the stage waggon could not cover more than an average of from two to three miles per hour (127/119). By 1850 this important east-west artery was only partially planked or macadamized. Every spring stretches of the road were virtually impassable (129, II/538; 274/67).

Consequently, the seasonal variation in overland travel, observed for the period before 1820, continued to prevail until the building of the railways around 1850. Midsummer and midwinter were still the only seasons during which one could travel with any degree of comfort. During the first season, travelling on horseback or in a light waggon was best; during the latter in a sleigh which was by far the best mode of land travel (116/54).

Almost all the heavy freight was not moved until the winter months, unless good water routes were accessible. The winter was the season when the farmers delivered their wheat. At each of the lake ports, every day a string of sleighs, perhaps a mile long, could then be seen waiting to unload (292/107).

After 1840 the transportation facilities improved considerably. Brown noticed a big increase in pleasure carriages. In 1842 Upper Canada possessed 980 of these vehicles; by 1848 the number had risen to 4,680! This rapid increase probably indicates the great improvement that had taken place in the main roads of the country (113/73, 74). In particular a substantial mileage of plank roads was built.

An important factor in the improvement of roads was the

change from statute labor, whereby the local inhabitants were responsible for the maintenance of roads, to the system of road companies which built roads and established tolls.

By 1850 the province had a highly organized system of stage-coaches. In 1837, stages ran six days a week from Toronto to Kingston, Hamilton, and Lake Simcoe. The Peterborough stage made, in 1840, three trips a week to Port Hope (337). Gradually, all the more important centres received connections.

Yet, in spite of all these improvements, waterways remained the chief means of communication before 1850. This not only led to the improvement of natural water courses and the building of canals, but also subordinated the road network as a feeder system for the water routes.

The road system

By 1850 only one road traversed the region in an east-west direction. This was the Dundas or Kingston Road. Only near Kingston and Toronto was there a good all weather road; the other sections were of poor quality. Only one daily stage ran between Kingston, Toronto, and Hamilton. The stage fare was twice as high as the fare for the steamers, which also plied daily between the three cities, calling at the main ports along the route. Steamers also left Toronto for Rochester and Oswego, and called at the various ports between Toronto and Port Hope (51). The amount of through traffic on the Kingston Road was therefore very small, and it was limited to passengers and mail. All goods were shipped by water.

Several other roads struck inland from the ports and served as feeders for the shipping on Lake Ontario. Those feeders generally were built by local initiative of citizens in the lake ports. Bitter competition prevailed among the various ports. In the east, Kingston was a focal point for feeder roads, but its sterile hinterland prevented the building of roads to the north. On the other hand, a reliance on the Rideau Canal may have made the need for feeder roads less urgent. Belleville had a more fertile hinterland and also the lure of iron ore deposits farther north, near Marmora and Madoc.

Competition between the ports of Cobourg and Port Hope for the trade of the Rice Lake-Otonabee area was very keen. In the late forties, both towns were rapidly improving their communications with the interior townships. The citizens of Cobourg displayed particular initiative and thrift. The immediate hinterland of the town, however, was limited owing to the late settlement of the oak plains. Port Hope has an easier access to Rice Lake, as the height of the intervening land is more than 200 feet lower. Port Hope could also expand its trading sphere in a northwestern direction to Lindsay and beyond. There was not much difference between the harbours of the two towns (328).

Farther west, there was a strong competition among Bowmanville, Oshawa, and Whitby. There, three ports tried to tap the trade of the Scugog district. Whitby was the most successful, as it possessed one of the best and most secure harbours on the north side of the lake. By 1850 a plank road led from Whitby to Port Perry on Lake Scugog and from there an ordinary road continued to Lake Simcoe. A steamer plied between Port Perry and Lindsay. Oshawa's communications with the interior were not as good as those of Whitby. In contrast to Whitby, however, it had waterpower facilities and its mill served a wide and rich district; Whitby township was reckoned to be the finest in the province (129, II/26). Farther to the east, Bowmanville and Newcastle also had feeders striking out inland, but their road connections were inferior to those of Oshawa and Whitby.

Around the middle of the century, Toronto had become the most important road centre. Here, feeders had been pushed in northeastern and northwestern directions. Most important, however, remained Yonge Street, which was in good condition as far as Bradford. From that point steamers plied between the various ports on Lake Simcoe. The road to Penetanguishene was still of poor quality and it remained of little value until 1847 (207/516). From Barrie, at the head of the Kempenfelt Bay, a shorter portage route led to the Nottawasaga River, and plans existed for a canal through the flat floored valley between the basin of Lake Simcoe and that of the Nottawasaga River.

To the west of Toronto, Port Credit, Oakville, and Dundas had the best road communications with the inland townships. A few common roads extended as far as Georgian Bay. The harbours on the north shore, west of Toronto, were poor, but the hinterland was rich, and artificial ports had been established. A company opened the harbour of Oakville in 1830, and around 1850 a plank road was built inland. There were plans to extend this plank road in the direction of Owen Sound in competition with similar roads from Fergus and Elora.

Dundas, at the head of the lake, was an old supply centre with excellent waterpower facilities. Even before 1820 it had a road connection with the Middle Grand settlements. Two good roads led from Dundas to the rapidly growing town of Guelph.

Thus the road network reflected the fact that transportation by water was the most important means of communication. Goods from the inland townships were sent to the nearest possible landing place to be forwarded by boat.

Canals

The importance of water transportation gave birth to various canal projects, such as the Welland Canal, the St. Lawrence Canals, the Rideau Canal and the Trent System. Only the last two are largely within the region.

The Rideau Canal contributed during a few decades to the growth of Kingston, because it opened up the hinterland of this city, particularly for logging operations. The canal was built by the British government for military reasons in order to establish a less exposed water connection via the Ottawa River with Montreal. It consisted mainly of the Cataraqui and Rideau rivers, which were made navigable by the building of 20 dams and 47 locks. The system was about 132 miles long and only 5 feet deep; it was completed in 1834. The canal was never used to any great extent for trade, because it followed a roundabout course and was much longer than by way of the St. Lawrence. The government established blockhouses along the canal and settled many groups nearby in order to strengthen its defence. For some time it carried a large amount of lumber, which was exported through Kingston.

The building of the Trent Canal to link the head of the Bay of Quinte and Georgian Bay via a system of rivers, lakes, and short canals was the result of the old concept of establishing a direct communication between the Upper and Lower Lakes. Despite the building of the Welland Canal, this project was kept alive until well into the 19th century. About 1820 the system was proposed by the Imperial Government as a colonization and military route, but the first work in the project was not completed until 1835, when the canals and locks at Bobcaygeon were ready. In the following years, other locks were finished and in the forties, timber slides were built in the Trent River between Rice Lake and Trenton. For a time, the government seemed to be more interested in the shipment of timber than in navigation. The work proceeded by fits and starts during the 19th century. In the 1860's a large timber slide was built at

Fenelon Falls. After 1880, there was a revival of the canal project and a few locks were built. In 1906, the Kawartha Lakes were connected with Lake Simcoe. The final section, that between Lake Simcoe and Georgian Bay, was completed with the building of two marine railways, which can carry vessels of fifteen tons, but as a shipping route it never gained much importance. Nowadays it is used by tourist craft. In the past, however, it carried tremendous amounts of timber, and this formed the basis for the lumber empire of Trenton.

At the head of Lake Ontario, Dundas obtained good connections with the lake through the building of two minor canals. In 1830, the first vessels passed through the Burlington Bay Canal which had been cut through the bay-head bar. Seven years later, the Desjardins Canal between Dundas and the Bay was completed, and Dundas, replacing Burlington, became an important shipping point, especially during the last decade before the building of the railways.

Such was the transportation system by 1850. The roads, canals, and lakes formed a closely integrated network, in which none was independent from the other two, but they were each others logical extensions. Later on, the relationship between the communications system and the distribution of the larger urban centres will be dealt with.

Agriculture

The products of the soil obtained through either agriculture or forestry continued to be the main source of wealth in Upper Canada. Around 1840, five of every six Canadians were engaged in one of these occupations (30/135). The demand for urban services and institutions necessarily came from the population engaged in those industries. As long as they remained in a state of self-sufficiency, urban life could not prosper.

The lakeshore townships continued to practice self-sufficient agriculture until the late thirties. This was mainly a result of the inadequate transportation system. Particularly in the remote or inaccessible districts, wheat was of little value. The pioneers near Lake Simcoe saw the value of their crops halved by the cost of transportation down Yonge Street (292/81).

Furthermore, the costs of shipping the goods to Montreal created a considerable price differential. In 1836, wheat prices in Upper Canada varied from 75 cents to 90 cents per bushel, yet in Montreal it was marketed at prices of from $1.00 to $1.50 a bushel (23, IV/590).

Thus, as a result of the deficient transportation facilities, the farmer in many townships received a low price for his product, and he was forced to practice a more or less self-sufficient type of agriculture. The improvements in the road network and the completion of the St. Lawrence canals, both of which occurred in the forties, led to notable changes for the farmer. To a greater extent he could obtain cash for his produce.

Wheat and lumber were the two important staple products. For both of them a cash payment could be obtained, and it was through them that the first accumulation of capital in the region took place. The two staples fitted very well in the pioneer economy. In many districts the lumberman preceded the farmer, and in other areas timber-making was a part-time occupation of the settler. Wheat enjoyed a favourable climate and did not require much capital investment, as labour-saving machinery was not available. Land was abundant and as soon as it was exhausted another piece could be taken. Consequently, the farmer planted wheat till he was forced to abandon it, owing to either a loss of markets, soil exhaustion, or the midge. The latter travelled up the St. Lawrence lowland and reached the Bay of Quinte in 1849.

Wheat was by no means the only crop which was cultivated, but it was the only one which could be sold. Several other crops were grown – peas, potatoes, flax, Indian corn, barley, oats, rye – but they were mainly consumed on the farm. Barley was grown for the breweries which had become very numerous by 1850. Potash continued to be an important export article till it was ousted by chemicals around mid-century.

Livestock raising remained a part of the self-sufficient economy and scarcely existed in Upper Canada in the thirties (292/126). Compared with wheat, livestock required a much higher initial investment and even near urban markets cattle raising was not profitable, because competition from the United States kept the prices low.

This staple producing economy was extremely weak. Everything depended upon Britain's willingness to give a preferential treatment to Canadian products and on the general crop conditions in that country. The British Corn Laws exerted a variable influence on the prosperity of the Canadian farmer. In the early twenties, when wheat prices in Britain were low, Canadian wheat and flour were barred. But from about 1825 on, the

Canadian products obtained good prices in the home country, and the Upper Canadian farmer was prosperous.

At the same time the Canadian market expanded. The construction crews working on the new canals and the large projects of the Canada Company offered a great demand for provisions. Finally, American competition decreased because of duties imposed on American foodstuffs destined for consumption in Canada, and also because of the rapid opening up of the western states which created an ever-growing home market for the American producer (292/45, 46). But the prosperity did not last long.

In the early thirties, Britain had a number of years with abundant crops and the Canadian farmer found himself again excluded from his traditional market. There were other markets such as the Maritimes and the British West Indies, but there American competition was strong. In 1835, a major depression hit Upper Canada and it, together with the troubled internal political conditions, brought the development of the region almost to a standstill. Durham reported in 1839, that, with the exception of the labouring class, most of the immigrants who had arrived during the last ten years were poorer than at the time of their arrival (3/132). During the late thirties, crops in Canada were scanty and it was not until 1840 that wheat was exported again to Britain in larger quantities.

The forties were plenteous years with rich crops. Britain's turn to free trade darkened the sky, but new markets were found, especially in the United States. During this decade the wheat acreage in Upper Canada increased by 400 per cent. The building of canals and roads, the easier flow of cash, the introduction of farm machinery, the steamers on Lake Otnario, new markets, all contributed to this expansion. The Toronto Board of Trade reported in 1845 that at no former period in the history of Upper Canada had the condition of the farmers been so prosperous as in that year (292/137).

By 1850, the farmer in the older townships had passed through the phase of self-sufficiency, mainly because of the improved communications. He more often received cash for his products. His greater prosperity and wealth were to be seen in the rapid succession with which various kinds of farm machinery were introduced. Thrashing machines and revolving hay rakes were in general use before 1850, and by that year many other machines had made their first appearance.

Rural Ontario had become a market for manufactured

goods and a wellspring for trade and commerce. The thirties were poor years, but the late twenties, and in particular the forties were good for the farmer and his demand for urban services increased accordingly.

Lumber Industry

When the Napoleonic wars had cut off supplies of Baltic timber, Britain became interested in the Canadian forests and gave a preferential treatment to timber imported from the North American colonies. The Ottawa Valley was the first main producing area, but soon after the disappearance of the fur trade on the St. Lawrence, in 1821, timber trading gained momentum on that river; by 1830, the lumbermen had reached the head of Lake Ontario (348/3).

The industry consisted mainly of the production of square timber for the British market. But gradually, the American market also opened up. The American side of the lakes was a hardwood region which did not yield a great deal of lumber, and with the rapid development of that country a demand for Canadian timber grew (348/89). The building of the Erie Canal and its feeder from Oswego made the American market easily accessible for Canadian lumber. The opening of the Welland Canal was another stimulus. The United States demanded mainly sawn lumber and so caused an increase in the number of sawmills in Upper Canada. Later on, when Canadian preference in the British market gradually came to an end as Britain turned to free trade, the American market began to open up, at first reluctantly and slowly, but much more rapidly after 1850. In conjunction with this change, square timber making dwindled and the sawmill began to prevail everywhere.

The Canadian timber most in demand was white pine (*pinus strobus* L), which was called the most useful timber in the world (10/275-276). The wood is light but strong and it is easily worked. It found numerous applications, from matches and venetian blinds to shipmasts, for which it was extremely suitable. The tree favours a sandy soil and Upper Canada had some exceedingly fine stands, among others in the Trent and Georgian Bay watersheds and adjacent districts.

Accessibility was also the prime factor which determined the early expansion of the lumber industry. Only the timber close to the waterways could be profitably exploited. Therefore, only the front townships could sell their lumber and increase their prosperity. The Rideau Canal district, close to Oswego and the Erie Canal system, constituted an extensive inland area from which large supplies were forwarded (348/99). The Trent system represented another gateway to the interior. By 1840, pine was shipped from as far as the head of the Kawartha Lakes, close to Lake Simcoe. The pine from the Lake Simcoe district itself was not shipped out until about ten years later, when the railways opened up the district. Much was done to improve the inadequate Trent system of lakes and canals for the floating down of the timber. Large slides were built to prevent damage to the logs. The "Big Chute," twenty miles north of Peterborough was famous (207/238). Peterborough itself prospered from 1840 on, owing to these logging operations.

Like wheat, lumber experienced considerable fluctuations in prices. For a long time wood remained a prominent item in Canadian trade, and for many a farmer logging was an additional source of cash income. In general, lumber was an important builder of large fortunes which, in turn, would become available for the broadening and expansion of the economic base of the province. Together with wheat, it was the main factor in the development of trade and manufacturing.

Manufacturing

The growth of manufacturing in Upper Canada was inevitably linked with the progress in agriculture and lumbering. The only raw materials available were those from the forest and the field. There was no other potential market for industrial goods than the predominantly rural population. As long as the farmer remained self-sufficient and as long as he did not have ample cash at his disposal, manufacturing could not flourish, and therefore could not stimulate the growth of towns.

Throughout the period between 1820 and 1830, the volume of manufacturing remained extremely small, and the goods produced were of an inferior quality. In 1833, Dunlop advised immigrants to bring with them various goods, as they were either much better or cheaper compared with those manufactured in Canada. He put clothes in general in this category and listed also cooking utensils, clocks, books, hosiery and above all, boots and shoes. Dunlop did not think highly of Canadian leather; he stated that one pair of English shoes would easily outlast three made in Canada. According to him, as a general rule, everything made of metal, such as iron parts of farming tools, should be taken along, "for iron mongery is very dear" (116/14). Several other contemporary writers state similar views.

During the entire first half of the century, farmers continued to make their own soap, candles and sugar. Spinning was largely done on the farms and many had still their own handlooms.

The *Canadian Economist* of August 8, 1846, gave a review of manufacturing in Upper and Lower Canada (10/301-302). It stated that Canada had not yet produced any manufactured goods, except potash, which were of such a quality that they could compete in foreign markets. In general, manufacturing, in the modern meaning of the word, was almost non-existent.

Throughout this period (1820-1850) manufacturing remained a village handicraft in small workshops. Closely linked with the largely self-sufficient agriculture, it partially or wholly processed materials provided by the farmers. Its services extended over relatively small areas, as the inadequate transportation network made it difficult to ship goods and raw materials, particularly flour and lumber, over long distances. Consequently, because of a limited market, the workshops did not grow into large factories. Throughout those decades, the number of employees per establishment remained small (Table I).

TABLE I – Industrial establishments and average number of workers in 1851 in South-Central Ontario

	employees per est.	establ.	number of ind. workers
Gristmills	3.5	283	990
Sawmills	2.4	756	2,570
Carding and fulling mills	1.7	56	151
Woollen factories	9.6	42	445
Distilleries	2.2	37	118
Tanneries	4.5	91	500
Foundries	14.6	34	530
Breweries	4.1	16	82
		1,315	5,386

The above table is based on the census data for mills which had sent in their returns. The census also reported the total number of mills, and these figures were used together with the average employment figures to estimate the total number of workers in each industry. This total number of industrial workers also includes the employers.

From the table it appears each mill employed in general fewer than five persons. Woollen factories and foundries showed a higher figure. If the large woollen mill in Cobourg (p. 77) were excluded from the calculations, the average employment in this group of mills would fall to 5.3. To a certain extent this is also true for the foundries. In general, this last category included the highest number of large establishments and with the exclusion of a few of the bigger employers, the average would still remain close to ten persons per foundry. The average employment as given for the breweries also is rather high, probably because only the better-established, large producers sent in their census returns.

As has been pointed out in the previous chapter, the handicrafts and workshops are closely linked with the general distribution of population. Their size is limited by the number and prosperity of the nearby inhabitants. With prosperity remaining the same, these small industrial establishments increase in proportion to the population. Essentially, they are service industries, and they follow the general spread of population. As such, they contribute little to the overall growth of population, although their presence made a district more attractive to new settlers. Also, by being concentrated at certain points, they helped the growth of small service and market centres.

According to the census of 1851, South-Central Ontario had in that year 1,500 industrial establishments. But it should be remembered that the authors of the census did not consider the industrial returns accurate. Most numerous were the sawmills and gristmills, 756 and 283 respectively for South-Central Ontario. All the other establishments were much smaller in number. The mills listed in table I constitute almost 88 per cent of the total number of industrial establishments in South-Central Ontario. The 12 per cent not included in the list included oatmeal mills (20), carriage factories (19), planing mills (11), lath factories (10), potasheries (9), cabinet factories (9), boot and shoe factories (9), and others.

It should be noted that the service industries did not increase in size with increasing population density and improved road network. The industries in York County (by 1851 the county with the densest population) had an average employment which was similar to, or even smaller than, that of the entire region. The presence of Toronto did not have any influence on the size or number of the establishments in the county. In Toronto, only the gristmills and the foundries had an employment which was larger than the average for the region. The city had in 1851, 3 gristmills with a total of 11 employees and 5 foundries with 112 workers.

Some of the small service industries grew into larger establishments. This largely depended on the personal initiative of the owner of the workshop or mill. Personal initiative made a blacksmith shop into a foundry and the foundry into an engine and machine factory, or pushed the saw and gristmills into production for wider markets as soon as opportunities arose.

Enterprising persons established mills near favourable sites and promoted the growth of small towns around them. Salem stagnated in its growth after the sudden death of the man who was the driving force behind its industrial and commercial development (191). For a similar reason, nearby Elora lay dormant between 1833 and 1843 (191). The vision and initiative of a leading mill or store owner were of vital importance for the growth of many a small town.

As far as the use of steam power is concerned, it should be noted that its early use was not confined to the larger urban centres, where one would expect a greater accumulation of capital. The census of 1851 recorded 61 steam grist and saw-mills in South-Central Ontario. Of those, only 55 per cent were situated in the townships bordering on Lake Ontario which had 69 per cent of the places with more than 200 inhabitants in the region. On the other hand, the remaining 45 per cent of the steam mills were found in the inland townships which had only 31 per cent of the larger centres. The steam mills were not concentrated therefore, in the front townships which had most of the larger urban settlements. Such small inland centres as Bondhead, Holland Landing, Richmond Hill, Prince Albert and Bridgenorth (on Chemung Lake) had steam mills. In part, this was a result of the presence of cheap fuel.

However, the small service industries were not the only ones which could be found in South-Central Ontario in 1850. It has been noted earlier that already before 1820 a few larger establishments existed (p. 52). Gradually the conditions for the rise of larger plants improved. Agriculture and lumbering began to provide important raw materials. Labourers could be drawn from the immigrants which arrived in ever increasing numbers. Many of them were skilled craftsmen, such as British textile workers. Finally, the home market began to expand as the province was opened up and cash payments began to prevail.

At first, the home market was rather isolated from the outside world by the St. Lawrence barrier. The high costs of imported goods, owing to the long distance and transportation difficulties, justified the manufacturing of goods in Ontario itself. Isolation tended to encourage industrial growth. But this did not last very long. As the communication system between Upper Canada and the outside world improved, it became easier for British and foreign goods to enter the Ontario market and compete with local manufacturing. As early as the early forties, Smith pointed out how dominant British imports were. He wrote that business of every kind was carried on extensively in Canada, and that most articles were as cheap here as in England, with merely the addition of the transportation costs. On many articles the duty was lower than in England and, therefore, they were cheaper in Canada. He mentions that one wholesale house alone was understood to have imported goods during the season of 1844 to the amount of £210,000 (130/251).

This meant severe competition for the rising manufacturing industries in Ontario, but in spite of this, several larger plants were established, also in South-Central Ontario. Their number, however, remained small before 1850. A paper mill was established in Belleville in 1831. Two years later, it was reported that Toronto had an elaborate engine works operated by steam power. It employed about 80 men and produced steam engines (10/296-297). At about the same time, another plant in Toronto manufactured "substantial and beautiful" carriages which were said to be equal to those built in London (10/299).

Several times attempts were made to establish an iron industry near the ore deposits at Marmora, about 30 miles north of Trenton. But the attempts were not successful, even though the government placed large orders to promote the industry. The high costs of transportation, the inefficiency of the production, and competition and lower prices in the market caused all undertakings to fail (284/53).

The woollen industry was more successful. Gradually more sheep were raised, and several small woollen mills were established. Some grew into important plants, such as the one in Cobourg which employed about 170 persons (31). It seems that some very good textiles were produced in Ontario in the forties. In the first provincial exhibition in 1846, tweeds, blankets, flannel, and other materials were shown, which were said to be equal to any imported products (230/634). Undoubtedly, skilled immigrant labour had contributed considerably towards this success.

The census of 1851 also mentions the existence of some large foundries; Dundas possessed two, one with 120 employees and another with 30. Kingston had at least four establishments – machinery and shipbuilding – employing between 20 and 50 persons.

As far as town growth is concerned, the large manufacturing establishments were of far greater importance than the service industries. Unlike the service industries, the larger plants caused the population to increase as they enlarged the opportunity for employment. Therefore, they may be called propelling industries. The service industries follow population increase, but the founding of propelling industries stimulates population growth. Propelling industries may be established in sparsely populated or unpopulated areas and their existence will result in an increase in population. An example of such a propelling industry is the establishment of an aluminium industry at Kitimat in British Columbia.

Unlike the service industries, propelling industries produce for a wide – provincial, national or international – market. To a certain extent, they may be considered as "exporters," because they bring money from the outside into the district in which they are located. Service industries, on the other hand, do not increase the volume of money in the area over which they extend their services (347).

Often, however, a service industry became propelling. A local sawmill began to cut for the American market; a small flour mill turned to the production of flour for the British consumer; a local tannery grew into a leather and shoe factory selling its products Ontario wide. Most of the agricultural implement factories, later on in the century, began as small local blacksmiths and repair shops.

Being essentially "exporters" it is obvious that the propelling industries preferably located in centres with good transportation facilities, especially larger centres which already had an important local market. Toronto was the most important of these, and had the additional advantage of having a class of wealthy citizens and higher government officials.

Through a lack of statistical data, it is impossible to make a sharp distinction between service and propelling industries, but industries which show a great amount of concentration in their distribution can be classified as propelling. Toronto and Kingston had the largest number of these industries.

The 1851 census reported for Toronto among others, one axe factory (38 empl.), one iron and brass factory (17 empl.), one glue and oil factory, one oil cloth factory, one patent leather factory, one mustard and spice mill, one ginger and syrup mill, one looking glass factory. Some of the more important industries in Kingston were two steam engine and machinery factories, respectively employing 20 and 50 men, one copper works (8 empl.), one iron works (22 empl.), one marine railway and shipyard (50 empl.), one match factory. Belleville, Cobourg, Streetsville, and Dundas were the other centres which had one or more large manufacturing establishments.

Toronto's industrial development by 1851 was different from the rest of South-Central Ontario only in that its industrial production displayed a greater variety. The establishments in Toronto did not have a larger average employment than those in other places.

As a whole, manufacturing remained of minor importance during this period as a factor in urban development in South-Central Ontario. In total there were about 1,500 individual manufacturing establishments in the region, according to an incomplete census. Of those, 1,315 establishments had a total of about 5,400 industrial workers. The total employment in manufacturing was probably between 6,000 and 6,500, as compared with a total population in South-Central Ontario of approximately 369,000.

The industries were largely of the service type, but propelling industries were gaining in importance. The latter grew with the improvement in the transportation network, but especially with the opening up of the home market. The service industries were not builders of large population agglomerations, but operating in unison with other services, they contributed to an urban pattern of small central places. The propelling industries were not yet important enough to cause deviations in that pattern.

Trade and Finance

Export and import trade

For Canada as a whole, lumber remained the most important export item for many years; in 1834, two-thirds of the total value of Canadian exports to Britain still consisted of lumber. But, according to Innis and Lower, grain and flour had by 1850 replaced wood in value of exports (10/274). By that time, South-Central Ontario had already received a considerable income from the shipment of wheat and flour to the United States. Calculations based on data taken from Smith's work (129) show that, in value, wheat and flour in the trade with the United States were between four and five times as large as lumber and timber. South-Central Ontario exported about 400,000 barrels of flour and close to one million bushels of wheat to that country. It is not known how much was sent to Montreal and other British ports, as those shipments were not required to be reported.

For many years, Canadian trade with the United States consisted of the sending in transit of British goods. But in the thirties, the export of Canadian lumber across Lake Ontario to the States began to gain importance. Vast quantities of lumber were being prepared in 1836 on the Ottawa River for shipment via the Rideau Canal to Oswego and New York. Also, small quantities of grain were forwarded in that direction (10/251, 252). In 1840, Oswego received 1.9 million feet of Canadian lumber; ten years later, this had increased to 60 million feet (348/101, 116).

The wheat export to the United States (292/177, 178), developed much later and suddenly became of importance during the late forties, when Canadian wheat was exported from 1847 on. American millers used Canadian wheat for blending with the poor Upper-lake wheat to make good flour. In addition, much wheat was sent in bond to New York.

Besides wheat, flour, and lumber, a variety of other products was shipped, in spite of the tariffs. Among those were livestock, meat, hides, malt, wool, shingles, staves, potatoes, rye, barley, furs, etc. Manufactured products had practically no part in the foreign trade. Cobourg exported, in 1850, hardware which was valued at £39.15.0 and there was an export of textiles from that port (p. 77). The iron manufactures shipped from Toronto were valued at £23.10.0 (64; 129).

As a result of these new trends in trade developments, the small ports along the north shore of Lake Ontario enjoyed a period of great prosperity after 1840, and grew rapidly. In 1843, Whitby exported 28,562 barrels of flour, 29,674 bushels of wheat, and 353,500 feet of lumber; in 1850 these figures were respectively 35,337, 107,101, and 1,745,004 (129). In 1850 the young port of Oakville shipped 13,430 barrels of flour,

165,839 bushels of wheat and 4,518,500 feet of pine boards.

It is not possible to obtain reliable statistics on the trade of the various ports around 1850. Smith and the Directory for 1851 (129; 64) give a few data, but they are incomplete and not given for all ports. This is also true for the statistics provided by Andrews (277) which have been given in table II. The only

TABLE II – Trade with the U.S. in 1851
Value in £ (277)

	imp. from U.S.	exp. to U.S.
Kingston	743,232	421,016
Bath	9,384	21,428
Napanee	22,120	43,196
Belleville	98,524	147,368
Trenton	—	—
Picton	42,732	17,808
Milford	1,584	10,480
Wellington	2,352	22,884
Colborne	7,496	944
Grafton	—	3,992
Cobourg	125,464	71,612
Port Hope	71,728	100,408
Bondhead	—	—
Newcastle	3,928	—
Darlington	14,676	29,960
Oshawa	—	—
Whitby	26,456	201,164
Toronto	1,525,620	327,368
Port Credit	8,556	181,268
Oakville	40,760	122,880
Port Nelson	—	—
Burlington	—	—
Dundas	—	—
Penetanguishene	252	3,736
Sutton	3,984	—

merit of the table is that it generally indicates the relative importance of the various ports, although no figures are given for such an important lumber port as Trenton.

The biggest exporter in South-Central Ontario was still Kingston (trans-shipment trade), followed by Toronto, Whitby, Port Credit, Belleville, Oakville, and Port Hope. Wheat, flour, and lumber were by far the most important goods exported. The largest wheat ports were Oakville, Toronto, Whitby, and Port Credit. Kingston, Belleville, and Trenton were the busiest lumber ports.

The import trade from the United States was very different. The commercial interests in Canada were always in favour of free import of American goods in order to attract American exports, especially from the western states, to the St. Lawrence system. This free trade had come to an end in 1822, when the Canada Trade Act imposed duties on American products. But the Colonial Trade Act of 1831 reversed this policy, and the duties were repealed. It was hoped that the grain trade of the western states would be channeled into the St. Lawrence and thus increase the commercial activity in Canada.

American wheat milled in Canada could be imported in Britain as Canadian flour and enjoy the same preferential treatment. This stimulated the Canadian milling industry, particularly in the early forties, when colonial wheat obtained easy access to the British market. The forwarding trade and the milling industries in the lake ports prospered and many large mills were erected. Unfortunately, this lasted only a few years, because in 1846 Britain repealed the Corn Laws; the short boom period came to a sudden and unforseen end. Property values in the mill ports fell as much as 50 per cent between 1845 and 1848. In some of these towns 75 per cent of the businessmen became insolvent (30/137).

Besides agricultural produce, other American products gradually invaded the Upper Canadian market. In 1839, the *Montreal Gazette* wrote that certain American textiles had entirely superseded imports from England. It said that American iron tools completely superseded Birmingham and Sheffield goods. The American tools were better and cheaper (10/243, 244).

Concentration of trade

Unlike the export trade which was shared by a great number of ports, the import trade was channelled into the two main ports, Toronto and Kingston. They ranked far above the other ports of South-Central Ontario (table II). Toronto had, by 1851, already established itself as the main distributing point. It had access to the most densely populated districts of the region, and from Toronto steamers sailed to all other ports on the lake. Ports such as Port Credit, Oakville, and Whitby were among the most important exporters, but their proximity to Toronto kept their import trade relatively low. Foreign goods reached them via Toronto importers and wholesalers. With increasing distance from Toronto, the import trade of the ports became relatively more important. Port Hope had a much more favourable ratio between import and export, while Cobourg had an exceptionally high import trade compared with its exports and such a large exporter as Whitby. Yet, it was not only distance from Toronto which gave Cobourg this special position in the import trade. Already in 1832, Picken noted: "The trade of Cobourg is increasing rapidly, more through the spirit and enterprise of its merchants, than through its natural advantages" (124/155). Farther east also a few other ports had relatively large imports compared with their export trade, especially Picton in Prince Edward County.

Importing and wholesaling began to be concentrated. There were many busy ports on the north shore of Lake Ontario, but it was much more economical if one of them would specialize in importing and would maintain relations and connections with foreign suppliers. It was only natural that this trade should concentrate in the capital, the largest city and market with the biggest banks and one of the best ports. Thus Toronto became at an early date the main wholesale centre of the region.

As far as its immediate hinterland is concerned, Toronto was not much better off than the other ports. Its hinterland was not much larger than that of Port Hope, Whitby, or Oakville. It was more intensively occupied and more densely populated, but in size it was comparable to the others. It did not extend beyond Lake Simcoe, and before 1850, practically no freight was shipped from the Upper Lakes via Yonge Street to Toronto.

From an article in a newspaper of 1835, it appears that the old concept of drawing a large volume of trade from the far west through the Upper Lakes to Toronto was still alive. It was pointed out that a substantially good road should be built and also a railroad "having for its object the rapid and cheap transit of the persons and produce of the distant countries, avoiding the delay and uncertainty of the circuitous route of Lake Huron, the St. Clair, Erie and the Welland Canal" (10/39). If this were done, it was expected that Toronto would become as important as Buffalo and would be able to compete with any city on the continent of America (10). Actually, not even the smallest trickle of trade came through to warrant these expectations. Smith reported in 1846 that it was eleven years since the collector of customs at Penetanguishene had registered an entry (130). In 1850, the total value of imports and exports handled by that port amounted to slightly more than £200 (64). The trade from which since early days so much had been expected never contributed to the growth of Toronto in the era before the building of the railways.

Toronto and Montreal

In addition to the important shifts in the external trade, which affected urban development in South-Central Ontario to such a great extent, there were also profound modifications in the pattern of trade routes, particularly in the Lake Ontario region. The importance of the powerful flow of traffic through Lake Ontario has been discussed in connection with the early rise of Kingston (p. 46). The American cities on the Atlantic Seaboard looked upon this diversion of trade from their hinterland with envious eyes and became disturbed about it (10/235). In particular New York was expanding its hinterland and a sharp competition developed between it and Montreal for the trade of the western states and Upper Canada. From the 1820's on, these two large ports struggled for the trade of Toronto which gave the latter the opportunity to gain a certain independence from both of them.

New York struck firmly with the building of the Erie Canal in 1825. As the Welland Canal was not opened until 1829, most of the trade from Lake Erie and farther west went through the new canal to the Hudson and down to New York, making Buffalo the big trans-shipment point. To what extent the trade on the St. Lawrence decreased may be gathered from the amount of customs revenue collected in the port of Quebec (10/384). In 1820, the amount of revenue collected was £95,086. The revenue increased to £127,854 in 1825, the year the Erie Canal was finished. After that, it largely remained unchanged, and by 1838, it actually had dropped to £115,956.

New York not only attracted the trade from Lake Erie but also from Lake Ontario by way of the Oswego feeder canal. This canal linked the port of Oswego on Lake Ontario with the Erie Canal and was completed in 1828. When the Welland Canal was opened, Oswego rejoiced, because as long as the St.

Lawrence canals were not built, the outlet through Oswego was highly attractive (348/100).

These changes in the flow of trade and in the transportation system had far-reaching consequences for the two largest towns of South-Central Ontario, namely Kingston and Toronto. Kingston suffered a setback through the loss of trans-shipment, although shipping together with the naval and military establishments still remained the principal support of the city (129). Toronto, on the other hand, took another step on the road to metropolitan dominance as it obtained another outlet to the ocean and became more independent from Montreal. This in turn contributed to Toronto becoming the chief city of Ontario and to its phenomal growth in this period. The American canals offered an alternative outlet to the ocean and made Toronto and Upper Canada less dependent upon Montreal. And Toronto was ready to exploit these possibilities.

Upper Canada, being an inland province, did not possess a tidewater port and was at the mercy of Montreal. The merchants of Upper Canada had no direct dealings with exporters in Britain; the Montreal merchant was the mediator and took a commission on all exports and imports to and from Upper Canada. The Montreal merchant was always the creditor, and in the eyes of the Upper Canadian his charges were too high. He was an advocate of free importation of American agricultural produce, while the Upper Canadian farmers wished tariffs imposed. As early as the 1820's, Upper Canada began to resent the monopoly enjoyed by Montreal. In 1829, an Upper Canada paper noticed with satisfaction that the country traders were importing foreign goods directly. This relieved them, it said, from the necessity and expense of the semi-yearly trips to Montreal, and eventually would "eclipse the Lower Canada Emporium" (10/244).

In 1835, merchants of Toronto met in order to consider the possibility of importing European goods through the United States (10/177, 178). Upper Canada felt it had been hampered in its development and that the merchants of Montreal had enriched themselves at the expense of Upper Canada. It did not look upon the St. Lawrence as the natural highway of the province. Many persons considered the route to New York much cheaper than that to Montreal (10). By 1850, Toronto and the other ports had begun to lure the country dealer away from Montreal. The Robert Sargant Company advertised that they imported their goods directly from the manufacturers and could thereby offer considerably lower prices to country dealers and the trade in general than any other house. A wholesale and retail confectioner offered to supply country dealers on the lowest terms (64/438, 436).

Finally, the American Drawback Act of 1846 made it possible to send Canadian goods in bond through the United States without paying duty. At the same time, the consequences of the free trade policy of Britain were felt. Lord Elgin, the governor-general, reported to the home government: "Peel's Bill of 1846 drives the whole of the produce down the New York channels of communication, destroying the revenue which Canada expected to derive from canal dues, and ruining at once mill-owners, forwarders and merchants" (30/138). By 1850, more Upper Canadian wheat and flour were being sent in bond to New York than were exported down the St. Lawrence (292/176).

The consequences of those developments were extremely damaging to Montreal. In addition to the loss of the Upper Canadian trade, the port also declined as a handler of American grain. After the repeal of the Corn Laws and without the preference, it became more economical to send American grain by way of the Erie Canal. By 1850, Montreal's hegemony over a large sector of its hinterland, including Upper Canada, had been broken. Between 1841 and 1851, the population of the city decreased by about 10,000 persons. High expectations were built on the St. Lawrence Canals, which were completed in 1849, but this was about twenty years after the opening of the Welland Canal and too late to harm New York. The western trade had become accustomed to the Erie Canal route and what was more important, New York was ready with its railway plans. The commercial interests of Toronto were pleased to see the monopoly of Montreal being broken and readied themselves to strike at the financial hegemony of that city.

From barter trade to banks

The lack of currency and the accompanying system of trade by barter was, in the period before 1820, one of the main factors limiting the growth of towns in that period. The demand for urban services was extremely small. But the expansion of the export trade and the general improvement of the economic conditions in the forties changed all this. The flow of money began to increase and towns and cities began to prosper. In the twenties, the settlers still handled little cash. A new hat shop was opened on King Street in the capital of Toronto in 1826, and in an advertisement the proprietor offered his goods "either for cash, or for the following articles of country produce – whiskey, flour, pork, beef, pot and pearl ashes" (229, I/503). As late as 1842, wheat was considered as cash in Toronto to pay for groceries and other products (12, II/245). From the directory of 1851 (51), it appears, however, that cash sales were then the rule in Toronto. There may have been exceptions, as some merchants found it necessary to mention in their advertisements that all their dealings were in cash.

In the ports on the lake in general, wheat merchants had paid cash since the late twenties, and by 1850 cash was paid for all sorts of produce. This was also true for an inland town such as Guelph. But in the interior townships, the barter trade probably continued to be common: In Peterborough there were, in 1851, at least eight dealers in dry goods (51). Six of them certainly, and possibly all eight, dealt also in country produce, while none of them mentioned cash payments, in contrast to similar merchants in Port Hope and Cobourg. In Guelph, a dealer in groceries, china and glass took country produce in exchange at market prices.

Throughout the first half of the 19th century, the scarcity of money was a general complaint. All imported American goods had to be paid for in cash. The United States had an abundance of foodstuffs of her own and could not take Canadian produce in exchange (10/257, 258). But the only way that Upper Canada could obtain cash was through the sale of its flour and lumber, through the execution of public works, such as the building of canals, and from what immigrants transferred to the country. In 1831/32 new arrivals deposited not less than £300,000 in the Bank of Upper Canada (286). This is a considerable amount, if one remembers that in 1819 it had been impossible to raise £20,000 when the bank was founded.

In the later thirties the Upper Canadian pine forests started to attract American capital (10/253), and in the forties cash began to flow more abundantly than ever before. Exports were resumed and also the American market opened up for Canadian produce.

Trade in general showed very little specialization and the barter system as a whole had a very injurious effect upon the economic development of the country. The country merchants dealt in almost everything which was produced or needed in the townships; they had to handle and ship products with which they were not very familiar or which they could not take care of properly. Flour often turned sour through improper packing, and "Canadian Sour" was a common product on the British markets (131/85). Thus, the barter system even reduced the possible flow of cash into the country.

The developments in the field of banking are a good indicator of the rise of Toronto over its rivals in Upper Canada and its growing independence of Montreal. Through doubtful means Toronto had become the exclusive banking centre of the province with the founding of the Bank of Upper Canada. The close relationship between the bank and the government, both being run by the Family Compact, enhanced the credit of the bank considerably. It handled all the financial business for the Upper Canada government. By means of its close ties with the government, the Bank of Upper Canada succeeded in blocking the establishment of other banks till as late as 1832 (286).

The prosperous years from 1828 to 1832, however, saw the rise of plans for several new banks, and one of them was successful; the financial interests of Kingston obtained a charter for their Commercial Bank in 1831. It revealed the influence and commercial strength of that city particularly, because by 1835, the capital of the Commercial Bank was of the same size as that of the Bank of Upper Canada. In the late thirties several new bank charters were granted, and by 1850 all places of some importance in South-Central Ontario had banking facilities. The monopoly of the Bank of Upper Canada had been broken, but in 1833 it secured the Upper Canada share of the financial affairs of the British government, and succeeded in breaking this monopoly of the Bank of Montreal (23, IV/627). The Bank of Upper Canada owed this success largely to its political influence with the home government. The Family Compact continued to build up Toronto's financial strength as much as possible. Yet, in the country as a whole, Montreal remained financially the most important centre. It was not until the 1860's that in financial affairs a more nearly equal balance was established between the two rivalling cities.

Urban Centres in 1851

Various considerations led to the selection of 1851 as the year for which the urban development should be analyzed. In this year, the first Upper Canadian Census was published and also Smith's *Canada, "Past, Present and Future,"* two sources which made it largely possible to obtain uniform data concerning the various settlements; together with other sources they provided the material for the construction of the maps (fig. 7, 8). The year 1851 also marks the end of a period in the development of transportation, as it falls just before the building of the first railways in South-Central Ontario; it exhibits an urban pattern which had grown in close relationship to a communication system depending on water and roads. From the point of view of economic development, the pioneer period with its self-sufficient economy was drawing rapidly to a close, as agriculture had started to become more mechanized. The development of trade and finance underwent considerable change during the forties, particularly as a result of easier access to the American market. The middle of the century finally witnessed the beginning of a more ample flow of capital, the shortage of which so seriously had hampered the general development of the region. Some of these changes had already started in the early forties, while others did not become fully effective before the late fifties. Urban growth, however, is the result of the combined influence of those changing factors, and thus the year 1850 appears to be best suited for making an inventory of urban growth.

Growth and distribution of urban centres

The total urban population in 1851 was still small. In all of Canada, 15.0 per cent of the population lived in incorporated places. For Ontario, the percentage was approximately the same – 16.2 per cent. The counties in South-Central Ontario, however, displayed considerable diversity. Counties such as Dufferin, Halton, Lennox and Addington, Peel, and Victoria possessed no incorporated places at all. York County, on the other hand, had an urban population of 61.2 per cent.

The two largest cities were Toronto and Kingston with, respectively, 30,775 and 11,585 inhabitants. (Outside South-Central Ontario there was only one large city of similar size, namely Hamilton (14,112). At that time, Ottawa had 7,760 and London 7,035 inhabitants.) The region did not have centres in the population range of 5,000 to 10,000, and only five were in the category of 2,000 to 5,000. These were Belleville, Cobourg, Dundas, Port Hope, and Peterborough. Table III gives the population figures of the larger urban centres for the years 1830 and 1851.

In total, South-Central Ontario in 1851 numbered twenty-four places with 500 or more inhabitants. Of this total, seventeen were on or near Lake Ontario and had easy access to lake shipping. But the remaining seven also had relatively good connections with the lake. Peterborough was at the head of navigation on the Otonabee River and profited from roads from Rice Lake to Port Hope and Cobourg. Barrie, Bradford, and Newmarket had easy access to Yonge Street and Toronto Harbour. Also, Streetsville, Georgetown, and Guelph had good road connections with Lake Ontario ports. The same was true for the expansion of settlement in general, as transportation possibilities or accessibility was one of the main factors in urban development during the first half of the century.

The development of this urban pattern had been extremely slow. Accurate statistics on the size of the various centres in the decades before 1850 are difficult to gather, but various contemporary writers give an account of the urban development in specific years. In 1832, the Surveyor-General Bouchette wrote that the front part of all the townships from Kingston to Toronto were, with a few exceptions, well settled, and that there were a few small villages, rather distant from each other. He listed as the most important of these Belleville, Cobourg, Port Hope, Darlington, and Whitby (110, I/86). By 1830, Kingston was still the leading city (Table III). Cobourg, the gateway to the Otonabee district, came third after Toronto.

Twenty years later, in 1851, nearly all of these places had more than doubled in population. Only Cobourg and Newmarket failed to do so; their increase was less than 100 per cent. This slower growth was mainly due to unfavourable transportation facilities. When the various ports began to build good roads inland, Cobourg was at a disadvantage compared with Port Hope. The latter could by-pass Rice Lake and grew therefore at a faster rate than Cobourg, which saw its way to the north blocked by Rice Lake. A ferry service was tried without success. Smith pointed out that the only solution for Cobourg would be to bridge the lake (129, II/209).

Newmarket had similar problems. It was located near a waterpower site on the East Branch of the Holland River, about four miles from the head of navigation at Holland Landing. When shipping on Lake Simcoe increased, the point of transshipment moved from Holland Landing to the Yonge Street crossing of the deeper and straighter West Branch of the river; and Newmarket became more isolated. It also must have suffered because it was a mile to the east of Yonge Street. The result was that Newmarket grew rather slowly between 1830 and 1850, while Holland Landing lost its initial impetus, and

TABLE III – Urban centres in 1830 and 1851

	1830	1851
Toronto	2,900	30,775*
Kingston	3,800	11,585*
Belleville	1,500	4,569*
Cobourg	2,000	3,871*
Dundas	1,000	2,500
Port Hope	1,000	2,476
Peterborough	500	2,191*
Yorkville	—	2,000
Guelph	450	1,860*
Bowmanville	—	1,650
Picton	500	1,569*
Oshawa	500	1,142
Whitby	500	1,100
Napanee	—	1,000
Trenton	—	950
Barrie	—	800*
Newmarket	500	800
Streetsville	—	750
Oakville	—	700
Bath	—	700
Georgetown	—	650
Colborne	—	650
Bradford	—	600
Newcastle	—	600

The places marked with * were administration centres in 1851. The figures have been obtained from a number of different sources. In cases of discrepancies, the average was taken or the most reliable source was used.

Bradford rose rapidly. Newmarket increased its population by about 60 per cent during those two decades, but Bradford developed from a single tavern in 1829 to a prosperous village with 600 inhabitants around mid-century.

Administrative and other service functions

A few places displayed an exceptionally rapid increase in population. Toronto had in 1851 ten times its 1830 population, and during the same period, the population of Peterborough and Guelph more than quadrupled. The growth of those towns illustrates well that with the establishment of new settlements, the centre which starts first and which becomes a regional focus grows most successfully. Toronto, Peterborough, and Guelph were established as regional centres at a time when the area around them was virtually unpopulated. Peterborough was selected as the headquarters for the Otonabee district, Guelph for the activities of the Canada Land Company, and Toronto, not only as headquarters for the Yonge Street section, but also as the capital for a newly-formed province. Their administrative functions made them the centre of interests, and as such they attracted the more ambitious and more enterprising elements from their region, and, in the case of Toronto, from the entire province. Other centres also saw their growth stimulated by the presence of the administrative offices for the district in which they were located (Table III).

In the early forties, the district town Picton, in Prince Edward District, had the following government and district offices: Judge of District Court, Sheriff, Clerk of Peace, Treasurer, Inspector of Licenses, Collector of Customs, Crown Lands Agent, District Clerk, Clerk of District Court, Deputy Clerk of Crown, and Superintendent of Schools (130). These offices drew the population of the district to the centre, and therefore stimulated its commercial and social development. As soon as a place had been selected to be the capital for a county or larger unit, it began to flourish.

Kingston is a case in point. In 1841, this city became the capital of the united provinces of Upper and Lower Canada. The city expanded rapidly, but when, three years later, the seat of government was removed to Montreal, Kingston lost about 1,700 inhabitants (113/160; 129).

The location of the county seat had similar effects, although on a smaller scale. When the county town for Wentworth was expected to be established at Crook's Hollow, trade and immigration expanded and the surrounding country was settled rapidly. A number of valuable mills were erected and the small settlement of Greensville sprang up (87). Holland Landing was the capital of Simcoe County from 1821 to 1837. It was there that the elections took place, the registrar of lands had his office, and all official business was transacted (213, II/1). In 1837, Barrie became the county capital.

In addition to the actual administrative function, there was also the "gateway" or "supply base" function. This played a part in the rise of a large number of places, although they never became an official administrative centre. The immigrant settlers came from countries with a well developed urban tradition. From the very beginning, they felt, in spite of their self-sufficient economy, the need for a minimum amount of urban services and institutions. The result was that a point with favourable transportation facilities became a base which served as a gateway and supply centre for the tract of land being settled. Bradford, Newmarket, Orillia, Beaverton, and Cannington were such bases in the Lake Simcoe area. Others were Port Hope, Newcastle, Bowmanville, Oshawa, Whitby, Port Credit, Oakville, and Dundas.

The transportational framework was the most important factor in the founding of these administrative centres and "gateway towns." It also was the main factor in their subsequent rise as small regional service centres. They became central places and the services they provided – administrative, transportational, commercial, social, etc. – were focussed upon the demands of the population in their respective umlands. The prosperity and growth of these service centres were entirely dependent upon the economic development of the region. Thus we see that many places grew rapidly after the middle thirties, when profound changes began to develop in transportation, agriculture, manufacturing, and trade.

This is best illustrated by the growth and expansion of Toronto, which during those decades still served only Southern Ontario, and thus reflects the general unfolding and opening up of the region.

Toronto

Toronto grew rapidly during this period. In 1830, its population probably amounted to 2,900; by 1851, it had increased to 30,775.

It is of interest to follow the metamorphosis of the city during those decades by quoting the accounts of a few contemporary writers. Howison wrote in 1825: "The town in which there are some good houses, contains about 3,000 inhabitants. There is but little land cleared in its immediate vicinity, and this circumstance increases the natural unpleasantness of its situation. The trade of York is very trifling; it owes its present population and magnitude entirely to its being the seat of government; for it is destitute of every natural advantage except that of a good harbour" (121/70).

Galt, the sponsor and administrator of the Canada Land Company, emphasized the unpleasantness and called York in 1828 "one of the vilest hypochondriac places on the face of the earth" (198/94). However in the thirties, the population increased rapidly, due to large scale immigration. York became the city of Toronto in 1834 and had more than 9,000 inhabitants. The city gained much economic strength during these years and its commerce became more important than its function as a capital. ". . . the seat of government was moved to Kingston in 1841 . . . . Had this event taken place ten years sooner, it might have had a serious effect upon the prosperity of the town, but in 1841 Toronto had become a place of too great a commercial importance to feel much ill effect from the removal of the government offices, and the loss of the expenditure of a few thousand pounds per annum" wrote Smith in 1845 (130/193).

The appearance of the city changed considerably during these years. Bonnycastle wrote in 1841: "I was greatly surprised and very much pleased to see such an alteration as Toronto has undergone for the better since 1837 . . . a city in earnest . . . gaslit, with good plank side walks and macadamized streets, with cast sewers and fine houses of brick or stone. . . ." (109, I/107, 108).

Waterpower

In the location and growth of a great number of urban centres, waterpower facilities played an essential part. A good mill site was a focal point in newly-opened districts, for it provided essential services. It was frequented by the farmers of the surrounding countryside and as such it was a favourable site for the location of other services. Often farmers had to wait a few days before their grain could be milled, especially during busy periods, and hotels and inns were built to accommodate them. Other services were soon added: a store, a tavern, a tannery, a waggonmaker, a physician, etc. Such a centre was also the most suitable location for churches (of which there were a great number) and schools.

Yet, waterpower was not essential for the rise of towns; actually, it was of less importance than transportation facilities. Toronto and Kingston, the two largest towns, grew without the advantages of abundant waterpower. Many of the smaller centres also developed distant from mill sites. Accessibility and roads were more important for them. There were several water-power sites in the Richmond Hill area, but the village of that name rose on Yonge Street without the benefits of a mill site (p. 96). Grafton, seven miles east of Cobourg, had at least nine mills within a radius of seven miles (51); yet none of those sites developed into a village comparable to Grafton, which was on the Kingston Road and had a small port on the lake. Agglomerated urban settlement could develop without the benefit of waterpower, but not without good road communications.

This is evidenced by the existence of numerous cross-road villages. As the name implies, those centres did not develop near waterpower sites, but at road intersections. They comprised a number of stores, a tavern, churches, a school, artisan shops, etc., but no factories on account of the lack of waterpower. In general the cross-road villages remained smaller in size than the mill villages. However, one has to be careful in ascribing this to a lack of waterpower. A late start is probably a more valid reason. The mill villages sprang up early, in general at the time of, or soon after, the beginning of settlement in a district; they were a focal point from the very beginning.

The cross-road villages, on the other hand, grew out of the needs of the population, when settlement had already reached a certain density, and traffic had developed. Cross-road villages, therefore, had a late start and as soon as the transportation facilities improved they were the first to be by-passed, as the customer preferred the better facilities or wider choice to be found in the older and larger mill villages.

Central places

The urban pattern of 1851 consisted of a large number of small service centres or central places whose growth was determined largely by transportation facilities, population density and waterpower resources. These centres were focal points for trade and transportation, for workshop manufacturing, and a variety of other services. These towns and villages were predominantly non-rural settlements, as the active farm population in them was always very small. A large number of these centres were never incorporated, and there is no information about them in the censuses. Even their population is unknown, it being merged with that of the townships. To overcome this difficulty, a classification of the centres, both incorporated and non-incorporated, was developed for this and following periods. The basis of the classification is the selection of certain key-services (351).

The number of key-services which can be used as an indicator is rather limited owing to a lack of reliable data uniformly available for all centres. Thus, it was not possible to take mills or other manufacturing establishments as a basis for the classification. The sources are not accurate as to the number of mills in each locality. Especially for the unincorporated places it is difficult to determine whether the establishments are in the settlement or not. The Directory for 1851/52 lists for Richmond Hill twelve saw and gristmills, but all of them were outside the village proper.

Services to be taken as criteria had to be located within the settlement, and information had to be available uniformly for all places. It was also desirable to have indicators which could be used for the compilation of maps for later years so that better comparison would be possible. Similar considerations were adhered to when data were collected for the maps of 1881, 1911, and 1951.

The indicators finally chosen for 1851 were carefully selected from a total of 21 professions and establishments for the presence of which the places had been investigated. As professions, the legal and medical ones – attorneys, barristers, notaries public, physicians and surgeons – were considered most suitable. Other professions were often practised in conjunction with something else, but only the main profession would be listed. The legal and medical professions, however, had to be properly trained and licensed and are in general listed accurately. They were widely distributed and their presence in a place is a good indicator of its status.

In addition, banks and newspapers were selected as criteria. They also were widely distributed and information on them in general is accurate, often in special lists. The Directory for 1851/52 (51) was the main source for these criteria.

It was not possible to use shops as indicators of the service status of the towns and villages. By and large, the shops sold a great variety of widely different goods, without being listed as dealer in such goods. Printing establishments often sold books, yet were not necessarily recorded as booksellers.

A place which listed a member each of the legal and medical profession, a bank and a newspaper is called a fully-fledged town. In case one of these indicators is missing, the place is called a sub-town. The missing one is always either the bank or the newspaper. Places which have only two of the four indicators are called urban villages. They lack generally both bank and newspaper. Finally, the places with only one indicator – nearly always a physician – are called rural villages.

In eleven cases, however, a special decision had to be made, when it was improbable that a service was missing. Then the other services offered by the place and its number of inhabitants were taken into consideration and compared with other settlements. Whitby was classified as a town although the Directory does not list a bank there. A comparison with Oshawa and a consideration of its commercial function warrants this decision. Also, when a place had between 200 and 500 inhabitants, and it did not have any of the indicators, it nevertheless was classified as a rural village. It is assumed that they had at least one of the services, e.g. a physician. There are ten of these villages.

Being essentially service centres, the places show in their distribution and number a very close relationship with the population density. The highest concentration occurs in the zone with more than forty persons per square mile, and they rapidly decrease in number when the population is less than forty persons per square mile. The self-sufficient economy with its shortage of cash reduced the need for urban services in those already sparsely populated back townships.

The places with more than a thousand inhabitants were all fully-fledged towns. Transportation, in particular, had contributed to their growth; they had the best roads. Eight of the thirteen had administrative functions. It was only natural that they would have the most diversified services; they were easily accessible and the people had to visit them for their dealings with the government. Yorkville is the only place in this category which did not become a fully-fledged town. It remained an urban village, because as a suburb of Toronto, it apparently used the banking and newspaper services of the larger centre. Barrie was the only fully-fledged town which had less than a thousand inhabitants. The administrative and transportational functions had made it the regional centre for the area between Lake Simcoe and Georgian Bay.

Port Hope may be taken as an example of the growth of a fully-fledged town. Settlement started in 1793, and in 1798 mills were erected, after which it grew as a milling and service centre. Around 1825, it possessed four general stores, two saw and gristmills, four distilleries, a few blacksmith shops, an ashery, a tannery, a fanning mill, a wool carding machine, cut-nail works, a hotel, taverns, tailor's shop, and others. At that time, it had about 800 inhabitants. During the late twenties and early thirties, the town dredged the river mouth and it became a jumping-off point for the settlers on their way to the Otonabee area or to the Lindsay district. As such, it obtained an important supply and gateway function. In the thirties, it still had a profitable whiskey trade, but gradually the export of lumber became more important. The hinterland was opening up and large quantities of fine shipmasts were exported. Soon after, the shipment of wheat began to gain in volume. In 1844, the port shipped more than 58,000 bushels of wheat and 8,454 barrels of flour. The milling industry was of minor importance. It had only one gristmill and another was in course of erection. In addition, there was one foundry, one brewery, four tanneries, five distilleries, one ashery, eighteen stores, six taverns, one druggist, one bookseller, four bakers, one livery stable, one printer, four waggon makers, two cabinet makers, one watchmaker, seven blacksmiths, three tinsmiths, eleven tailors, ten shoemakers, four saddlers, one school for boys, two ladies' seminaries, two bank agencies; it also had five government and districts offices (130). This town with a population of about 2,000 had become a typical service centre with a very colourful variety of professions and shops, which catered to the clientele of the town and a wide region behind it, reaching as far as Peterborough and Lindsay. It shared the administrative functions with Cobourg, but it had its own more specialized educational facilities. The service function, trade and transportation were the factors which counted in the growth of the town. During the following years it prospered with the continued settlement of its hinterland, which was opened up by better roads.

With the exception of Barrie, there were no banks in places with fewer than a thousand inhabitants. In these centres, the store-keeper or merchant provided banking services. Napanee and Streetsville both lacked a bank, but they possessed a newspaper; this placed them in the class of sub-towns.

The development of Streetsville was rather unusual, as it did not have an administrative function, nor was it close to navigable water. The village started early (1818), and it grew rapidly as a milling and business centre in a good farming country on the till and clay plains west of Toronto. But the rise of many other small places and the growth of Toronto, together with the improved roads to that city, prevented it from becoming a fully-fledged town by 1850. Yet its newspaper was evidence that it was still a regional focus of some significance.

On the other side of Toronto, to the north and east of that

city, good roads gave the capital control over those areas and prevented the growth of sub-centres.

Trenton ($\pm$ 950) and Newmarket ($\pm$ 800) were two larger centres which did not grow beyond the status of an urban village. Trenton was a large exporter of lumber, but it lacked a rich wheat-producing hinterland. It was also too close to Belleville with which it had to compete. Newmarket was in rivalry with Holland Landing, but particularly with fast growing Bradford.

Fergus and Elora were jumping-off places for roads in a north-western direction and so had a gateway function.

The general distribution of the service centres reveals unmistakably the dominant part played by transportation and accessibility in general. A line of fully-fledged towns and minor service centres hugs the shore of Lake Ontario. A second line runs north from Toronto to Lake Simcoe and Barrie. The unimportance of transportation beyond Barrie is revealed by the rural village status of Penetanguishene; as a supply centre, that point was of no importance. The service centres along these two transportation routes are rather closely spaced. Each of the larger service points has arbitrarily been provided with an umland of 4.5 miles[1] and even then there was considerable overlapping. The regions serviced by these places were narrow tracts of land stretching sometimes quite far inland. The road network of 1851 is partly a result of the relationships between service centres and their respective umlands.

Also away from these two main transportation routes, the distribution pattern of the many smallest service centres is largely linear. The rural villages tend to be closely spaced on the roads leading to the larger centres on the lakeshore.

The pattern of service centres in 1851 was to a considerable degree unstable. Along the main transportation routes the places were crowded too close together and farther inland larger centres were lacking. This condition was due in part to the lay-out of the transportation network and, in part, to the low density of population. Changes in these two factors after 1850 led to profound changes in the distribution pattern of service centres in general.

The establishment of many small service centres resulted in the development of a colourful and varied regionalism in the

---

[1] This distance was relatively easy to travel back and forth in one day.

province. There were a large number of towns, much more equal to one another than ever would be the case again. Each was the central place for a small territory which had little contact with other towns or regions. Lord Durham described this pattern in his famous report in 1839: "The province has no great centre with which all the separate parts are connected, and which they are accustomed to follow in sentiment and action; nor is there that habitual intercourse between the inhabitants of different parts of the country which . . . makes a people one and united . . . there are many petty local centres, the sentiments and the interests . . . of which are distinct, and perhaps opposed . . . this isolation of the different districts from each other was strikingly apparent in all attempts to acquire information in one district respecting the agricultural or commercial character of another" (3/104). An urban pattern, however, was rapidly developing just as it was in Durham's England, where a few large cities influenced wide areas.

The First 70 Years of Urban Growth

The German saying "Hat der Bauer Geld, hat's die ganze Welt" depicts in a few words the main element in the rise of cities and towns during this period. As long as the settlers remained largely self-sufficient there was very little need for specialized urban services and a non-rural way of life in general.

However, with the improvements in the transportation facilities and the expansion of foreign markets, a general rise in the standard of living took place. It was of the utmost importance that the population should be fully drawn into the money economy. The turning point came in the late thirties and early forties, when the trade with the United States began to expand. It is from then on that we find conditions favouring town growth in South-Central Ontario.

Toronto in particular benefited from the improvements in the general economic conditions. As the capital and the biggest individual market with a good harbour, it saw a concentration of trade within its boundaries.

Its geographic situation enabled Toronto, during the latter part of this period, to lay the foundations for its future metropolitan dominance over an area where the hinterlands of the two rivalling ports of Montreal and New York overlapped.

4. The Building of the Railways

Settlement in the Ottawa-Huron Tract

Until the fifties, the main flow of settlement avoided the Shield, and the population isopleths (fig. 7) closely paralleled its edge. The southern part of Frontenac County was the only exception. Here, the Frontenac axis had been occupied under pressure from the demand of the markets of Kingston and other urban centres farther east and probably also as a result of the Rideau Canal development. In general, however, settlement had halted abruptly as soon as it touched the pre-cambrian Shield. Harvey, a township straddling the boundary of the Shield, received its first settlers in 1832. Yet, in 1851, it was still virtually unsettled, and by 1881 it numbered only 1,114 inhabitants. The township of Emily, on the other hand, just to the south-west of Harvey, but well south of the edge of the Shield, was opened for sale in 1821. In 1851, it had a population of 2,763, and in 1871 it reached its maximum population of 3,790.

By the fifties, however, the conditions had changed and two factors in particular stimulated the settlement of the pre-cambrian zone: the shortage of land in the rest of Southern Ontario and the northward advance of the lumber industry. During the eighteen forties, there had been a great increase in immigration. Consequently, by the middle fifties most of the crown lands in Southern Ontario had been disposed of. The clergy reserves were secularized by an act in 1854, and soon all the good land had been taken up by settlers. As a general need for new land arose, the government turned to the Shield area between the Ottawa Valley and Georgian Bay, the Ottawa-Huron Tract (see also p. 56).

In order to make this new territory accessible, a plan was worked out for the building of colonization roads. This was not a new approach. The building of roads as a means of promoting settlement had been practised since Simcoe's regime. Later, roads had been built outwards from such places as Guelph, Elora, Fergus, and Shelburne. In a similar manner a number of roads were built northward from points near the edge of the Shield, while others were projected in a east-west direction (fig. 9). From the main roads, a large number of shorter roads branched out.

These colonization roads often followed bush trails. One of them, the Peterson Road, which ran in a general eastern direction from Gravenhurst, had been opened as a military highway in the years 1812/15. Now, it was re-opened as a colonization road.

The government made the roads fit for waggon traffic, after which it was the task of the settlers to maintain and to improve them. Often, however, the government left the road in a very rough condition.

Eventually, eight main roads ran in a general northern direction. They were the Muskoka, Victoria, Bobcaygeon, Buckhorn, Burleigh, Hastings, Addington, and Frontenac roads. Two roads ran in east-west direction – the Monck Road and the Peterson Road. In the years from 1853 to 1860, a total of 481 miles of colonization roads were built in Upper Canada (10/530).

The land on both sides of the roads was given to settlers in free grants of 100 acres on a few light conditions. Within four years, twelve acres had to be under cultivation, a cabin erected, and the settler had to reside continuously on his land.

The government believed that the Ottawa-Huron Tract contained extensive sections of fertile farm land. But there were also officials who were doubtful about this. Before it was finally decided to build the Muskoka Road, several authorities went so far as to advocate the establishment of a vast Indian Reserve in the Muskoka and Parry Sound districts.

In order to attract settlers for the new land, the government advertised extensively in foreign newspapers. Yet the number of new immigrants remained low. Most of the newcomers were attracted to the open prairies of the West, where no forest had to be cleared and the fertile soil lay ready to be ploughed. Consequently, the Ottawa-Huron Tract was mostly settled by farmers from the older parts of the province. One of the exceptions was a small group of Germans who settled along the Addington Road. Another was that of the Canadian Land and Emigration Company, which was formed in London. It purchased ten townships of the Crown Lands Department in 1865 (fig. 9). The Company, however, was short-lived. Yet it founded the towns of Minden and Haliburton, and it repaired 25 miles of the old Peterson Road.

One of the factors which retarded the settlement of the Canadian Land and Emigration Company holdings was the Free Grants and Homestead Act of 1868. Free grants were no longer restricted to land on the colonization roads, but whole townships were set apart en bloc to be given away as free grants. A settler with children under 18 years of age received 200 acres free and was permitted to buy an additional 100 acres at the rate of fifty cents per acre. The settlement duties were light (152). These free grants diverted the prospective settlers of the Canadian Land and Emigration Company, especially to the Muskoka District where many townships were set aside for that purpose.

Railroads also were extended into the Ottawa-Huron Tract. In 1868, a charter was obtained for the building of a railroad which reached Haliburton in 1878. The government considered it as a colonization road and granted $12,000 per mile for the enterprise. In addition it received a bonus of $55,000 from the District of Haliburton and it was also encouraged by the Canadian Land and Emigration Company.

In spite of all these attempts the settlement remained a failure. Several circumstances are responsible for this. First of all there is the inherent inhospitability of the Shield towards farming. The scarcity of arable land was increased even more as a result of human activity. Tremendous forest fires raged annually over wide areas, burning bridges and fences, but worst of all destroying the humus cover which blanketed the bedrock. Together with the increased erosion resulting from the clearing of the forest, it made farming impossible in many places. The acreage of bare bedrock increased considerably and occupies at present 11 per cent of the Ottawa-Huron Tract (166/266). Secondly, roads generally followed the higher ridges, while the most suitable farmland was found in the valleys. Thirdly, the farmer was not allowed to cut the valuable pine on his land for commercial purposes. Thus he missed his first most important cash crop. The pine was cut by licensed lumbermen.

In addition, the expected market for agricultural produce did not prove to be reliable. It had been thought that the new settler would find a ready market in the lumber camps. But when the communication system improved, it was easy during the winter season to ship food supplies from elsewhere in the province. The pioneer settler could not compete with products grown in areas with much more favourable climate and soil conditions. In 1859, sixty lumbermen along the Hastings Road obtained their supplies mostly from Madoc and Belleville and not from the pioneer settlers in their own neighbourhood (292/296).

Though the colonization roads were a failure as far as actual farming is concerned, they were a success for the logging industry. They made accessible the magnificent pine stands of the district at a time when the American market was opening up widely. Lumbering and not agriculture became the most important business, although settlement had started for the purpose of farming. The farmer found employment in the logging camps during the winter season and he also was dependent upon them for a market. With the decline of the lumber industry, the farmer lost his only available market and an opportunity to supplement his income during the winter months. Consequently, many farms were abandoned. On others, the farmers continued to struggle for a very meagre and miserable existence.

The cutting of the pine forests was done in an extremely reckless and wasteful manner. Young trees were destroyed and the possibility of a future forest crop was not considered. Forest fires caused irreparable damage. This not only led to serious soil losses but also to alarming changes in the composition of the forests. The repeated fires burned all the seeds of the white pine; its root system was destroyed as the fire penetrated two feet into the ground. In the new forest, which grew up, poplars and birches, spreading through windblown seeds, dominated by far. At present only about 5 per cent of the forest consists of pure coniferous stands, while in 1850 about 65 per cent of the forests of the Ottawa-Huron Tract was excellent white pine.

The government recognized the failure of the attempt to settle the Ottawa-Huron Tract and, in order to protect some of the remaining pine stands, it established Algonquin Park in 1897. This park covers an area of 2,741 square miles and is largely outside South-Central Ontario as defined in this paper, but it includes the two north-eastern townships of Haliburton County.

Although the colonization scheme did not achieve the desired goal, it nevertheless led to the appearance of a number of towns. Large urban centres were not established, because a balanced farm-forest economy which could have provided a basis for such a development did not come about. Neither does the Ottawa-Huron Tract contain valuable mineral resources. In the early days, the mineral wealth was often thought to be tremendous. It was reported in 1877, that a gold nugget had been found at Gravenhurst, and a small gold rush to this place occurred. Until the present, however, there are no important settlements in the part of the Ottawa-Huron Tract within our region which are due to the exploitation of mineral resources.

Of major importance, however, was the expansion of the

transportation network. The colonization roads contributed to the growth of the places at which they began. This had been true for places like Guelph, Elora, Fergus, and Shelburne, but now also Washago, Fenelon Falls, Bobcaygeon, Madoc, and Tamworth went through similar developments. Like the ports on Lake Ontario in earlier decades, these places served as a headquarters and supply base for the new settlements in the tracts of land beyond them. They missed, however, the water transportation facilities of the ports and soon their supply function was partly taken over by a new centre farther down the road and closer to the new settlements. Such a pattern of successive supply bases came into existence north of Lake Simcoe.

For a short time, Orillia served as a base and gateway for the Muskoka district. Some settlers walked forty miles to that supply point to buy provisions or to mail a letter (79/14). But when the government began in 1858 to build the Muskoka Road, Washago replaced Orillia as a gateway point.

Washago became a busy supply point and a centre for logging operations, as it had a big sawmill. Washago's boom period in turn ended, when, in the early eighties, the Grand Trunk railway, which had its terminus for a time at the village, was extended to Severn Bridge. Soon the latter was more important than Washago.

In the meantime, Gravenhurst, 22 miles north of Washago, had grown after 1865 into a supply centre for the Muskoka Lakes. For a time, it had a considerable trade and a tremendous shipment of timber and lumber. In the late seventies, Gravenhurst had seventeen sawmills. It was, however, at that time already overshadowed by Bracebridge, which was ten miles farther down the road, and situated in a small basin of good alluvial soil. The latter had excellent waterpower facilities and was at the head of steam navigation, but its water communications were not as favourable for logging as those of Gravenhurst. The town had three tanneries, one of them – Beardmore's tannery – was one of the largest and most modern in North America at the time. The town also had woollen mills, and it became the county seat; thus Bracebridge, supported by its prosperous farming umland, became the main business centre for the Muskoka district and for the whole country as far north as Lake Nipissing (204/17). The amount of business done, including the sales in stores and the income of the hotels, was in 1877 estimated at $254,000 a year, although its population was then just over 1,000 (152/77).

For several decades, Bracebridge's position remained unchallenged. Huntsville, 22 miles to the north-east of Bracebridge, destined to eclipse Bracebridge, was in the late seventies only a small hamlet. Thus the supply function migrated northward as settlement expanded and the road was extended. The older centres retained an umland which was only a small part of the extensive region originally served.

Elsewhere in the Ottawa-Huron Tract, many other small urban centres sprang up at mill sites on the colonization roads or at the intersections of those roads. They all declined, however, as soon as the pine stands had been cut and the lumber frontier moved farther away. There was no industry to sustain them. Later, many of them were revitalized with the development of the tourist industry. Only the places which had gained enough momentum during the lumber era to attract other industries, or were at points which enjoyed special transportation facilities withstood the decline of the lumber industry. Some even continued to grow. Gravenhurst, Bracebridge, Huntsville, Bobcaygeon, Fenelon Falls, Madoc, Tamworth, and Bancroft may be considered as such. Washago, Severn Bridge, Coboconk, and others at one time handled enormous quantities of lumber, yet never grew beyond the hamlet stage. Numerous are the hamlets, such as Uffington, ten miles to the east of Gravenhurst, which developed in a pocket of relatively fertile land, found a market for their produce in the lumber camps, but stagnated and declined after the lumber era.

The attempts to settle the Ottawa-Huron Tract and the logging industry also had their effects upon urban centres in the rest of South-Central Ontario. This will be discussed in another section of this chapter.

The Population Pattern in 1881

The density of population in South-Central Ontario has been reconstructed for the year 1881 (fig. 10). In making the map, the population of places with fewer than 200 inhabitants was taken as being rural and as spread out over the townships. These very small centres were to a large extent non-rural in character, but it is impossible to acquire information as to their size. On the other hand, to subtract them from the rural population would probably not alter greatly the general trend of the isopleths, since they were fairly regularly distributed over the countryside. The classification of the larger places is based on statistics obtained from the census for 1881 and Lovell's Ontario Directory for 1882.

By 1881, practically all of the region, called South-Central Ontario in this paper, had been penetrated by white settlers. Several townships on the Shield had so few inhabitants that for census purposes they were added to neighbouring townships. Only the townships in the northern half of Muskoka and Haliburton did not record any population at all.

The section centered on Toronto with a population of more than 60 persons per square mile had not changed very much since 1851. It extended slightly farther up Yonge Street, but in area it had remained approximately the same.

The zone with between 40 and 60 persons per square mile almost enclosed Lake Simcoe by 1881, and a small outlier, almost linked with the main zone, surrounded Peterborough. Those two northward projections reflect the progress of settlement before 1850. On the other hand, the rather late settlement of the Scugog district is reflected in a zone of lower population density. In these cases it was apparently accessibility rather than the quality of the land which continued to determine the pattern of 1881.

Similarly, to the west and south-west of Lake Simcoe, the 40-isopleth had the same trend as the 20-isopleth in 1851 and the 40 to 60 zone corresponds with a longer settled and therefore more accessible zone. Within this zone, however, there was a circular area west of Toronto with a lower population density in 1881 than 30 years before. The density in this area was just under 40, and was a result of rural depopulation which had begun in those townships. The same phenomenon led to an enlarged low-density area in Prince Edward County.

The 20-isopleth continued to parallel more or less the margin of the Shield. The main exception was in Frontenac County where it continued to reflect the forced development of the period before 1851. The presence of nearby urban markets and the east-west transportation routes continued to push settlement on the Frontenac axis and the margin of the Shield. Transportation routes also caused the lobes of denser settlement which, enclosed by the 10-isopleth, jutted out into the Shield. They closely reflected the main colonization roads which had been built to open up the Ottawa-Huron Tract.

This population pattern, however, was not only the result of trends which had set in before 1850, but also of important changes which occurred after that year in transportation, agriculture, lumbering, manufacturing, and trade. On the other hand, these changes in unison with population density profoundly affected and determined town growth. These changes in the transportational framework, and in the general economic geography of the region will therefore be analyzed first.

The Economic Structure in 1881

The census of 1881 reveals that in that year in the province as a whole almost half of the population still listed farming as their main occupation (table IV); 20.6 per cent considered manufacturing as their main occupation and 7.1 per cent, commerce and transportation.

Compared with the province as a whole, South-Central Ontario was in 1881 slightly more urbanized. This was mainly due to the fact that Toronto is included in the region. The agricultural group was about 4 per cent smaller, while manufacturing and commerce together were more than 3 per cent stronger. Those differences between the province and the region are relatively small, and the most striking aspect is that both occupational structures are more or less similar.

TABLE IV – Economic structure in 1881

	Ontario %	South-Central Ontario %
Agriculture	48.3	44.2
Manufacturing	20.6	22.1
Commerce	7.1	8.1
Domestic	5.3	6.2
Professional	3.7	3.9
Not classified	15.0	15.5

In the gradual and slow development towards a non-rural economy, and thus to a stronger sub-stratum for urban growth, the expansion of the transportation network was of the utmost importance. So far, accessibility had been an essential factor in economic development, but during this period the revolutionary changes in the transportation system would affect urban growth more deeply than ever before.

Transportational Changes

Railways

The middle of the 19th century marks an important break in the development of transportation in Canada. Before 1850, waterways were the chief means of communication and only a few short portage railways – in total 66 miles – were built before that date, as compared with about 10,000 miles in the United States. The second half of the century, however, saw a tremendous expansion of the railway network, and railways largely replaced roads and waterways as a means of transportation.

Railway construction in Canada began rather late, because so much capital had been invested in the building of canals and it was thought that the canals constituted a good transportation system. As in the United States, the first railways were projected to supplement the water routes. The building of railways, however, became a necessity after the expansion of the American rail network south of the lake, just as the Erie Canal before had forced the improvement of the St. Lawrence River. Without railways, the St. Lawrence route and Montreal would not be able to compete with the American transportation system.

At the end of the first half of the 19th century, Toronto had succeeded in gaining a considerable amount of independence from Montreal; it had become a budding metropolis, engaged in the organization and expansion of its hinterland. Toronto could do this because she had obtained easy access to New York as an alternative outlet to the ocean, and the city benefited from its location in the zone of maximum friction between the hinterlands of those two formidable rivals on the Atlantic Seaboard. In the late forties New York was the more powerful of the two as far as Southern-Ontario is concerned. This was revealed not only by the larger volume of trade which went to New York, but also by the first railway developments in Southern Ontario (fig. 9).

Several railways had been chartered in Ontario before 1850. Among the oldest was the Great Western, which was incorporated as early as 1834, but its charter lapsed and was revived in 1845.

The line was built in the early fifties and ran from Niagara via Hamilton to Windsor. This section was completed in 1854 (table V). At the end of 1855, a branch line to Toronto was completed. The Great Western was mainly financed by British capital. It was, however, always believed that the line was under strong American influences and the American railways converging upon Buffalo. This American influence placed it in opposition to the Grand Trunk which was the line from Montreal to Toronto, and later to Sarnia (23, X/407).

The Grand Trunk, on the other hand, represented Montreal's bid for the control of the Ontario hinterland; it was an attempt to draw the trade from the western states to the St. Lawrence and to retrieve it from New York. The line began construction in 1853, when the building of the Great Western was already in full swing, and it reached Toronto a year later than the Great Western. It was not until November, 1859 that the Grand Trunk was completed as far as Sarnia. Thus, Toronto received, at about the same time, rail communications with Montreal on one side, and the Niagara frontier and the American trunk lines on the other. This development shows clearly the favourable position occupied by Toronto between the competing spheres of influences of Montreal and New York. This strategic position protected Toronto from being entirely drawn within the sphere of either of them; it enabled Toronto to attain a semi-metropolitan predominance and to carve out a metropolitan region of its own. During those years, Toronto acted more resolutely than Montreal to combat the pull exerted by the Niagara frontier.

Buffalo made a powerful bid for the western trade via Lake Huron. The Buffalo and Lake Huron Railway was chartered, and construction on the line from Fort Erie to Goderich started as early as 1852. But the line, promoted by Buffalo citizens, was not very successful. Financial difficulties soon developed, because the tracks were poorly laid. It was a serious disadvantage that it only carried trade during the season of navigation, since it collected very little local trade.

Toronto competed successfully with Buffalo and completed early in 1855 the Northern Railway which ran from Toronto to Collingwood. Soon this railway began to carry a considerable volume of trade. Toronto did not participate in the construction of the Grand Trunk line, which was always considered as a Montreal affair – something like a foreign enterprise. The Northern, however, was entirely the result of Toronto initiative and a Toronto venture. On the other hand, when considered within a wider framework, the Northern, striking out from Toronto, was also the result of the increasing influence of New York in the struggle with Montreal. The other lines built during

TABLE V – Main railway lines in Southern Ontario 1850-1860

	Opened
Great Western	
Hamilton-Niagara	Nov. 1853
Hamilton-Windsor	Jan. 1854
Hamilton-Toronto	Dec. 1855
London-Sarnia	Dec. 1858
Northern Railway	
Toronto-Collingwood	Jan. 1855
Grand Trunk	
Toronto-Montreal	Oct. 1856
Toronto-Sarnia (via Guelph)	Nov. 1859
Cobourg and Peterborough Railway	May 1854
Port Hope and Lindsay Railway	Dec. 1857
Buffalo and Lake Huron	
Fort Erie-Goderich	Jan. 1858

the fifties in South-Central Ontario have to be considered in a similar light.

The lakeshore towns were, like Toronto, not primarily interested in a trunk line, but in feeders which would make them the gateway to a deeper and wider hinterland that would increase their trade with the American ports. Essentially, these feeder lines were nothing other than tentacles of the American transportation network, which was extending its lines across the St. Lawrence and across Lake Ontario. The Ottawa-Prescott line, east of Kingston, was projected by American interests for the movement of lumber, and was intended to be operated in connection with the railway from Ogdensburg on the American side of the St. Lawrence (316).

Port Hope and Cobourg were the only two ports which built feeder lines before 1860. Both ports were in very strong competition and it was with the building of railways that Port Hope became the victor. Cobourg put a rail line across Rice Lake to Peterborough. The bridge over Rice Lake, however, could not sustain the pressure of the ice in winter and since Cobourg could not finance the building of a causeway, for several years communication on Rice Lake was maintained by steamers. The Port Hope and Lindsay Railway, which was completed in 1857, in the same year built a branch line into Peterborough. Cobourg ceased to be a gateway to the Otonabee district.

In the ten years between 1850 and 1860, Canada built 2,000 miles of railroad. This was more than the country needed at that time, and consequently during the next ten years practically no new lines were built. The lines which had been completed found themselves in financial difficulties. Tracks had been poorly laid and the operating costs proved to be much higher than had been expected. In many places, the lines had not been built to tap all the possible local traffic, since through traffic had been the main consideration. They were away from towns and short spurs had to be built to link them with ports such as Port Hope, Cobourg and Kingston.

As far as heavy freight is concerned, the railways could not compete with water transport.

Finally, an evil so common in Canadian railroad building had already revealed itself – needless duplication of lines. The lines of Port Hope and Cobourg were too close together. West of Toronto, there was at that time no need for the Grand Trunk line to Sarnia. The Great Western suffered from rate wars among the American lines south of Lake Erie and its competition with the Grand Trunk seriously weakened both lines. The two lines were amalgamated in 1882.

Also, many municipalities which had engaged themselves in railroad building faced serious financial difficulties. Port Hope and Cobourg with 2,476 and 3,871 inhabitants respectively in 1851, had borrowed $1,240,000 on which there were $625,000 arrears of interest (23, X/414). Much speculation had occurred and many new buildings were erected in places on railroads. Day mentions the "great building mania" in 1854/55, when the Grand Trunk was in the course of construction. Five years later, property had depreciated over 100 per cent and some speculators had been ruined (115, II/60).

The lull in railway building came to an end during the late sixties. The abrogation of the Reciprocity Treaty (p. 130) brought a decline of through traffic and a need arose for more feeder lines. At the same time, the railways were generally considered to be essential for the opening up of the interior parts of the province, in particular for establishing connections with free grant lands in the Ottawa-Huron Tract. In 1871, the provincial government introduced a system of subsidies under which allowances from $2,000 to $4,000 per mile could be granted.

In South-Central Ontario, this period of renewed railroad construction was characterized by a sharp competition among the towns. The lake ports made zealous efforts to enlarge their hinterland, while the inland centres competed in attracting lines in their own direction. In this struggle, the granting of bonuses to the railways by the competing towns was the main weapon. All railways received liberal financial aid and many municipalities, in their anxiety to secure railway connections, gave far beyond their means (219/148). The largest towns were the strongest bidders, with Toronto outbidding them all. Toronto gave $350,000 to the Toronto, Grey and Bruce (Toronto-Orangeville-Owen Sound); $150,000 to the Toronto and Nipissing (Toronto-Stouffville-Coboconk); and $350,000 to the Credit Valley (Toronto-Orangeville and Woodstock) Railways. The inland town of Lindsay with a population of 4,049, in 1871, paid together with the township of Ops, $80,000 to the Midland Railway (Port Hope-Midland); Lindsay granted also $85,000 to the Victoria Railway (Lindsay-Haliburton) and another large bonus to the Whitby Railway (219). Milton, a town of 891 inhabitants in 1871, voted a bonus of $30,000 to the Credit Valley, while the county granted another $75,000 (77). It is understandable that the railways often followed tortuous courses with sharp turns, in order to obtain the grants from the competing municipalities.

In many cases land speculation had forced up land values to such an extent that the railway station was erected a short distance from the town. Chisholm, the founder of Oakville, asked the railway company for $50,000 for land he owned. The result was that the station was erected a mile or so outside the town. Often this hampered the further expansion of such a town. A new settlement grew near the station (Oakville Station, Burlington Station, Grafton Station, etc.), while the old town tended to grow in the direction of the station. If the two settlements were not too far apart, they would merge. Often much economic and social rivalry existed in these divided towns between the two sections. Both sections tended to compete for establishments or services and nearly always this led to a delay in decisions.

A new series of divided towns developed later in the 20th century, when the big arterial highways were built. Oakville saw a new section rising near the Queen Elizabeth Way. Whitby shifted from its original site near a creek to the railway, and later, its growth was directed towards the highway (353).

Toronto, the largest commercial, industrial, and financial centre as well as the provincial capital, gradually became the hub of an extensive railway network. It was the railways which put the city in a position of effective control over a large part of the province. They contributed fundamentally to the growth of metropolitan dominance of the city. The first developments towards that position occurred before 1880. By 1880, Toronto had pushed its lines in north-eastern, northern and western directions to such points as Coboconk, Sutton, Gravenhurst, Collingwood, Owen Sound, and places in South-western Ontario. The Northern had two steamers plying between Collingwood and Fort William, touching at various intermediate ports. In all these communications Toronto initiative and influence were strongly represented (224). The Toronto, Grey, and Bruce, and the Toronto and Nipissing were largely the result of the ambition and initiative of Toronto businessmen.

But the city was flanked on both sides by powerful and aggressive competitors. Hamilton, which had early become a railway centre, made a strong bid for the trade of the Georgian Bay ports. In the sixties, it already had a line to Milton and from there it reached Barrie in 1878, the section Barrie-Midland having been opened two years earlier. Collingwood was reached in 1879. Hamilton penetrated deeply into territory claimed by Toronto's Northern.

From the east, the Northern was subjected to keen competition from the Midland Railway. This Port Hope and Lindsay line reached Beaverton in 1871, and Midland in 1875. Between the two railways rivalry was strong over the lumber trade of Simcoe County and Muskoka. But the Northern had more feeders and remained the stronger of the two (348/179).

Whitby and Belleville were also active railroad builders. The development of a hinterland for Whitby had been retarded because of the relatively late settlement of the Scugog district. Port Hope had connections with Lindsay which were much older than those of Whitby, and when the railroads were built, Whitby found its hinterland again restricted, both by Toronto and especially by Port Hope. It was also a disadvantage that the Whitby Railroad reached Lindsay rather late, in 1875. Partly this was a result of the protracted struggle between Whitby and Oshawa as to which of the two would be the terminus of the line. Oshawa and other towns refused to support the railway. As early as 1857, this controversy led to a division of Whitby

Township into an eastern and western section. When the Whitby line finally did reach Lindsay, Port Hope had already had a rail connection with that town for eighteen years, and a considerable flow of trade had become accustomed to that route. Whitby, as a railway builder, did not constitute a serious threat to Toronto's rising hegemony.

Belleville was linked by rail to Peterborough in 1879. The Trent system had remained inadequate for the shipment of lumber, and Belleville established a direct link with the lumber capital Peterborough. Belleville also had a rail connection with Madoc, the terminus of the Hastings colonization road.

Kingston was, by 1880, the only large town from which no railroad struck inland. The Rideau Canal provided a good communication with its lumber producing hinterland and just as this was true for Trenton, the need for a railway was not considered as urgent as for the other lake ports. The town, however, also tried to tap the pine resources of the Ottawa Valley. In 1871, a charter had been obtained for the Kingston and Pembroke Railway, but the line was not completed until the middle eighties. Kingston received much competition from ports farther east on the St. Lawrence. Prescott and Brockville tapped the forest wealth of the Ottawa Valley through the building of railways as early as 1854 and 1859 respectively.

Most unfortunate were the big wheat exporting towns between Toronto and Hamilton. They suffered the fate which Whitby barely escaped, but which sooner or later would befall all lake ports: they found their hinterland traversed and tapped by feeder lines of larger neighbouring ports. It meant the decline of such prosperous ports as Oakville and Port Credit.

In general the railway network of South-Central Ontario in 1880 was strikingly similar to the road network of 1850. There existed still only one main east-west line, the Grand Trunk, and a number of other lines striking inland from the major ports. The sectionalism which had developed before 1850 was still somewhat reflected in the rail network of 1880. But, by that time, the pattern was changing rapidly and the future trends were indicated by the transportational network west and northwest of Toronto. Here the lines converged upon Toronto; eventually the entire network would be focussed on that city.

Roads

From the transportation point of view, the railroads were the most important factor in the further development of the urban centres. The stage coaches disappeared and there was no need for big arterial highways. Accordingly, after 1850, very little improvement in the general condition of the roads took place. Even at the close of the 19th century, there were almost no roads which were good during all seasons. Discussing the condition of the roads in 1896, Glazebrook quotes from a report by the provincial road instructor: "It is doubtful if there is a mile of true macadam road in Ontario outside a few towns or cities. There are miles of roads which are covered with dirty gravel or rough broken stone, and are popularly supposed to be macadamized. To-day the majority are little better than trails. From the middle of October until the end of December, and from the first of March to the end of May, a period of five months, by far the greatest part of the mileage of the province is mud, ruts, and pitchholes. There are at least two months when the roads are practically impassable" (325/442-443).

It was not until the advent of the motor car that Canada built macadamized roads on a large scale. Before 1914, practically no hard-surfaced highways existed in the Dominion. As late as 1915, motorists got stuck in mudholes on the main highways of the province (325/445).

Where no rail communication was available, travelling by water was preferred to road travelling. Actually the amount of travel by road declined as the rail network expanded. The stages could not compete with the railroads and consequently a general decline of the number of hotels and boarding houses set in. In 1871, the province still had 4,124 such establishments, but by 1881 this had declined to 4,094. In Ontario County, the number declined from 116 in 1871, to 77 ten years later (33; 34). The disappearance of these services from the hamlets and villages contributed to their decline.

In general, the villages and small towns which by this time had not become important or fortunate enough to attract a railway and which remained dependent on roads were doomed. This was widely recognized and the reason why the larger and economically stronger ones tried so desperately to excel each other in the granting of bonuses to the railways. As far as the urban centres were concerned, the railway was a matter of growth or decline. It was not until the motor car became widely used that places away from the railroads could develop and take part in the general process of urbanization.

Canals

Canal building in South-Central Ontario had never been very extensive. After 1850, it ceased to operate as a factor in the urbanization of the region. Besides a few improvements in the Trent System, the only new addition was the building of the Murray Canal. This canal traversed the isthmus at the head of the Bay of Quinte and was completed in 1890. On the other hand the Welland and St. Lawrence Canals continued to be of great significance to the ports on Lake Ontario.

The Welland Canal (10/478-486) had attained a depth of ten feet in 1853. This was increased to twelve feet in 1883; but its locks remained too narrow. Passage through it was very slow. In part this was due to an inefficient and monopolized towage system. It was reported that in 1860 one-third to one-fourth of the vessels could not pass the canal and that nearly three-fourths of the propeller steamers were too large for it. In 1871, the Oswego board of trade reported that three-fourths of the tonnage of the Upper Lakes could not pass the Welland Canal (10). Between 1850 and 1880, the large vessels on the lakes increased rapidly in size and number, yet the Welland Canal remained practically unchanged. The difficulties of the Welland Canal strengthened the position of ports such as Hamilton, Toronto, and Port Hope. It gave them an opportunity to attract a considerable share of the grain shipments of the Upper Lakes by rail from the Georgian Bay ports.

The inadequate depth of the St. Lawrence Canals continued to maintain Kingston as a trans-shipment point. In 1850, the St. Lawrence Canals had a draught of nine feet; this was increased to a depth of fourteen feet by 1905. During this entire period of 55 years, grain that passed through the Welland Canal had to be transferred to river barges, Erie Canal boats, or to railway boxcars at the foot of Lake Ontario (323).

The transportational changes during this period were of the utmost importance for the further growth of cities and towns. Toronto obtained ready access to large parts of the province. Urban development was not any longer restricted to waterfront sites, and places with an inland location saw their possible markets considerably expanded. Most important was perhaps the fact that the railways pulled the farmers of the back townships out of their self-sufficient farming and gave them access to outside markets. The farmers became now fully involved in the money economy. This development will be discussed in the next section.

Agriculture

By 1850, the farmer in the older townships had become fully involved in the money economy. He had begun to buy machinery and thus had begun to practise a more modern type of farming. After 1850, conditions changed rapidly. The railways opened up the back-country, reduced the shipping costs of the products and helped the farmer of the interior districts to break through his system of self-sufficiency. Writing about the decade of the 1850's Jones states: "So extensive were the changes that, in dealing with this area, the present-day student feels that he is concerned, for the first time in Upper Canadian history, with an agricultural economy essentially modern in its characteristics" (292/215).

For Ontario as a whole, wheat continued to be the most important product between 1850 and 1880. The highest wheat production ever obtained was in 1882 with a total production of 40.9 million bushels. In particular, the Crimean War had greatly stimulated the production of this grain. Brampton, Burlington, Prince Albert, Whitby, Port Hope, and many other towns were thriving wheat markets. The expansion of wheat production, however, was entirely due to the productive capacity of the newly-settled parts of Southern Ontario. In the older townships along the Lakes Ontario and Erie, wheat farming declined continuously. The midge and soil exhaustion forced the farmer to turn from the product which had stimulated so greatly the development of the transportation network and of urban centres. In South-Central Ontario, barley gradually replaced fall wheat.

By the late sixties, barley had become the staple crop in the older settled districts of South-Central Ontario. In particular, the Bay of Quinte district was a large producer. Prince Edward County produced in 1881, 876,432 bushels of barley and only 35,473 bushels of fall wheat. In 1851, the barley production had amounted to about one quarter that of wheat. Ontario barley found a ready market in the brewing industry of upstate New York. It was considered indispensable for the production of good American beer (292/240, 241). The barley export to the United States continued till the Mackinley Tariff became effective in 1890, after which the trade was reduced to a trickle and the brewing industry in upstate New York was ruined.

Barley, however, never gained the exclusive position wheat had enjoyed for so many years. With the decline of wheat, mixed farming became the general practice, and by 1880 it was fully established as the common form of agriculture. Traditionally one of the leading wheat producing areas, Peel County – at that time comprising the three southern townships of the present county – still produced, in 1881, 359,767 bushels of fall wheat. But it also produced 83,419 bushels of spring wheat, 437,545 bushels of barley, 491,628 bushels of oats, 97,377 bushels of peas and beans, 153,297 bushels of potatoes, and a variety of other products (34).

The Civil War played an important part in the development of the mixed farming economy in Southern Ontario (292). It did not increase the demand for Canadian wheat owing to the rising production of the western states, but it created a great demand for barley, oats and in particular for Canadian livestock, butter, and cheese. This export trade brought a considerable amount of cash into the country.

In the meantime, the Canadian urban population also became an important market for animal products. The railways made possible the shipment of perishable goods over longer distances. Here and there, specialization occurred. Market gardening had started to develop on the outskirts of urban communities after 1850. Small fruits and vegetables became of importance between Toronto and Hamilton. By 1880, the Oakville district had become one of the leading strawberry producers of the Dominion. In that year, 126,000 quart baskets per season were shipped from the station at Oakville (292/ 322). Prince Edward County was, in 1881, the largest hop producer with a production of 136,266 pounds. Hastings, East Northumberland, and Prince Edward were among the larger factory-made cheese producers. This district numbered 86 cheese factories employing 267 adult workers. The value of the total production was $703,488 or 15 per cent of the total provincial production (34). Belleville and Picton ranked among the largest cheese markets of the Dominion. In general, however, the number of milch cows remained relatively small; in 1871, the province numbered 638,759 milch cows and in 1881, 782,243. York County, in which Toronto is located, even showed a decline in the milch cow herd from 22,513 in 1871 to 21,096 in 1881. The production of fresh milk for the urban population was by 1880 still very small and the quality of the product left very much to be desired (10/562, 563). On the other hand, Simcoe County was still one of the more important winter wheat producers, with a production of more than 900,-000 bushels.

During these thirty years between 1850 and 1880, rural

Ontario underwent profound changes. All the good land had been cleared, even to such an extent that many farmers lacked a woodlot and had to buy cordwood for their own use. In 1851, not one-third of the land owned by farmers had been cleared and the forest still limited the view in most areas, but by 1881, the landscape looked open and bare. In certain districts anxiety developed after 1871 about the disappearance of the forest resources. Shade trees were planted along roadsides and lanes and some attempts were made to protect the woodlots (258/9).

The farmers gained a considerable degree of prosperity and comfort. The rigors of pioneering were gone. The log houses began to disappear. By 1880, about 45 per cent of the farmers occupied houses of brick, stone, or excellent frame construction; about 54 per cent had first class barns, stables, and sheds (292/306).

The growing importance of the farmers as consumers of manufactured products is best illustrated by the increase of the use of farm machinery. Farm labour was scarcer than ever. Not only was it still relatively easy to obtain land, but now the railway construction and the lumber industry created a great demand for labour. At the same time, with the disappearance of the hardwood and pine stumps, land was easier to work; in part this was due to improved stumping machines. The census recorded for 1871, 36,874 reapers and mowers and 13,885 horse rakes in use in the province. By 1880, about 90 per cent of the farmers in the older settled districts were using agricultural machinery (10/541-544). The effect of this rapid increase in the use of farm machinery was a large-scale development of a farm implement industry. In the middle sixties, the demand for farm machinery was so strong that it was remarked that the manufacturers had difficulty in producing enough (292/309).

At first, the use of American-made machinery was extensive, but soon the repair shops began to manufacture on their own, imitating the foreign models and improving on them. Already as early as 1869, there were so many Canadian-made implements that American machines had become a rarity (292/202). This strong and increasing demand for machinery along with the greater demand for comfort from the farm population stimulated the development of manufacturing.

By 1880, all the land south of the Shield had been cleared and here the forest did not constitute any longer an additional source of income. More than 44 per cent of the population of the region listed agriculture as their main occupation. Farming was the basic industry of the population and had become a truly modern industry south of the Shield by 1880. Its produce stimulated trade, manufacturing, and transportation. The rural population had gained in wealth and provided a rapidly expanding market for consumer goods.

The Lumber Industry

Between 1850 and 1880, the logging operations moved rapidly northward, deeper into the Ottawa-Huron Tract and the Georgian Bay watershed. The building of the railways made it possible to tap the pine stands of those northern regions and to carry the lumber to the important shipping points on Lake Ontario. During the fifties, Simcoe County became the largest lumber producer of the province. In 1851, its production was practically nil (3.8 million feet), but in 1861, the production was almost 208 million feet, compared with the 63.5 million feet of Peterborough, the second largest producing county. However, the railway stimulated the lumber shipments from Peterborough, which had been handicapped by the limited value of the Trent system for the movement of logs. The exports from the town rose three or four million feet a year to 20 million during the first year of the railway (348/115).

In the Lake Simcoe-Georgian Bay district, the Midland and Northern Railways competed bitterly for the lumber trade of that area. The route of the Midland cut right across that of the Northern. The latter railway tapped the rich pine stands on the sandy plains in central Simcoe and added them to the hinterland of Toronto. In Simcoe County, Barrie, Belle Ewart, and Bradford became important saw-milling points. This activity, however, did not continue for very long as the supply areas for the towns in Southern Simcoe were relatively small. Collingwood, Midland, and other ports on Georgian Bay could draw on the timber resources of a much wider area as large quantities of logs were floated across the Bay to those ports. Farther east, the colonization roads poured large quantities in terminal points such as Severn Bridge, Coboconk, Fenelon Falls, Bobcaygeon and farther down into Lindsay, Peterborough, Harwood, Hastings, Trenton, Belleville, and Deseronto. After 1878, Lindsay profited from its rail connection with Haliburton.

This rapid expansion of lumbering led to a tremendous growth in saw-milling and lumber trade, which in turn led to the start and growth of many towns. Soon after 1850, the saw-mill developed rapidly into a larger and more efficient unit with an ever increasing production (348/43-52). Until the middle of the century, almost all the cutting was done in the small local mill, but with the increasing demand for Canadian lumber in the United States, the mills became larger and often American inventions and capital were introduced. A local miller with initiative and vision could expand his mill. Many entirely new mills were erected close to the lumber areas.

During this period of change, the steam mills gained rapidly in number. After the building of the railway, a steam mill could be erected at the most suitable site. Refuse was burnt as fuel. In 1850, only 154 of the 1,567 mills in Upper Canada were driven by steam. By about 1875, however, steam was in general use and water mills were erected only in very few cases (348/47).

Some mills attained a tremendous production capacity. The steam sawmill of Gilmour and Company at Trenton was, in 1873, considered to be one of the finest in the Dominion (10/515). It employed over 100 men and had a capacity of 100,000 to 110,000 feet a day (1863). Another steam sawmill at Trenton had a total of 75 upright saws and employed 60 to 70 men. In twelve hours it could process 340 18-inch logs, or 60,000 feet, and 20,000 feet of lath. In 1878, it was said that as much as 20,000,000 feet of sawn lumber were cut in one season by the steam mills in and near Trenton (78). The lumber industry was undoubtedly the main reason for the growth of that town.

A large scale American establishment was the mill of Sage and Grant at Belle Ewart (213, I/324-325). Americans erected this mill in 1852, and for a time it was one of the most extensive in the province, having a capacity of about 15 million feet annually.

In 1874, there were 57 mills north of Lake Ontario with a capacity of 285,000,000 feet. In addition, there was a large number of smaller mills. In the early seventies, North Simcoe had 49 mills with a capacity of 182,000,000 feet annually (10/515, 516).

The lumber industry brought prosperity to many towns in the back counties and some of them gained enough momentum to attract other industries so that they survived, when the lumber trade declined. Belle Ewart became overnight a booming village. Midland on Georgian Bay did not develop until it became a railway terminal. Soon the hamlet acquired more mills and it became a large saw-milling centre. Its greatest development, however, did not come until after 1880. Penetanguishene,

Victoria Harbour, Waubaushene, Collingwood, and Gravenhurst experienced similar developments. The lumber industry
was also the source for a lively trade and as such contributed
greatly to the activity in the ports on Lake Ontario. This lumber
trade will be dealt with in another section of this chapter.

Other Primary Industries

Fishing was carried on in most of the settlements on the lakes.
In general, however, it was a small scale industry and played
only a minor part in the expansion of the villages and towns on
the lakeshores. The most important district for fisheries was
Prince Edward County. Here, 232 men – about half of the total
in South-Central Ontario – were employed in the fishing industry. The total number of boats was 131 (34). Another concentration was in North Simcoe which reported 94 men
employed in fishing with 52 boats. This district led in total yield
of fish, mainly white fish and trout.

The other primary industry to be mentioned is mining.
However, this did not lead to any important urban development
either. Iron ore was produced on a small scale in some of the
eastern districts of the region, such as Hastings North and Addington. Larger in volume and more widespread was the production of building stone. By far the largest producing district,
also in the whole province, was Cardwell. This district comprised four townships northeast and southeast of Orangeville.
The total production of the district amounted to 740,880 tons
in 1881. Other important producers were Hastings East (51,200
tons) and Lennox (31,700) (34).

Manufacturing

After 1850, manufacturing developed under greatly changed
conditions compared with those during the first half of the
century. Waterpower was replaced by steam, and coal took the
place of wood as a fuel. Profound changes came as a result of
the building of the railways. Transportation became cheaper
and was not subjected any longer to seasonal interruptions. Coal
could easily be shipped to inland towns. A much larger concentration of industry became possible and was encouraged by
the new transportation network. All the more important towns
suddenly became potential markets for the manufacturer. The

home market itself increased through the expansion in agriculture and growth of population. The inflow of American capital and the Civil War were instrumental in the founding and expansion of many establishments. Thus the woollen mills prospered during the Civil War years, when the supply of raw cotton was cut off. Most important was probably the fact that a favourable tariff fostered industrial growth. During the Civil War, the American government imposed a war tax on American goods, while Canadian manufacturing also enjoyed the shelter of the Galt-Cayley tariff of 20 per cent. The latter continued from 1858 to 1866. Under its protection the boot and shoe industry and the agricultural implements industry became firmly established (25). Also the woollen industry benefited considerably from a protective tariff. It was reported to have ousted imported woollen goods from the Canadian market (27). The first three years of the seventies were very prosperous but, in 1874, a period of stagnation set in. At the end of the decade, full protection was established with the introduction of the National Policy.

Although the conditions which influenced manufacturing underwent profound changes after 1850, manufacturing preserved by and large many of its characteristics from the preceding period. In the first place, the proportion of the population engaged in manufacturing remained rather low throughout this period. In 1881, 22.1 per cent of the working population of South-Central Ontario and 20.6 per cent of that of the entire province was employed in manufacturing (34, II).

Secondly, the size of the establishments continued to be small. In general, the manufacturing establishments were of the small workshop type and had fewer than 5 workers per establishment. Of 27 of the most important industries on the basis of employment, only eight had an average employment of more than ten workers per establishment. These eight industries with their average employment were as follows: foundries and machine working (14); agricultural implements (22.7); printing offices (13); car and locomotive works (135); hosiery (19); fittings and foundry, in brass, iron, lead, etc. (14); cotton factories (160); tobacco working (19).

Finally, the industries were scattered (fig. 11). The only major concentration was in Toronto, which in 1881 had 10.7 per cent of the persons employed in manufacturing in the province, though only 4.4 per cent of its population.

After 1850, the average size of the manufacturing establishments, although still small, was bigger in the larger cities and towns than in the rest of the region. This trend was most pronounced in Toronto, but it was also to be found in smaller centres such as Kingston. The average Toronto bakery employed 8 workers (provincial average 3 to 4), the average Toronto boot and shoe shop 16 workers (provincial average 2 to 3), the cabinet and furniture shop 22 (4 to 5), the carriage maker 8 (3 to 4), the saddle and harness maker 4 (2), and the average Toronto tailor shop 24 workers (6 to 7). In part, the larger size of the Toronto establishments was due to the fact that Toronto was a large city where the purchasing power was much higher than elsewhere in the province. In part, however, the larger size was also due to the fact that Toronto served a much wider area than any other city, mainly as a result of the expanding rail network. Thus the larger establishments in Toronto were a corollary of its rise as a metropolitan city.

Types of industries

For the province as a whole, sawmilling was in 1881 still the largest employer. In South-Central Ontario it was the most important industry on the basis of employment in 16 of the 31 census districts (fig. 11). The census, however, points out that the sawmills often worked only a few weeks and few ran more than six months (34, III). This seasonal operation reduced their importance as an employer of labour considerably. North Simcoe, Muskoka, and West Hastings were the most important districts for this industry. In these areas, the sawmills could easily be supplied with logs, especially in North Simcoe where logs were shipped from across Georgian Bay.

The second largest employer was the men's clothing industry. In general this industry was regularly distributed; as a typical service industry, its distribution pattern reflects the density of population. In both Kingston and Toronto it was the largest industrial employer. It was especially important in Toronto where it employed about 1,500 persons, or almost 12 per cent of the total employment in industries.

For the province as a whole, the census listed blacksmithing as the third largest employer. In its distribution this industry also followed closely the pattern of population density. Within South-Central Ontario, it was the most important type of manufacturing in only four census districts. These districts had practically no other industries of importance and were, to a very great extent, rural. They were Frontenac, Northumberland East, and Wellington Centre.

Of a similar nature were boot and shoe manufacturing and carriage making, the next largest employers. Like blacksmithing, they were widely distributed. In no census district were they the largest employers.

The making of wool cloth, an industry which ranked sixth in importance of employment in the province as a whole, was, in South-Central Ontario, the most important industry in Wellington South (Guelph) and in Peterborough West (Peterborough). It was also of importance in York West and Peel.

Location of industries

For almost all industries, Toronto was by 1881 the largest employer of the region. Some of the exceptions were sawmilling, blacksmithing, and woolcloth making. But, although Toronto by 1881 had become the most important centre for manufacturing, its manufacturing establishments employed only 10.7 per cent of the total manufacturing employment in the province, and only about 32 per cent of the manufacturing employment in South-Central Ontario. Several other places possessed industrial establishments which compared favourably with those in Toronto, or had industries not represented in Toronto at all. This is evident from the following summary which is based on a large number of sources (Table VI). Where available, the number of workers has been given; in other cases the industry is mentioned only when it is thought to be of unusual importance. The summary is for the years around 1880, and does not give a picture of the situation at any specific moment.

Although Toronto had become, by 1881, the largest centre for manufacturing, several factors contributed to the preservation or rise of industries in South-Central Ontario outside the city. Most important was probably the development of the larger industries from small service workshops. Often they had grown in relation to local raw materials. Hardwood, especially maple, was important for the manufacturing of organs and pianos. The same was true for the furniture factories. Woollen mills relied on the wool production of the surrounding areas. Leather, boot, and shoe industries had grown as a result of a large supply of hides, and of hemlock and oak tanning bark.

In the expansion of the small establishments into large industries personal initiative played a vital part. Before 1850,

TABLE VI – Survey of more important industries in
South-Central Ontario around 1880

Acton	glove factory (35 to 50); sole leather tannery; tannery for sheepskin leather.
Belleville	furniture factory; axe factory (45); 2 locomotive shops (200).
Bowmanville	organ and piano factory (175); furniture factory.
Bracebridge	tannery ($\pm$ 100).
Brampton	agricultural implements plants ($\pm$ 140).
Cobourg	car and locomotive works (175); woollen mill.
Collingwood	foundry and boiler shop; shipyard.
Dundas	2 cotton mills (532).
Georgetown	paper and wallpaper factory ($\pm$ 60); boots and shoe factory ($\pm$ 90).
Guelph	knitting mill ($\pm$ 120); agricultural implements ($\pm$ 160); musical instruments factory (115); lumber mill; sewing machine factory (160).
Kingston	shipyard (50); cars and locomotives, engines (350); steam engines; musical instruments; cotton mill opened in 1882 (200).
Lindsay	sawmills.
Oakville	pump factory.
Orillia	carriage works.
Oshawa	malleable iron works; agricultural implements.
Peterborough	woollen mill (120); agricultural implements plant (50); sawmills.
Streetsville	woollen mill.
Toronto	3 agricultural implements (322); printing offices; bookbinding; 2 distilleries (113); trunk and box making plant (111); 2 corset factories (263); fire-proof safe factory (75).
Trenton	lumber mills.

there were many foundries and blacksmith shops and many an enterprising operator built his establishment into a factory for agricultural implements, a carriage factory, etc. Blacksmiths repaired imported American farm machinery and finding that they could improve on them began to build them themselves. Thus Massey's blacksmith shop at Newcastle grew into a factory for agricultural implements. Massey produced the first mowing machine in Canada in 1852, the first self-rake reaper in 1863, and the Massey harvester in 1878. The Robson Leather Industry of Oshawa started as a small tannery in that town in 1836. Elsewhere small towns offered specific advantages. In 1878, G. Mclaughlin left his shop at Enniskillen and set up a carriage factory in Oshawa. Mclaughlin most likely was attracted by the supply of malleable iron which could be obtained from the establishment of Joseph Hall, an American who had set up a factory for agricultural implements there in 1858. Later on, Hall began to make his own malleable iron, for which he brought in skilled workers from Troy in New York State. He also imported skilled machinists. Oshawa had two other implement factories, two carriage factories and one more foundry at the time of Mclaughlin's arrival. The supply of skilled labour must have been an additional attraction for Mclaughlin.

The province had many competing railway companies and this led to the establishment of railway industries in several centres, among others in Kingston, Cobourg, and Toronto.

Until the 1870's, the market facilities, the capital and labour supply available in a city the size of Toronto were apparently not always the main factors considered in the location of industries. Partly, this was the result of an optimism accompanying the building of the railways. It was generally believed that a railway would solve all problems, that raw materials could be obtained easily, and that manufactured goods could be shipped anywhere. Every place with a rail connection was thought to be capable of growing into a large centre. These expectations not only led to a large scale and irresponsible system of bonus granting, but they also encouraged industrial developments in smaller centres. During this period, many American industrialists came to Ontario and established industries there. Several of them, however, selected smaller towns and by-passed Toronto. In 1859, Cositt's Agricultural Works came to Guelph from the United States and developed into an important industry. Guelph had, in these days, just over 3,000 inhabitants. Charles Raymond of Massachusetts also came to Guelph and founded a sewing machine factory. In 1860, a miller from New York State erected a flour mill in the town (10/595, 602). A Rochester firm established a branch factory for agricultural implements at Oshawa (27/149). The arrival of Hall in that town has been mentioned before. Also, industries moved from one small town to another, and sometimes even to a smaller municipality. Knitting mills which had started in Belleville were moved to Paris in South-west Ontario, in 1867, where they became an important establishment (10/610). Belleville was, in 1871, one of the larger urban centres of the Dominion and had a population of 7,305. Paris was in that year only a small village.

On the other hand, before 1850, Toronto had already become a centre for industrial establishments of which there were only a few, often only one, in the whole country. This development became more pronounced after 1850, and by 1881 a large number of these establishments were concentrated in that city. They produced a wide variety of goods, such as billiard tables, glue, gold leaf, lasts, mathematical instruments, paper bags and boxes, roofing felt, scales, shirts, collars and ties, steel barb fence, surgical appliances, tents and awnings, and wire. There were also chemical establishments, aerated water manufacturers, carving and gilding shops, a gun-making shop, coffee and spice mills, and a cork cutting establishment. Only in a few cases were these establishments large. A trunk and box manufacturer employed 111 workers, and a plant for fire-proof safes, 75 workers. In general, however, the plants were small.

Service and propelling industries

During this period the service industries continued to decline, while the propelling industries slowly increased in importance. Before 1850, the industries by and large had belonged to the first category. The transportation and economic framework, however, changed considerably between 1850 and 1881. The service industries nevertheless remained the most important during this period. This is evident from the fact that 19 of 27 of the most important industries, on the basis of employment, employed on an average fewer than ten workers per establishment. To those 19 belonged the industries with the largest total employment such as sawmilling, men's clothing, blacksmithing, boot and shoe making, carriage making, wool cloth making, dress making and millinery, flour and gristmilling, cabinet and furniture making, etc.

It is practically impossible to make a distinction between service and propelling industries. Some of the service industries listed above had establishments which served a regional market and therefore had partly become propelling. This was true for Toronto in particular, where many establishments served a province-wide market. This is evident from the larger average employment in the establishments. The average boot and shoe shop, the cabinet and furniture shop, the tailor shop in that city had an employment several times larger than the average establishment in the province (p. 124). In part, these service industries had become propelling, but it is not possible to determine to what degree they were so.

On the basis of distribution and average size of establishment it may be concluded that the following manufactures by and large had also become propelling industries: agricultural implements, car and locomotive works, cotton factories, shipyards, bookbinding, edge tool, distilleries, engine building, and musical instrument making. A firm at Oshawa developed an export trade in agricultural tools (scythes, hoes, forks) to Europe after 1870 (10/595).

Undoubtedly, Toronto was the centre in which the propelling industries had begun to play an important part in the growth of the city. Propelling industries were also of importance in the growth and prosperity of several other towns, as can be gathered from the survey on p. 127. These towns are shown on fig. 11.

During the decades between 1850 and 1880, manufacturing remained largely of the service type, and thus continued to constitute part of the general service function fulfilled by cities and towns. The importance of those industries is reflected in the status of the urban centres as central places.

Trade and Finance 1850 to 1881

Importance of the American market

From the late forties on, prosperity in Canada depended largely upon the trade relations with the United States. When that country practised a policy of restrictive tariff legislation, during the last three decades of the 19th century, the results for Canada were so serious that it has been said that the Dominion found itself in an "almost chronic depression" during those decades (293). For most of the period between 1850 and 1880, however, the trade relations between Canada and the United States brought prosperity and expansion to Canada. The intimate trade relations between the two countries induced Canada in 1853 to adopt the American dollar instead of the pound sterling for its currency system.

In 1854, a trade agreement, the Reciprocity Treaty, was

concluded with the United States. It brought free trade in agricultural and forestry products, minerals, and fish. The Americans received navigation rights on the St. Lawrence and on the canals between the Great Lakes and the Atlantic Ocean. Through this Canada hoped to draw more American trade into the St. Lawrence. The Canadians were granted similar rights on Lake Michigan. The agreement stimulated the lumber industry in Canada, and also caused large quantities of wheat, barley, and other produce to be shipped to the United States. But the treaty was not the only cause for the prosperity in Canada. The Crimean War, the construction of the railways, the Civil War all created a great demand for Canadian products.

The Reciprocity Treaty did not cover manufactured goods and criticism in the United States mounted steadily, especially when Canada's tariffs were raised. By 1859, the duty on most manufactured products was already as high as 20 per cent and on a few items more (10/641). The treaty was abrogated in 1866. However, the American demands during the first years after the Civil War were so big that the new 20 per cent tariff did not cause much harm. Gradually, the American demand levelled off and after a few years, there was for instance a recession in the lumber trade. In 1873, the exports of lumber were valued at $29 million, but by 1878 they had declined to $13 million (348/152). In the seventies, the foreign trade suffered considerably from the international depression of 1873, which continued till 1879.

Within Canada itself, the demand for new markets led to an increased desire for trade between the provinces and as such contributed to the development of Confederation. At the same time, it was more and more voiced that the larger home market be reserved as much as possible for Canadian producers. Later, in the seventies, the demands for protective tariffs became very strong and the result was the creation of the so-called National Policy.

Orientation upon American ports, Kingston

By mid-century, the East-West trade had become deeply embedded in the Erie route to the ports on the American Atlantic Seaboard. The opening of the St. Lawrence Canals did not alter this pattern. The trade diverted to the American seaports in 1856 amounted to over six million tons compared with a scant 600,000 tons which went to Canadian seaports (299/

214). Canada attempted to collect a larger share of the western trade through the building of railways and the granting of free navigation on Canadian water routes to American shipping. But the results remained disappointing. In part this was due to the inadequacy of the Welland Canal and, in part, to the fact that the trade had become accustomed to the Erie route. Nor were the railways very effective in their competition for western traffic. It was reported that in 1859 the railways carried an aggregate of 197,209 tons of freight eastward. However, the arrivals of grain at the two ports of Buffalo and Oswego alone averaged between 1854 and 1859, 1.3 million barrels of flour and 27.5 million bushels of grain. The average shipments from Canadian ports seaward were during those years only 205,821 barrels and 672,625 bushels (10/492). Canada and eight western states sent, in 1856, 57 million bushels of grain eastward. In that same year, Montreal received 589,767 barrels of flour and 1.3 million bushels of wheat. This shows that a tremendous volume of trade was sent from the old Montreal hinterland to the American ports. Ten years later, in 1866, 110 million bushels were sent eastward, but Montreal received only 975,295 barrels of flour and 7.5 million bushels of wheat (299; 19). By far the major part of these receipts came to Montreal by water. In 1869 Montreal received 524,773 bushels of wheat via the Grand Trunk Railway and 6.9 million bushels via the Lachine Canal (19/90). During the first six years of the decade of the seventies, the movement of goods by the Welland Canal increased, but during the last four years it declined at an average of 14.4 per cent for each year. On the other hand, the shipments eastward on the two trunk railways of New York State increased by 62.7 per cent in 1870 and by more than 300 per cent by 1879 (10/485). Compared with the huge amount of trade which went eastward via the Erie Canal and the New York railways, the trade by way of the St. Lawrence and the Canadian railways was extremely small.

Neither did the St. Lawrence route succeed in attracting the import trade for the American West. According to the Select Committee of the Legislative Council in 1861, goods to the value of only $21,505 passed through Canada with United States destination during the previous year (299/216). New York remained the importer for the western market. This port was accessible all the year round and it had frequent sailings to Britain and other European ports. Much more than Montreal, it was a focal point for international shipping routes. Competition had led to a reduction in the freight rates to and from New

York. The St. Lawrence route was more hazardous and required higher insurance rates and additional expenses for towing and pilotage. Finally, American fiscal regulations also tended to discourage western merchants from importing their goods via the St. Lawrence (299/217).

It is understandable that the Americans tried to monopolize the imports for their home market. But a large part of the Canadian imports was also routed by way of American ports. In 1866, Canada imported goods to a total value of 53.8 million dollars. Of this total, 12.7 million dollars passed through the United States in bond, 14.6 million dollars worth was produced in the United States, and goods to a value of 2.2 million dollars were purchased in the United States, but were not produced in that country (299/218).

The trade through Lake Ontario between the western states and the Atlantic Ocean, augmented by trade from Hamilton, Toronto, and other ports, was of vital importance to Kingston. All the grain that passed down the Welland Canal between 1850 and 1905 was trans-shipped at the foot of Lake Ontario. During those 55 years, about 50 per cent of the freight that came down the Welland Canal left Lake Ontario by way of the American ports of Oswego and Ogdensburg for the United States east coast (323). The competition of these two American ports and the fact that by far the bulk of the wesern trade went through the United States prevented Kingston from becoming a major trans-shipment and distributing centre at the foot of the lake. This general pattern of trade also reveals to what extent the Ontario and western producers had become orientated towards American outlets, particularly Toronto which, because of its relation with American ports, especially New York, became practically independent from Montreal.

Commercial expansion of Toronto

After 1850, Toronto began for the first time in its history to benefit from a transit trade via the Toronto passage. The city had gained enough economic strength to push its rail lines to Georgian Bay. At last, the old expectation of a large volume of trade from the Northwest gradually became a reality. This old plan of diverting the western trade to the Toronto passage had been one of the main reasons for the building of the Northern Railway (325/165). In the fifties, conditions were much more favourable; the railway could compete effectively with the

Welland Canal which suffered from several handicaps, and Toronto had become an important trading centre of its own. Significantly, when the Lake Michigan ports began to export, their trade had not yet become accustomed to one particular channel as had the fur trade before. Wheat was a new commodity, requiring new and different means of transportation. The western states explored different routes to the eastern seaboard for their grain, and Toronto was ready to make a bid for a share in that trade after the building of the Northern.

As soon as the railway reached Nottawasaga Bay, Collingwood became an important trans-shipment point. It grew from a mill hamlet in the early fifties to a town with 4,445 inhabitants in 1881. Collingwood was not only the terminus of the Northern Railway, it also became the terminus of a tri-weekly line of steamers to ports on Lake Michigan and a weekly line to Green Bay. The first regular line of steamboats in connection with the railway began to operate in 1857. A large grain elevator, built in 1871, quickly transferred the corn from the Chicago steam barges into railway freight wagons. In 1861, the trade at Collingwood was said to amount to $2,500,000 (10/293, 294). Until the completion of the Canadian Pacific Railway, the Northern formed an important route to the Canadian West. Around 1881, two shipping lines were engaged in the iron, copper, and silver ore trade of Lake Superior and in the immigrant and general carrying trade of Port Arthur and Duluth (4, II/592). In 1880, the Collingwood harbour received 3,868,-455 bushels of corn, 633,419 bushels of wheat, and nearly 2,000 tons in general freight. There were 20,770 tons of freight sent to Chicago, and almost 10,000 tons to other ports. Three steamship lines operating from the harbour carried a total of 28,460 passengers (83).

Other ports on Georgian Bay also built up a considerable grain trade. Soon after 1872, Midland completed its first elevator. In later years other elevators were built at Tiffin, Victoria Harbour, and at Midland itself.

The flow of grain coming through these ports made Toronto and also Hamilton important exporters of grain. Toronto became a major grain market, and its grain prices tended by 1865 to determine those in the smaller ports (292/235). The development of Toronto as a grain market led also to the formation of the Toronto Exchange in 1855. It was organized partly as a stock exchange but mainly as an exchange for the trade in wheat, flour, and other farm products.

Toronto was the largest exporter of Canadian wheat across

the lake to the United States. In the years 1866, 1867, and 1868, it shipped a total of 1,090,580 bushels, compared with 417,136 bushels shipped at Hamilton, and 111,497 bushels shipped at Kingston (19/18).

In 1860, about 29 Toronto schooners were engaged in the grain carrying trade. The largest, the *Omar Pasha*, had a carrying capacity of 14,000 bushels of wheat (230). Toronto's grain trade was almost entirely with Oswego and other American ports. In 1859, only 2 per cent of the flour and wheat shipments went to Montreal and Quebec (10/492).

The Northern Railway brought to Toronto not only an important grain trade but also a tremendous lumber business. Huge quantities of lumber came to the city from the Georgian Bay shores via Collingwood. In the early seventies, North Simcoe had 49 mills with a capacity of 182,000,000 feet, of which 140,000,000 feet were sent to Toronto (10/516). Only a small part of the Georgian Bay lumber trade went by way of the lakes and through the Welland Canal to Oswego (348/179). But Collingwood and other Georgian Bay ports also sent lumber to Chicago, which became an important market as a result of the opening up of the American West.

Also, the other ports in South-Central Ontario had a share in the grain and lumber trade. Port Hope, Cobourg, Trenton, and Belleville had a large export, but Toronto, Kingston, and Collingwood were the most important. Table VII gives a summary of the amount of shipping owned by residents in the various districts.

The shipping registered in Frontenac and Kingston may be considered as one unit of 67 ships with a total of 15,703 tons. The high concentration of shipping at the foot of the lake illustrates the importance of the trans-shipment function performed there. The other major concentrations of shipping in 1881 were at Toronto, the Georgian Bay ports, and outside the region, Hamilton. The large tonnage of Simcoe North was mainly in hands of the shipping interests centered at Collingwood and Midland.

By 1881, the railway network had already created a considerable differentiation among the Lake Ontario ports. Many of them continued to have some trade but the proportion of their share was much smaller than in 1850. The ports between Toronto and Hamilton only owned a large number of small crafts. The great wheat exporters, Port Credit and Oakville, had lost all importance. Whitby, the rival of Toronto around mid-century, also had lost all its economic independence. Only

TABLE VII – Number of vessels and tonnage in
South-Central Ontario in 1881 (34)

	Vessels	Total tonnage
Frontenac	26	5,986
Kingston City	41	9,717
Prince Edward	27	4,802
Hastings West (Trenton and Belleville)	12	1,442
Northumberland West (Cobourg)	16	2,218
Durham East (Port Hope)	16	3,108
Ontario South (Whitby and Oshawa)	7	989
Toronto	30	8,138
Peel (Port Credit)	24	846
Halton (Oakville and others)	7	603
Simcoe North (Collingwood, Midland and others)	39	10,109
Hamilton	28	8,502

TABLE VIII – Duties and other revenues collected during the
fiscal year 1879-1880 (53)

	dollars		dollars
Belleville	43,248	Newcastle	2,418
Brighton	867	Oakville	3,453
Cobourg	11,421	Oshawa	11,661
Colborne	8,667	Penetanguishene	1,877
Collingwood	28,835	Peterborough	10,122
Darlington	20,936	Picton	4,859
Dundas	19,897	Port Hope	10,679
Guelph	57,059	Toronto	2,500,266
Kingston	157,219	Trenton	2,443
Lindsay	3,388	Whitby	4,126
Napanee	1,152	(Hamilton	718,717)

Port Hope and Cobourg still had a higher concentration of
shipping, while Trenton and Belleville had almost none.

The amount of shipping owned at the various ports does
not, of course, reflect the amount of trade carried by them. It
illustrates, however, the rise of Toronto and Hamilton as the

main centres and the relative decline of the other ports. Table VIII gives a better illustration of the actual amount of business of each port. Toronto and Hamilton are the large importers of foreign goods, but Kingston still has a considerable share, and Collingwood is the main trade centre on Georgian Bay.

By 1850, the import trade was already beginning to be concentrated at Toronto. This trend continued between 1850 and 1880. In 1858, Toronto's foreign imports had a total value of $3.5 million, in 1884, it was $18.6 million, and in 1889, $23.4 million (113/172).

It was only natural that with the growth of the city as an independent importer of foreign goods its wholesale trade would expand. More and more, Toronto's commercial travellers competed with those of Montreal and reduced Montreal's hinterland for wholesale trade. The Bank of Toronto reported in 1870 that more and more wholesale firms transferred their business to Toronto (224/103). In particular the next three years saw a tremendous increase in the volume of wholesale and retail trade. Palatial commercial buildings were erected by some of the leading wholesale firms. Scadding and Dent say that ever since that time the Toronto city merchants have practically ruled the provincial market (198/258). The number of commercial travellers in Toronto increased from 114 in 1871, to 390 in 1881, or by 242 per cent. In Hamilton the increase amounted to 182 per cent, in Kingston 180 per cent, in Northumberland West (Cobourg) the number rose from 3 to 8, in Durham East (Port Hope) from 1 to 4, but in Ontario South (Whitby and Oshawa) it declined from 8 to 7 (33; 34). These trends reveal the increasing importance of Toronto as a centre for wholesaling, thus illustrating another aspect of its ascendence towards a metropolitan city. The increased competition with Montreal was shown, when the Montreal branch of the Commercial Traveller's Association withdrew itself from the national organization. The Toronto branch had been organized in 1873 and numbered 500 members.

Toronto as a financial centre

Between 1850 and 1880, the money economy spread from the front townships over the rest of the region. The railways played a major part in this development. In the first place their building brought a large amount of cash into the country. Between 1853 and 1857, £15,000,000 currency was spent in Upper and

Lower Canada (23, X/408). Secondly, the railways broke the isolation of the inland townships and made it possible for the farmers to obtain cash for a wide variety of products. Large amounts of cash entered the country through the sale of products on the American market. The lumber industry was another main source which brought much ready money into circulation. Soon the population of the back townships could pay cash for manufactured goods and all kinds of services, which in turn stimulated the urban centres in those townships.

The larger amount of capital in the country, the expansion in agriculture, trade, and manufacturing were accompanied by an increase in the number of banks and their branches. By 1881, banking facilities had become widely spread. Toronto had not succeeded in preserving its former banking monopoly in the province.

Gradually, however, the larger Toronto banks absorbed several of the smaller regional banks. The Gore Bank with its headquarters at Hamilton was absorbed by the Canadian Bank of Commerce in 1870. The Niagara District Bank amalgamated in 1875 with the Imperial Bank, an offshoot from the Bank of Commerce. The Canada Land Company moved its headquarters from Guelph to Toronto. Later in the century, in 1899, the Canadian Life Assurance Company moved its head office from Hamilton to Toronto. Thus Toronto became the financial capital of Ontario. This, however, did not develop without a bitter struggle with Montreal (224; 286; 215; 10).

This struggle had its origin in the failure of the historic Bank of Upper Canada. Almost all government funds were transferred in 1863 from this bank to the Bank of Montreal, its rival. The collapse of land and railroad values led to the failure of the bank in 1866. In Ontario, this failure was ascribed to the financial policy of the Bank of Montreal and the event aroused a great deal of resentment against that Bank. In 1867, the other large bank, the Commercial Bank, failed. Again, the failure of this bank was considered to be entirely the result of the attitude of the Bank of Montreal and its president, King. The Ontario banks began to fear the monopolistic position of the Bank of Montreal. In the meantime, the Canadian Bank of Commerce had been founded by McMaster and others. Its board of directors was closely connected with the import and export trade via New York, and as such they were particularly interested in breaking Montreal's hegemony.

The struggle reached an acute stage in the late sixties in connection with the drawing up of a new national banking policy. The Bank of Montreal had much influence with Galt, the Minister of Finance, and Toronto financial circles feared that if King's view-points were to prevail, Ontario banking would be crippled. Toronto became determined to break Montreal's financial hegemony. In this, the city was successful. The Toronto group won, and the new General Banking Act of 1871 made it possible for the city to expand its financial power and to gain complete financial control over its hinterland.

This financial independence of Toronto was of vital significance for its growth towards metropolitan predominance. The new financial strength served to stimulate and foster the expansion of trade, manufacturing, and transportation in Toronto and its region. It served to integrate city and metropolitan region.

Toronto also obtained new banks. In 1871, the Dominion Bank was established and in 1873 the Imperial Bank. The city also had its own programme of railroad financing, and it made a powerful bid for the charter of the C.P.R. The Bank of Montreal nevertheless remained a giant. The total assets of the Ontario banks in 1880 amounted to $54.4 million; the total assets of all the Quebec banks was $108.9 million, of which the Bank of Montreal alone possessed $44.5 million.

By 1881, Toronto found its position as a financial and commercial stronghold considerably strengthened. Thirty years earlier, it still had powerful rivals such as Kingston and Whitby, but now it was the unchallenged leader of the province and a powerful competitor of Montreal, which had been forced to relinquish a large part of its control over the Ontario hinterland. After 1880, this new position of Toronto became fully evident in a re-arranged railway network.

Urban Development 1851 to 1881

The urban pattern of 1881 was the result of the changes and expansion which took place in transportation, agriculture, lumbering, manufacturing, and trade. The population engaged in these occupations required goods and services which were localized in urban settlements. Manufacturing in general was still of a service type catering to the needs of the nearby population. All urban centres, except the suburbs of Toronto, were economic, social, and cultural focal points for small districts. The economic, social, and cultural institutions and establishments constituted the basis for urban growth and development;

they determined the distribution pattern of the villages and towns.

Service centres and their distribution

The urban settlements of 1881 were classified as service centres. For this purpose the census does not provide the necessary data, and Lovell's Business and Professional Directory for 1882 was used as the main source. All places were checked for a number of services and institutions. Finally, five key services were selected to provide the criteria for a classification of the urban centres as central places: banks, weekly newspapers, county high schools, members of the legal profession, and physicians. Their presence or absence gives a good picture of the economic, social, and cultural function of the towns.

Places were classified as fully-fledged towns when they provided all five services. In case one of those was missing, the centre is called sub-town. In all cases, except one, the missing service was the high school. The only exception was Newcastle which did not have a weekly paper. The urban villages possessed two or three of the five services. Of 32 urban villages, 31 had a physician and 20 a newspaper; 12 had a barrister or lawyer, 7 a bank, and 7 a high school. The rural villages had only one of the five key services. In all cases this was one or more physicians. The rural villages were the smallest service centres classified. They had one or more stores and often a few service establishments. The urban villages were much more important as about two-thirds of them had a newspaper. This indicates their importance as small regional focal points around 1880.

There is not always a correlation between the service status and the number of inhabitants of an urban centre. Two places with about the same number of inhabitants may have a different service function. Thus, Deseronto with a population of about 2,000 was an urban village as far as service status is concerned, but Cannington with just over 900 inhabitants was a sub-town in the service classification. The demand for services increased with the growth of the municipality, but services appear sooner in a centre which attracts the population of a large surrounding district. In 1881, there were a considerable number of places with a population of 200 to 500 which had not yet reached the service status of a rural or urban village. On the other hand, many smaller hamlets which are not shown on the map (fig. 10) were already rural villages and appear on the map of the service centres.

The service centres, except the very small ones, have again been given an arbitrary umland of a 4.5 mile radius (p. 99). But even with this relatively small radius there is a considerable amount of overlapping. This overlapping occurs wherever the places are strung along important transportation routes, especially the railways. This linear pattern is most pronounced along the older railways, the Grand Trunk from Kingston along the lakeshore to Toronto and from there to Guelph, and on the railway between Toronto and Hamilton. Elsewhere on the map, overlapping was the result of places being close together on the rail lines. There were practically no service centres larger than rural villages which were not situated on a railroad. On and near the Shield, the colonization road took the place of the railway. Compared with 1850, a remarkable number of advanced service centres had spread over the inland townships. This was entirely due to the building of the railways. In the areas which were too far from the railways, the pattern of small rural villages, so common in 1851, continued to prevail. A zone without larger service centres ran through the rear of the lakeshore townships, and also east and west of Yonge Street, although most of those areas had a population density of more than 40 persons per square mile. The urban settlements serving those areas were by and large on the main transportation arteries which paralleled those zones. Consequently, the urban umlands were elongated and elliptical with their long axis perpendicular to the transportation route. In areas with less through traffic, the servicing pattern was less crowded and less elongated. The umland pattern of Lindsay, Omemee, Peterborough, Millbrook, Port Perry was the result of local trade and local market development, rather than through traffic.

Outside the Shield there were not many areas which were more than four or five miles distant from a service centre where at least the most common services could be found. As such, the distribution pattern of service centres was much more balanced than in 1851, when the interstices were a great deal more extensive. Many service centres had sprung up to fill those gaps and others would develop after 1881.

Not many service centres declined or disappeared between 1851 and 1881. Where there was much crowding of centres, which is evident from the overlapping circles on the map, much competition existed between them. The place with the best facilities tended to survive. Holland Landing was one of the service centres which disappeared. This urban village of 1851 could not face the competition from Bradford and Newmarket, both of which became fully-fledged towns. For a few decades an urban village maintained itself to the east of Holland Landing, but it still was too close to the two towns, and by 1911 it also had disappeared. The rural village slightly farther east had become an urban village by that time and a balance seemed to be reached. Oakville, an urban village in 1851, pushed aside two other service centres and became a fully-fledged town. It was the capital of a small prosperous fruit growing district.

Orangeville, 45 miles to the northwest of Toronto, may be taken as an example to illustrate the nature of a fully-fledged town in 1881. In 1851 it had barely started, as the surrounding country had been settled rather late. It developed around a mill site on a branch of the Credit River. In the seventies, two railways reached the settlement and stimulated its growth considerably; the population almost doubled in those 10 years, rising from 1,458 in 1871 to 2,847 in 1881. Some of the industries were partly propelling and had developed from service industries. By 1881, Orangeville possessed a flour mill, a woollen factory, two foundries, two sawmills, a steam planing mill, a large tannery, two brick manufactories, and two cabinet factories. The town did an important lumber business and shipped large quantities of timber and cordwood. Even more important was the grain trade, for which there were four large grain warehouses. A cattle fair was held monthly. There were some large hotels. Orangeville was also an important social and cultural centre; it had nine churches and three weekly newspapers were published in the town. Its financial affairs were taken care of by a branch of the Canadian Bank of Commerce. Such was the colourful and varied structure of this fully-fledged town in 1881.

The most diversified service centre, where the most specialized services could be obtained was, of course, Toronto, although no attempt has been made to show this on the map. In 1881, Toronto towered far above the other cities and towns in the province. Its situation and antipathy against Montreal had pushed it far towards metropolitan predominance and independence. The city had grown as a result of its relations with the American ports, especially New York, and not on account of its relations with the St. Lawrence outlet. This apparently was also expressed in the general appearance of the city. According to a traveller of 1858, quoted by Scadding and Dent, "The contrast between Toronto and the cities of Canada East was so marked and striking that it was some time before I could persuade myself that I was not back in the U.S. – a Yankee look about the whole place which it is impossible to mistake; a pushing, thriving, business-like smart appearance in the people and in the streets; in the stores, in the banks, and in the churches" (198/217-218). This account is probably exaggerated, but it serves to illustrate the nature of the city and its background. Not long after 1850, the balance of power between Montreal and Toronto was very close as is evident from the compromise choice of Ottawa as the capital for the new Dominion. This was followed by Toronto's success in the struggle over the banking legislation. The city began railroad financing in its own metropolitan region and also in this field, its ambitions soon clashed with those of Montreal.

In 1881, Toronto was the largest importer of foreign goods in the province and the most important wholesale centre. It possessed industries which were found nowhere else, neither in the province nor in the Dominion. Toronto had become the centre of Ontario education, with several colleges which were federated in 1887. The city was by far the most important printing and publishing centre of the province. Toronto had 32 printing establishments which employed 38 per cent of the workers in these establishments in the province. The city had 58 per cent of the bookbinders of the province and about 74 per cent of the persons employed in engraving and lithographing. The dominance over the province was however not yet completely established. This is clearly expressed in the railway network of 1881. A few other towns and cities had pushed their railways into the Toronto hinterland and attempted to divert the flow of traffic away from the city.

Toronto and Kingston were in 1881 still predominantly service centres. To measure this, we have only the occupational census for 1881 (table IX). In the table the service industries have been added together so that they may be compared with the industrial class. It should, however, be emphasized that in part the commercial and professional classes had a propelling aspect as far as those cities were concerned. The commercial and professional classes performed services which were regional or provincial in scope. On the other hand, it may be estimated that even in Toronto more than half of the industrial class was of a service nature. The sawmill settlements on and near the Shield were probably the only places in which propelling industries played a dominant part.

TABLE IX – Occupational structure of main cities in 1881

	Toronto	Kingston	Ottawa	Hamilton
Agricultural class	539	65	67	173
Commercial class	6,618	1,066	1,506	2,383
Domestic class	4,152	578	1,284	1,518
Professional class	2,162	543	1,418	715
Total service industries	12,932	2,187	4,208	4,616
Industrial class	13,646	1,795	2,829	6,633
Not classified	4,647	773	1,823	2,012

TABLE X – Urban centres in 1851 and 1881 in South-Central Ontario

	1851	1881
200– 500	41	57
500– 1,000	10	30
1,000– 2,000	6	25
2,000– 5,000	6	15
5,000–10,000	–	5
10,000–50,000	2	2

Urban growth and decline

The period between 1851 and 1881 was characterized by a vigorous growth of urban settlement. By 1881, South-Central Ontario had a dense pattern of places with 500 or more inhabitants. In 1851, there had been 24 such centres, but by 1881 their number had risen to 77. The biggest increase was in the places of between 500 and 5,000 inhabitants (Table X). Fifty-two per cent of the urban centres belonged in 1881 to that group as against 31 per cent in 1851. In 1881 there were relatively fewer incorporated places of between 200 and 500 inhabitants than in 1851. Their percentage had decreased from 65 per cent in 1851 to 42.6 per cent thirty years later.

The distribution pattern of 1881 also differed considerably from that in 1851. The lakeshore had lost its monopoly of the larger places. In 1851, only two inland centres had more than 1,000 inhabitants, but by 1881, there were 26. The country had become much more filled in with towns and, compared with 1851, it was much more in balance as far as the distribution of urban centres is concerned. For the first time in the history of the region, a large scale movement of raw materials, coal, and finished products to interior locations had become possible. By 1881, practically all places with more than 500 inhabitants were located on or near a railway.

The failure of the attempts to settle the Ottawa-Huron Tract is reflected in the absence of towns. The attempts, however, did contribute to the growth of a number of places on or near the border of the Shield. Penetanguishene, Midland, Orillia, Fenelon Falls, Bobcaygeon, Madoc, and Tweed were stimulated by the lumber industry and the extension of roads into the tract. Places farther south also enjoyed prosperity through the expanded logging industry. Collingwood, Lindsay, Peterborough, Trenton, Belleville, and others received large quantities of lumber from the northern districts. But the Shield itself saw very little urban development.

For the province as a whole, the urban population (incorporated places) rose from 133,463 to 375,848. Of a total of 23 places with 500 or more inhabitants in South-Central Ontario in 1851, 15 more than doubled their population during the following 30 years, and two others, Bradford and Picton, almost did so. The most vigorous growth among the 15 older towns occurred in Napanee, Trenton, Peterborough, Oshawa, Barrie, Toronto, and Guelph.

In several of these towns manufacturing contributed to their growth. But that this was by no means the only factor is evident from the growth of Barrie, which became a trading and service centre with a relatively small development of manufacturing. Its main source of wealth was the surrounding farm land, for which it served as market. This made Barrie's population rise from just under 1,000 in 1851 to 4,854 in 1881. Another example of how general service fostered the growth of a town is provided by Picton. This town increased its population from 1,569 in 1851 to 2,975 by 1881. Picton was the administrative, commercial, and social centre for its peninsula-county. The town did not possess big manufacturing establishments of extra-regional significance. As a central place, the town had to operate within the rather narrow scope of this island-like county; it was entirely dependent upon the productivity and the demands of the surrounding rural population. The county had been settled at an early date and expansion of demand could only come from a rise in the standards of living.

Those conditions did not favour tremendous growth, nevertheless the town almost doubled its population in those thirty years. This shows that between 1850 and 1880, the general service function in itself could be sufficient ground for important population growth.

In five of the 23 places in 1851 with over 500 inhabitants, the population increased by less than 50 per cent during these three decades. These centres with their population figures in 1851 and 1881 respectively were Kingston (11,585; 14,091), Cobourg (3,871; 4,957), Streetsville (750; 755), Weston (500; 750), and Dundas (2,500; 3,709). In general these places declined as service centres. Kingston, Cobourg, and Dundas lost much of their importance as trade and shipping centres. Dundas had been overshadowed completely by Hamilton, which became the focal point for the railways, while Kingston and Cobourg failed to expand their trade in proportion to the general increase in the volume of trade. Kingston especially lost much trade to the American routes. Most important, perhaps, the city missed an expanding consuming and producing hinterland. The only product shipped in considerable quantities was lumber. Kingston's population even declined from 13,743 in 1861, to 12,407 in 1871.

Cobourg did not lack a good hinterland, but it had difficulties in maintaining connections with it. The town began to decline in prosperity when the railroad bridge across Rice Lake proved unusable. At the same time, Cobourg met severe competition from Port Hope which was more successful as a railroad promoter, and from Peterborough which became an important regional capital in the area north of Rice Lake. Cobourg also carried a heavy railroad debt. During the early sixties the town went through a particularly bad period, when the harbour had no shipping and the lumber and wheat went via Port Hope (205). But the town had a few important propelling industries which in part balanced these losses.

Dundas was an old service centre in which the change towards manufacturing had probably progressed furthest. More than 500 persons worked in the cotton industry alone, a considerable number for a town with a population of just over 3,700. In addition to the cotton industry, the town had a large foundry which produced steam engines, a screw factory, farm implements works, a boiler shop, an axe factory, a paper mill, and other industrial establishments. Manufacturing had become an important and probably the main asset of this town. But it had not led to a spectacular increase in population. Its function as a central place was of minor importance; there was only one bank office, and only two weekly papers were published. Brampton with a smaller population had two banks and three papers.

Streetsville and Weston suffered as central places from their close proximity to Toronto, with which they had good communications. Weston, however, would soon grow as a prosperous suburb of the city, but Streetsville remained stagnant as a service centre. It is one more example of a small town which declined after the arrival of the railway. One of its propelling industries moved to Toronto (p. 171). The decline of Streetsville was already evident as early as 1850. W.H. Smith described it as follows: "Formerly a place of much business, but the improvement of the road to Toronto, and the gradual springing up of small places in its vicinity have shorn it of a considerable portion of its trade" (129, I/275). One of these small places was Brampton, which had railway connections at a much earlier date than Streetsville.

Bath was the only one of the 23 places mentioned before whose population declined after 1851. The decrease was about 30 per cent. At one time an important shipping centre, Bath was by-passed by the railway, although the Grand Trunk originally had planned to go through it. A local landowner asked too high a price for his property and the company changed the route (212). Napanee replaced Bath as the main service centre of that district (186/445).

It has been noted before that the smallest centres experienced a relative decline in number between 1851 and 1881. There are nine places with a population smaller than 500 on the 1851 map which do not occur on the map of 1881. They were all close to larger urban centres, and the better transportation facilities brought them into competition with the larger centres. Their service facilities were neither as diversified nor as broad as those in the larger towns, and so they declined. In a similar way a large number of the very small localities declined and disappeared. This development began already before 1881 in the older settled districts and became wide-spread throughout South-Central Ontario after 1880. This decline of the smallest service establishments, due to the improved transportation facilities, played a major part in the general decrease in rural population and will be discussed at greater length in the next chapter.

Finally, in addition to the 23 places mentioned above as having already become of some importance by 1851, there were several others which grew from insignificant hamlets in the fifties to places with 2,800 or more inhabitants in 1881. To this group belong Orangeville (population in 1881, 2,847), Brampton (2,920), Collingwood (4,445), and Orillia (2,910). Orangeville, Collingwood, and Orillia grew in connection with the general expansion of settlement and economic activities. The building of the railways was the main reason for their growth. The rapid rise of Brampton differs from the three other towns in that it developed in one of the older settled districts in Southern Ontario. On the till and clay plains west of Toronto, Streetsville had functioned for several decades as the main service centre. It was not reached by the railway until the seventies, while the Grand Trunk went through Brampton in 1856. This proved to be a tremendous stimulus for the small hamlet with a population of little more than 50 in 1853. It was in the centre of a good farming district and it became one of the largest wheat markets. In 1865, Brampton became the administrative capital of the newly-formed county of Peel. The main function of the town was in commerce and trade and in the provision of services to the surrounding districts. It had an extensive retail trade. Its commercial and social importance in the district is evident from the fact that it had two branch banks, three weekly newspapers, and five hotels. Agricultural fairs added much to the prosperity of the town. The industrial development in the town was of minor importance; the only outstanding establishment was an agricultural implements works which employed about 140 persons.

Conclusion

Such was the urban development between 1851 and 1881. In practically all cases of urban growth or decline the provision of services was the decisive factor. This service function was completely dependent upon the transportation facilities. To expand, a central place required good connections with a prosperous umland and a certain freedom from competition of the larger towns. Before 1851, it had been water and not road transportation; after 1851 it was the railway. In 1851, the larger urban centres were ports and trans-shipment points. Thirty years later, the main villages and towns were district and regional service centres. Their distribution is closely related to the railway network.

As far as manufacturing is concerned, propelling industries played only a minor part in the growth of urban settlement. There were no large centres in South-Central Ontario during this period whose growth depended entirely on propelling industries. Dundas was probably the most important exception.

By 1881, Toronto had gone a long way to gain metropolitan dominance over the province. Its position, however, was not yet fully established. Montreal and various centres in the province were still undefeated competitors. This is most evident in the further expansion of the railway network after 1881.

5. The Rise of Modern Manufacturing, 1881-1911

Distribution of Population in 1911

The dominant aspect of urban development during the three decades between 1881 and 1911 was the rise of modern manufacturing. Not only did central service function decline as a factor in town development, but through improved transportation facilities, many places lost their position as a service centre, and their population decreased.

By 1911, three years before the first world war, the settlement pattern had changed considerably (fig. 13). The map of population density for 1911 shows only those urban centres which were incorporated. No attempt has been made to include the unincorporated places. except for two, Frankford and Bala, which were incorporated during the next ten years. Altogether, there were probably between five and ten unincorporated places with more than 200 inhabitants which have not been put on the map.

Compared with 1881, the pattern of rural population density was much less varied. The districts with more than 60 persons per square mile had been reduced still further until they occupied only a small triangle around Toronto. On Georgian Bay, another small area with higher densities was found. By far the greatest change had taken place in the zone with between 40 and 60 persons per square mile. From the large areas with this population density in 1881, only a strongly tapered triangle was left between Dundas, Cook Bay, and Bowmanville. There was also a pocket around Peterborough, and one at the head of the Bay of Quinte. To the south of the Shield, by far the largest number of townships had a population density of between 20 and 40 persons per square mile. The 20-isopleth followed very closely the border of the Shield and had not changed much in position since 1881. This isopleth reflected the physical geography of the region in Frontenac County as well, where it now, in contrast with 1881, followed the edge of the Shield. South of Lake Simcoe, the isopleths continued the general trends which had become established before 1850. On the Shield proper, an additional isopleth has been drawn, in order to show in more detail the population density pattern in that area. Compared with 1881, the belt with between 10 and

20 persons per square mile is smaller, but the isopleth tends to follow the same general directions.

These changes in the population pattern were due to a variety of factors. In the main, they were the result of changes in the economic structure of the region. These changes will be analyzed first, as they, in conjunction with the changed pattern of rural population density, conditioned urban expansion and decline.

The Economic Structure

Just before the first world war, 31 per cent of the gainfully employed persons in the province worked in agriculture (169, table XVI), while in 1881 this proportion still amounted to 48.3 per cent. In other words, the non-rural occupations increased considerably in importance during those thirty years. Manufacturing, which included the building trades in 1881, declined from 20.6 per cent to 17.6 per cent in 1911; but, if we were to include the building trades again in 1911, then the percentage would rise to 23.1 per cent, which is still considerably less than the proportion employed in agriculture. Trade and transportation was the main occupation for 14.4 per cent of the gainfully employed population. This represented a considerable increase since 1881. In general the occupational structure of the provincial population had become much more urbanized, because the non-rural occupations in 1911 comprised about two-thirds of the gainfully employed population compared with about one-half in 1881. This change was accompanied by a big increase in urban population; in 1911, 52.5 per cent of the population in the province lived in incorporated places, as compared with 31.5 per cent in 1881. The amount of urbanization was even greater in South-Central Ontario owing to the expansion of Toronto.

Agriculture

The trend towards mixed farming continued after 1881, as it became increasingly more unprofitable to grow wheat. Soil exhaustion and blights had already reduced the wheat acreage, especially in the older settled counties. New circumstances arose, however, which accelerated the trend away from wheat farming. The Canadian West had begun to export wheat since about 1876, and the competition of Manitoba wheat became very strong with the completion of the Canadian Pacific Railway in 1885. At the same time, several other new producing areas poured their wheat on the world market, and consequently prices dropped sharply. Barley, the crop to which many farmers had turned when wheat growing became impracticable, also experienced difficulties in Ontario. First of all, there was the problem of soil exhaustion which tended to have similar results as earlier with wheat. Furthermore, the exports of barley decreased. In part, this was due to the increased use of substitutes for barley malt, but more particularly it was the result of the McKinley tariff of 1890. The United States raised the duty from ten to thirty cents a bushel. The new tariff caused the exports of other grains, flour, wool, and other products to stagnate. Wheat production in the province became negligible. During the first decade of the 20th century, it declined by 42 per cent. Barley began generally to be grown as a feed for livestock, together with oats and corn. In Prince Edward County, long a noted producer of barley, the production declined sharply. In 1881 the production had amounted to 876,432 bushels, but in 1911 it was only 173,009 bushels (38).

The decline in wheat production was accompanied by the development of mixed farming. The demand for a varied agricultural economy grew rapidly. The cities, with their growing industrial population, the mining camps, and the pulp and paper industry constituted an ever increasing home market, and consequently, after 1900 the export of many food products declined, in particular dairy products and livestock. In 1911, Canada began to import butter.

Gradually, mixed farming became more intensive and specialization took place in the form of fruit farming, dairying, stock raising, etc. Considerable progress was made in these specialized branches, and farming became more and more scientific. The fertility of the land which had suffered so much from relentless wheat farming was restored through good farming practices. Moreover, the government did much to raise the general standards of farming. An agricultural college had been founded at Guelph in 1871. Experimental farms and stations were established to demonstrate good farming methods. Free government publications were made available and travelling exhibitions were organized. The farmers helped themselves through the formation of co-operative organizations. As a result, the efficiency, quantity, and quality of farm production were greatly increased.

The dairy industry gained rapidly in importance. Cheese production had become well established by the early eighties. The decline in cheese production later on was due to the increased demand for milk in the cities. The quality of the latter product was enhanced considerably through many improvements in creameries and cold storage plants. The centrifugal cream separator was introduced in 1882. The demand for milk increased also as a result of the rise in concentrated milk and ice-cream production. Plants were established to supply condensed milk to the mining and pulp industries. After the turn of the century, ice-cream ceased to be a special treat and was recognized as a food as well as a refreshment. Better freezing methods and probably the reduction of the fat content of the ice-cream also greatly increased the demand (288/78).

The greater demand for milk led to a gradual increase of the dairy herd in the province. The increase continued until 1901, after which followed a slight decrease. The number of milchcows in the province rose from 782,243 in 1881 to 1,065,763 in 1901 and declined to 1,032,996 in 1911 (38). The acreage under pasture grew steadily. In 1911, it was already 25 per cent of the farm land. In general there was a big increase in the production of feeds, the coarse grains now being used for this purpose. Corn especially became the staple feed crop; it tended to replace mangels and other root crops. After 1880, silage became a common practice as a means of making feed for livestock, especially where the increased demand of the urban population encouraged winter dairying. Considerable quantities of animal feed became available also through the use of industrial by-products from the milling, cotton seed, corn oil, beet sugar, and other industries.

Other branches of the livestock industry expanded as well. The raising of hogs accompanied the expansion of dairying and the production of coarse grains. A large increase took place in the poultry industry. The number of horses increased when oxen were abandoned as draught animals on the farms. Many horses were needed in the lumber camps, and for a short time also for horse-drawn streetcars in the cities. Soon, the demand declined with the introduction around 1890 of the electric streetcars and the use of gasoline engines.

The production of fruits and vegetables was yet another type of specialized farming. The Oakville and Port Credit districts had early become large producers of small fruits, especially strawberries (p. 119). Along the entire lakeshore the production of apples increased rapidly. Oakville exported apples to Glasgow and Liverpool. Prince Edward County in particular became an important producer. This peninsula has a higher temperature in the summer and a longer frost-free season than anywhere else along the north shore of the lake. The apple production of the county increased from 308,848 bushels in 1881 to 473,533 in 1901, which was an all-time high and made the county one of the largest apple producers of the province.

During the first two decades of the period, the number of farmers continued to increase, but before the turn of the century a decline had set in. For the entire province the number rose from 206,989 in 1881 to 285,608 in 1891. By 1901 the number had declined to 185,415, but it increased again during the next decade; in 1911 it was 226,801. In a long settled county such as Prince Edward, the number of farmers increased from 1,903 in 1861 to a maximum of 3,884 in 1891, after which it declined to 2,211 in 1901 and increased again to 2,891 in 1911. Durham county had 3,386 farmers in 1861, 6,068 in 1891, 3,007 in 1901 and again 4,061 in 1911. Thousands of farmers and farmers' sons went to western Canada, where virgin land only needed to be ploughed to yield an abundant crop. At the same time, there was a large emigration of Canadians to the United States. Between 1880 and 1890, the number of Canadians in that country rose from 717,000 to 980,000 (25/152). Many others turned to the cities and took up professions there. Finally, the decline of the rural birth rate was still another factor which contributed to the decline of the farming population. The pioneers had had large families. The average number of children was 6.2 in 1851; in 1891 5.1 and by 1921 it had declined to 2.9.

The decline in the farming population was thus mainly the result of internal and external migrations. Farm abandonment did not play a part in this decline except on the Shield, on poor morainic soils and in a few other areas. On the contrary, during this period the acreage of improved land continued to increase in practically all townships in South-Central Ontario. This was true even in the older and longer settled counties. In Peel, the acreage of improved land rose from 205,261 acres in 1881 to 245,535 in 1911; in Durham from 238,192 to 273,171; and in Prince Edward from 162,056 to 189,279 acres.*

Such was the development of farming during the thirty years prior to the First World War. The relation between farm-

* Based on data obtained from the Ontario Research Foundation.

ing and urbanization had completely been reversed, compared with what it had been before 1880. During the early period, after it had broken the shackles of a closed economy, farming formed the basis of a lively trade, largely an export trade. It created an important flow of traffic and with the resulting increased prosperity, this formed the main basis for urban growth. Soon after 1880, the urban population had reached such a strength that it began to mould the agricultural land-use pattern at a time when farming had to turn to new sources of income. Dairying, hog, and poultry raising, the production of fruits and vegetables became the corner stones of farming, and they were greatly stimulated by the urban demand. This new and modern type of farming produced a tremendous quantity of products and again created an extensive trade. For now, however, the main market was at home and not outside the province as before 1880. On the other hand, modern farming also constituted a basis for industrial development in the same way as the earlier agriculture, but to a far greater extent. Its products had to be processed and refined, and the industrial consequences were relatively much more significant in the growth of towns than the old milling industry. Meat-packing plants gained rapidly in importance. This was also true for the canning of fruits and vegetables. Dairies became large establishments, preparing fluid-milk for the consumer and producing a great variety of other dairy products. Thus the developments in farming after 1880 were to a very great extent the result of the rise of a larger urban market, yet this new farming also produced tremendous quantities of raw materials, encouraging industrial expansion.

Lumber Industry

In South-Central Ontario, lumbering during this period was predominantly concentrated in the Georgian Bay watershed. The mills in Southern Simcoe did not have a wide area from which to draw. Lumber may have come from the north through Lake Couchiching, but the mill at Bradford closed in 1894, and the last mill at Barrie operated on a reduced scale until about 1900 (348/172).

Farther north, the mill centres received lumber from a much wider territory. The mills at Collingwood, Midland, Victoria Harbour, and other points on Georgian Bay were fed by large supplies of lumber which were rafted across the waters of the Bay. Great rafts of lumber came down to Collingwood from the Algoma and Parry Sound Inlets (4, II/596), and other large supplies came from Manitoulin Island; Collingwood became an important sawmill centre. Its production rose from 3,000,000 feet cut in 1898 to 23,000,000 feet in 1902 and 1905 (348/172). Midland however became the biggest centre. After the opening of the first mill in 1872, it gradually grew into a leading saw milling centre outranked in Canada by Ottawa only (348). From the beginning of the century, 60 to 70 million feet of lumber were cut in its mills. The supplies were obtained from the eastern section of the Georgian Bay watershed whence the logs were floated down the rivers and assembled in rafts at their mouths along the east shore of the Bay. Penetanguishene and Victoria Harbour were other important saw milling settlements.

The Georgian Bay ports, however, saw their supply areas tapped by the Northern Railway which was built northward from Gravenhurst; in 1886, it reached Callander on the east shore of Lake Nipissing. This line crossed the rivers along which the logs were moved to Georgian Bay, and tapped the forest resources of their watersheds to the east of the line. Bracebridge and Huntsville became major milling points on this railway where it crossed the larger streams. Gravenhurst remained the leading town. Its period of maximum production fell between 1883 and 1890, when fourteen sawmills were in operation, cutting up to 40,000,000 feet (348/175). In 1906, the output still amounted to about 28,000,000 feet.

For many years, the white pine country, opened up by the Northern Railway, ranked in production only behind that of the Ottawa Valley and the Georgian Bay proper. In the 1880's, hemlock was more and more considered as a suitable timber for lumber, and around the turn of the century the Muskoka District produced more hemlock than pine.

The expansion of the saw milling industry was considerably stimulated by government policies. Increasing quantities of timber were rafted across the lakes to feed the mills in Michigan, where the beautiful pine stands had become exhausted. Gradually, Canada increased the export duties on this lumber in order to develop the cutting industries within the country itself. In 1886, the export duty became so high that it induced Michigan firms to begin sawing in Canada. The Emery Lumber Company of Michigan began sawing by contract at Midland in

1887, and somewhat later it built a mill in that town (348/154). The prohibition of the export of sawlogs cut on crown lands in 1898 also encouraged the establishment of Canadian mills.

The sawmills near Lake Ontario faced serious difficulties when the lumber became depleted in their supply areas. Some of them moved their mills to fresh lumber districts, while others tried to continue as long as possible until they broke down. The Rathbun Company, an American firm which had established mills at Deseronto, migrated to the Muskoka District and began cutting at Gravenhurst (348/171). In other cases, the railways which were built northward into the Shield fed large quantities of timber into the southern mills and so prolonged their existence. Most spectacular was the project of the old Gilmour Company at Trenton (256). In 1892, the company purchased timber stands in the southwest corner of present-day Algonquin Park. It planned to float the lumber down the streams to Lake of Bays; from there a steam alligator would haul the logs over the height of land, after which they would travel in water-filled troughs down into Raven Lake; this had been raised by a dam so that its waters overflowed into one of the headwater lakes of the Trent. The logs had to travel a distance of about 200 miles before they reached the mouth of the Trent. This trip took many months and it was found that the lumber had begun to deteriorate by that time. The gigantic project was an expensive failure. After the completion of a railroad, the company built a mill and a village at Mowat, on the west side of Canoe Lake, in Algonquin Park. But not long afterwards the company went bankrupt.

For many years, Toronto enjoyed an extremely lively lumber trade on the route between Georgian Bay and New York. The railways built with Toronto initiative and capital sent large quantities of timber to the city; from there it was sent in schooners to Oswego. But Toronto suddenly ceased to be a lumber capital, when the tolls were removed from the Erie Canal in 1883. The charges on the Welland Canal remained and the lumber was shipped directly by boat to Tonawanda and Buffalo. Buffalo, the old rival of Toronto for the Upper Lakes trade (p. 110), obtained also a direct rail link with Georgian Bay after the completion of the line from Port Dover on Lake Erie to Wiarton; Toronto was by-passed (348/179).

From about 1900, the lumber industry ceased to be a major factor in the establishment and growth of towns in the region.

The forests became exhausted and no suitable trees were left. At the same time, there was a growing competition of the logging industry in British Columbia.

In South-Central Ontario, lumbering had contributed to the growth of the majority of towns and for several, it had been the main factor in their rise and subsequent expansion. The first to receive this stimulus were the ports on the shore of Lake Ontario. As the watersheds of the rivers draining into that lake generally are small, for many towns the period of lumber activity was relatively short. Only those with good transportation facilities in the form of a large stream (Trenton), canal (Kingston), or a railway (Toronto, Port Hope) continued to receive the benefit of a lively timber trade. Gradually the industry moved across the height of land and Peterborough, Lindsay, Bradford, Collingwood, and the towns near or on the Shield succeeded the ports on Lake Ontario.

With the depletion of the logging activities, the towns had to turn to other sources of income. South of the Shield, the problem was not a serious one; the land was good and they became trade and service centres. In the Georgian Bay ports, the western wheat trade soon gained in importance. More serious, however, were the results for the saw milling centres on the Shield. Many of them declined when the forests became depleted. But some of them, especially in the Muskoka district, turned to tourism; Gravenhurst, Bracebridge, and others became later in the 20th century important tourist centres.

Transportation

Expansion of the rail network

During the first years of the First World War, railway building came to an end in South-Central Ontario. After 1915, the network received only a few minor additions.

Most of the railways built after 1881 radiated from or focussed upon Toronto. In the early 1880's, a second main line was built between that city and Montreal. This railway (the Ontario and Quebec Railway) was projected away from Lake Ontario and ran from Toronto via Peterborough in a general eastern direction. The line was opened in 1884.

About the same time, the Northern Railway of Canada pushed its tracks beyond Gravenhurst through Bracebridge and Huntsville to North Bay in 1886. Shortly after 1900, a second line, the Canadian Northern, was built from Toronto, around the east side of Lake Simcoe to Parry Sound and beyond. The Canadian Northern had started as a small railway on the Canadian prairie in 1899. But it had expanded rapidly and the line from Toronto via Parry Sound was meant to link up eventually with its main network in the West. In the years 1906 and 1907, the Canadian Pacific also constructed a line from Toronto to Sudbury in order to connect the city with its main line to the Canadian West. The Toronto-Sudbury line branched off from the old Toronto, Grey, and Bruce line and went in a general northern direction via Parry Sound to Sudbury.

Just after 1910, Toronto received two more railways from the east. The Campbellford, Lake Ontario and Western Railway branched off from the Ontario and Quebec line, just to the east of Frontenac County, and ran in a southwesterly direction to Belleville. From here it ran practically parallel with the Grand Trunk line to Toronto. The line was completed just before the First World War. The second railway, a line of the Canadian Northern, followed almost the same route, but farther inland. It was laid out from Toronto to Napanee and from there in a northeasterly direction to Ottawa, via the tracks of the recently acquired Bay of Quinte Railway.

Thus by 1915, Toronto had four lines running in a general eastern direction, three of which were very close together, and three lines in a northern direction, two of which were directly aimed at the Canadian West.

After 1881, the eastern part of South-Central Ontario also saw considerable railway construction. It was traversed not only by the lines going to Toronto, but rail communications from Kingston, Napanee, Belleville, and Trenton to the northern parts of the region. The Kingston line was meant to tap the forest resources of the Ottawa Valley in competition with similar lines from Brockville and Prescott, two ports on the St. Lawrence River. The Kingston and Pembroke Railway was completed in 1884.

Farther to the west in South-Central Ontario, the trade from Georgian Bay was expected to become so extensive that another railway seemed justified. Consequently, the Georgian Bay and Seaboard Railway was constructed from Port McNicholl via Orillia and Lindsay to Dranoel on the Ontario Quebec line. Along its entire route the line paralleled the old Midland Railway. The line was completed around 1910, but it never carried much freight, as it could not compete with the older and well-established Midland Railway.

Toronto versus Montreal

The motives behind this expansion of the railway network between 1881 and 1915 were manifold and varied. Toronto had become the main focal point as is evident from the convergence of the inter-provincial lines upon that city. In the building of these major lines, the traditional struggle between Montreal and Toronto played a decisive part. The railway history of this period makes clear the balance of power between the two competing cities, and to what extent Toronto had advanced towards metropolitan independence.

It had always been a Toronto tradition to expect a large flow of trade from the Northwest, through Georgian Bay. This tradition was vigorously alive during the era of railway construction. In the late fifties and the sixties, the Toronto press urged the building of a direct connection with the Red River (224/57). In the early seventies, the *Toronto Globe* pressed for the completion of a road along the shores of Georgian Bay and Lake Superior to Thunder Bay. The same paper was a strong advocate of the opening up and the annexation of the Red River district and the Northwest. The Toronto Board of Trade maintained similar viewpoints (224). But Montreal's ambitions went in the same direction. Influential circles in that city continuously urged that Montreal should control the Canada Central from Montreal to Lake Huron in order to prevent the Toronto and Nipissing from having a monopoly in Northern Ontario and the diversion of the projected CPR line to Toronto (224). The conflict of interests between Montreal and Toronto reached a climax in the struggle for the charter of the CPR. For a while, Toronto and the Grand Trunk succeeded in blocking the plans of the Montreal group to build the CPR. But Montreal eventually triumphed and it acquired the charter for the new railway in 1881. The Montreal group which completed the CPR was backed by such powerful interests as the Bank of Montreal and the Hudson's Bay Company. Thus, the metropolis of the St. Lawrence had a trans-continental railway at its disposal, while Toronto was forced to remain satisfied with the Act's guarantee of equal rates with Montreal (216). Toronto, which had been so victorious in the controversy over the banking legislation, suffered now a serious setback in railway affairs.

It was not until the building of the Canadian Northern that Toronto had a trans-continental railroad similar to Montreal and the CPR. The building of the Canadian Northern was a Toronto enterprise; it was supported by the Canadian Bank of

Commerce and other Toronto financial interests. But Toronto did not receive the trans-continental connection until about twenty years after the completion of the CPR. When the railway, which reached the Pacific via the Yellowhead Pass, was completed, the Toronto Board of Trade gave the builders a banquet (216); this reflects the expectations and hopes of the industrial and commercial circles in that city.

In 1886, Toronto acquired a communication with the CPR at North Bay with the completion of the Ontario and Pacific Junction Railway north of Gravenhurst (an offshoot of the Northern Railway). Its northern extension, the Temiskaming and Northern Ontario Railway, was also a Toronto ambition for which it had secured the support of the province. The Temiskaming and Northern Ontario opened up the mineral districts of Northern Ontario, which contributed so greatly to the financial empire centred at Toronto. The line was jointly operated with the Grand Trunk Pacific, with which it was connected at Cochrane.

Over-expansion

It is evident from the railway network, as it had developed by 1915, that considerable over-expansion had taken place. Several competing lines were too close together with the result that they faced serious financial problems. A solution was found through a series of amalgamations which eventually left the province and the Dominion with two major railway systems. These amalgamations were accompanied by a large scale abandonment of railroads. This occurred mainly after 1915.

As far as Toronto is concerned, the amalgamations tended to reveal Toronto's weakness as a railroad financier compared with Montreal. The Grand Trunk and the Great Western were amalgamated in 1882. Gradually the Grand Trunk absorbed a series of other systems such as the Midland Railway and the Northern and Northwestern, both of which in turn were the results of amalgamations and consolidations. The Midland Railway had absorbed the Toronto and Nipissing, the Grand Junction and the Victoria Railway; the Northern and Northwestern was a consolidation of the competing Hamilton Northwestern and the Northern Railway. The Canadian Northern, Toronto's trans-continental communication, experienced financial difficulties and was taken over by the Canadian Government. Together with other lines, it formed the nucleus of the Canadian

National Railways, established in 1919. Four years later, the entire Grand Trunk system was turned over to the Government and became part of the CNR. The railways continued to serve Toronto, but the city had failed as a co-ordinator and transportation organizer within a large part of its hinterland; the headquarters of the CNR was established at Montreal.

Soon after its establishment, the CPR also acquired important lines in South-Central Ontario, including the Ontario and Quebec, a line which always had been friendly to the Canadian Pacific and which had absorbed the Credit Valley and the Toronto, Grey and Bruce. Other lines consolidating with the CPR were the Georgian Bay and Seaboard Railway and the Campbellford, Lake Ontario and Western Railway. By 1915, the railway network in South-Central Ontario was mainly in hands of the CPR and the Grand Trunk system.

The railway pattern, as it had developed by 1915, continued to be of a somewhat dualistic character. There was still the old system of railways leading inland from the various ports on Lake Ontario. But, superimposed upon that older network, was the new radial network with Toronto as its hub. The new radial pattern tended to prevail, as lines were abandoned. The small ports east of Toronto suffered the same fate as Oakville had before. They were cut off from their hinterland by the railroads focussing upon Toronto; this development was a major factor in their decline as ports.

Before 1915, not much abandonment took place. Only the Cobourg line was liquidated. After the disintegration of the trestle across Rice Lake, it had turned to the iron ore deposits situated to the northwest of Marmora by means of a communication by water and a light railway. But the ore deposits were tapped by another railway from the south (fig. 14). As far as the other duplicated lines are concerned, for the time being, the amalgamated or competing companies continued to operate them. But later in the 20th century, long stretches of rail were abandoned in South-Central Ontario (fig. 15). Several north-south running lines which had served as feeders for the ports on Lake Ontario were given up. To those belonged also the line from Georgian Bay to Lindsay, on which over a long stretch the service was discontinued. Also one of the three lines along the north shore of Lake Ontario was abandoned after the amalgamation of the Canadian Northern Railway and the Grand Trunk in 1923. Then, suddenly two parallel lines were in the hands of one company, an older double track line and a newly built single track one. The latter was abandoned between Toronto and Deseronto.

Thus Toronto became the hub for the rail network of Southern Ontario. Also the communications between the region as a whole and other regions of Canada eventually went largely via Toronto. However, Montreal had proved to be more powerful as a railway builder. At a much earlier date than Toronto, the St. Lawrence port acquired a transcontinental rail communication. Moreover, the Toronto and Ontario-built lines had become part of the CNR with headquarters at Montreal, and so that city became the seat of the head offices of the two gigantic railway empires.

Employment in transportation

The railways not only directly affected the growth or decline of urban centres, but they also became an important source for employment and manufacturing. Of the gainfully occupied persons in the province 3.6 per cent was in 1911 employed by the steam railways. Toronto, although it was such an important focal point for railways, had nevertheless a relatively low proportion of its gainfully occupied population employed by them. The Toronto percentage amounted to 2.6 as compared with 4 per cent for Montreal.

The railway employees were rather regularly distributed over the larger and smaller towns and by 1911 did not yet exhibit any concentration. The proportion in Kingston was 2.2 per cent, in Peterborough 1.5, in Guelph 3.6, and in Hamilton 2.4 per cent (37).

If employment in transportation is taken as a whole, then the distribution of the persons gainfully employed in transportation shows more variation. The proportion for the whole province was 7.7 per cent in 1911. In Guelph and Toronto the proportion was about the same, 7.8 and 7.1 per cent. But, for Kingston it was 9.3 per cent, and in Montreal the proportion was 10.4 per cent. In Kingston transportation was still one of the propelling industries, while in Toronto it was less important. Kingston had 289 persons employed in the various branches of water transportation, and Toronto had only 522, although its population was about twenty times that of Kingston. Other towns in which transportation was one of the propelling industries were Collingwood and Midland. No statistics, however, are available for those places.

Trade and Finance

Unlike transportation, trade and commerce were concentrated in the larger centres, especially Toronto. In 1911, this city had 17 per cent of the provincial total of gainfully occupied persons, but the proportion employed in trade and commerce amounted to 35 per cent of the provincial total. Kingston, on the other hand, had only a relatively small number employed in these occupations, although, as far as transportation is concerned, it was relatively more important than Toronto.

TABLE XI – Persons gainfully occupied in trade and commerce in 1911 in Toronto and other cities (37)

	Trade and commerce	All occupations
Toronto	39,129	169,520
Kingston	1,422	7,218
Peterborough	1,144	7,331
Guelph	968	5,924
Ontario	111,783	991,013

Kingston was a trans-shipment point, while the capital was a distributing centre.

Toronto's position within the province as a retail centre had been considerably strengthened by the rise of the large department stores of Eaton's and Simpson's (301). Timothy Eaton came to Toronto in 1868 from St. Mary's. All goods in his store were marked and sold for the price listed. Eaton soon gained a strong position, as he bought his merchandise on long-term credits and disposed of them for cash only. He rigidly adhered to his principle that the customer was always right. He organized vigorous advertising campaigns and by 1881 Eaton's dry-goods store had expanded into a department store with forty employees. The firm sold a wide variety of merchandise. Three years later, the first catalogue was published and the mail order business was inaugurated. This meant severe competition for the store-keepers in small rural centres. Customers in isolated rural districts could select merchandise from a well-illustrated catalogue and have it sent to them by mail. Later, the big department stores extended this service through the establishment of mail order offices in the larger cities and towns of the province. This development is another example of how the large city undermined the economic foundations of the other towns.

Banking also was to a considerable extent concentrated in Toronto. In 1911, the city had 1,541 persons occupied in banking, or 25.7 per cent of a provincial total of 5,975 (37). The Toronto Stock Exchange had been incorporated in 1878, and the city was the unchallenged financial and commercial capital of the province. Compared with Montreal, the city had actually a larger number of persons occupied in trade and finance than that city, despite its smaller population (table XII).

TABLE XII – Employment in trade and finance in
Montreal and Toronto in 1911

	Montreal	Toronto
Trade and commerce (includes banking)	37,239	39,129
Banks	949	1,541
All occupations	184,257	169,520

Toronto had built up its powerful position in these economic activities through a lively trade with American ports. This trade had been originated and stimulated by the handicaps of the St. Lawrence River route and the influence of the Erie Canal. But after 1880, the trade with the United States underwent a considerable change. In 1883, Toronto ceased to be a lumber capital and with the agriculture of the region turning more to a production for the home market, the export of farm produce fell rapidly. The export of manufactured goods was stifled by tariff regulations. Ever since the Civil War, the United States had maintained relatively high tariff rates. There were a few fluctuations but the general trend towards protection remained strong in that country. It culminated in the passing of the McKinley Act, in October 1890, which practically excluded many manufactured products, especially textiles. Very high were the duties on agricultural products. Later, in 1897, another increase of custom duties became effective under the Dingley tariff. The tariffs resulted in a serious reduction in trade with the United States. Among the ports on Lake Ontario, Toronto, however, found compensation in an expansion of manufacturing and in an increased trade with the rest of the Dominion.

Manufacturing 1881 to 1911

General conditions

By 1881, modern manufacturing was still relatively unimportant in urban growth. During the next thirty years manufacturing continued to expand, but it was not until after the turn of the century, that it began to play a major part in the development of urban settlement. A wide variety of factors, notably tariff policies, new markets, and new supplies of raw materials, stimulated the industrial development in South-Central Ontario.

During the six years of depression following the panic of 1873, the demand for protective tariffs became increasingly stronger. In the Federal Session of 1874, it was pointed out in a report how the Americans had a larger home market and how they sold their surplus goods in Canada, often below cost prices. The wool manufacturers complained about the importation from Europe of low-priced woollen cloths, made primarily from shoddy (230/645). The cotton manufacturers, although able to compete successfully with English imports, were undersold by American cotton (27/243). After the general election of 1878, the National Policy, as the policy of high protective tariffs was called, was rapidly put into force. The import duties were increased considerably; especially favoured were the textiles. In 1881, a duty of 45 per cent was levied on imported blankets; clothing paid 35 per cent; cloths, coatings, and tweeds 32 per cent. The rates on furniture and clocks were raised to 35 per cent. Pig iron had been free previously, but under the National Policy a duty of two dollars a ton had to be paid. Machinery and other items of iron and steel paid from 25 to 35 per cent.

The National Policy soon led to the desired results. Innis and Lower give many examples of industrial expansion which was due to tariff protection (10). The report on the effects of the National Policy claimed that of a total of 54 woollen mills, 19 had been started since 1879 and that employment had increased by 91 per cent. Ten out of 20 knitting firms were started after 1879 and their employment rose 185 per cent. The cotton industry enjoyed similar benefits from the protective tariff system. In 1885, 13 out of 17 cotton mills were claimed

to have been started after 1878, with an increase in employment of 210 per cent. A new cotton mill was opened at Kingston
in 1882, employing 200 workers. A considerable expansion
occurred in foundries and plants for agricultural implements.
There were 45 foundries in 1884, 12 of them having started
after 1879, with an increase in employment of 83 per cent.
Eighteen of the 57 farm machinery plants in 1884 were established after 1879 and the number of workers increased by 87
per cent during those years.

In later years, the tariff system was amended on several
occasions, but the general trend of the import duties remained
upward.

Another important consequence of the tariff policy was the
establishment of American branch plants in Canada. Quite
early, individual Americans had come to Canada to establish
industries, but now the new plants remained affiliated with a
mother firm in the United States. Of the 1,350 American industries in Canada at the end of 1934, 5 per cent was reported
to have begun operation before 1900, and 11 per cent between
1900 and 1909 (17/19).

The home market, thus protected, was also expanding
rapidly. The market in the Maritimes had been opened up by
the building of the Intercolonial Railway and the development
of ocean steamship traffic from Montreal. In 1874, firms in
Ontario exported stoves, farm machinery, steam engines, knitted
goods, and other products to the Maritime Provinces (10/719).
This soon was followed by the opening up of Western Canada
where wheat, and mining and lumbering operations rapidly
gained in importance. In the nineties, Manitoba had practically
no manufacturing and in years of good harvests, large quantities
of farm machinery, dress goods, furniture, pianos, wines, etc.
were shipped to the West, mainly from Ontario. In particular
the Ontario manufacturers of agricultural machinery found
their western market almost insatiable (298). The province had
54 of the 77 agricultural machinery plants in the country. The
mining operations in British Columbia drew large amounts of
supplies and mining machinery from the east.

After 1881, the changes in agriculture and the development
of mining elsewhere in Canada made available large quantities
of raw materials for processing and manufacturing. The improvement in the quality of livestock led to the growth of the
slaughtering and meat-packing industry. In 1911, 31 of the 70
plants in Canada were located in Ontario, mainly in Toronto,
Hamilton, and London. Ontario also had six of the eleven

condensed milk plants in the Dominion, 63 of the 65 evaporated fruits and vegetables plants, 66 of the 82 establishments for fruit and vegetable canning, and 68 of 87 plants for woollen goods in Canada (37). Within the province, a large number of those industries were found in South-Central Ontario.

Finally, industrial development in the province in general was stimulated by the rise of iron smelting in Hamilton, Midland, and other places. Ontario manufacturers had been dependent upon imported pig iron. But by 1911 ten of the 18 smelting plants in the Dominion were located in Ontario. The first modern furnace at Hamilton was opened in 1895. Four years later a small furnace began to operate at Deseronto and another was established at Midland in 1900.

Types and distribution of manufacturing

For the province as a whole, saw milling was by 1911 still the biggest employer with 9 per cent of the workers employed in manufacturing. In South-Central Ontario it was the largest employer among the industries in 12 of the 27 census districts. It was mainly concentrated in the northern parts of the region. In Dufferin 30 per cent of all manufacturing workers were employed by sawmills, in Frontenac 38 per cent, Muskoka 46 per cent, Ontario North 30 per cent, Peterborough East 25 per cent, Simcoe East 46 per cent, Simcoe North 22 per cent, and in Victoria and Haliburton 35 per cent.

The foundry and machine shops in South-Central Ontario were of special importance in Guelph, Toronto and district, Oshawa, Peterborough, and Midland. These were all, except for Midland, older centres in which personal initiative had largely been responsible for the rise of the foundries and machine shops. By 1911, Midland had become a small centre for metal working. The industry had been especially stimulated by the building of a blast furnace with federal subsidies, in 1898. The furnace had a daily capacity of 125 tons and processed iron ore from the Helen mine in Northern Ontario. About ten years later, in 1909, a larger new blast furnace was built with a capacity of 250 tons per day. Both Midland and Collingwood were considered to be favourable sites for iron smelting. Coal and ore could be cheaply assembled and also the marketing conditions were regarded as favourable especially with respect to the Northwest. Collingwood tried to obtain an iron industry in 1901 by offering a large bonus ($115,000) and exemption from taxation (284/236). The blast furnace, however, was not built on account of financial difficulties. Another company began with the production of rolled wire rods, bolts, nuts, etc.

Of the remaining industries only a relatively small number showed important concentration in localities outside Toronto. Peel County had five establishments for the manufacturing of tiles and bricks, employing a total of 315 workers. Prince Edward County had a considerable concentration of fruit and vegetable canning establishments – 12 plants employing 1,299 hands. There were also 11 plants for the production of evaporated fruits and vegetables, with 175 employees. Flour and grist milling was concentrated in Peterborough where three establishments employed 530 persons. Halton County was noted for leather industries and the manufacturing of gloves and mittens. Four leather plants employed 582 workers. Acton was the main centre.

Compared with the conditions around 1881, the region had relatively declined in industrial importance, while Toronto's industrial rise had continued along the trends set in the 1870's. The Toronto area, which includes the city and the immediate surroundings, had, in 1911, about 70 per cent of the workers employed in manufacturing in South-Central Ontario (fig. 16). In 1881, this proportion had been about 32 per cent. Some of the largest industries of the province were now almost entirely concentrated in that city; thirty years earlier, that had been only the case for the less common industries, which were small establishments. The most remarkable concentration was that of factory-made women's clothing. Toronto had 60 of the 68 establishments in the province and employed 68 per cent of the employees in that industry. The industry employed predominantly female workers of which there was a large supply only in Toronto. The city was also the largest market for the finished products and the main distributing centre for the province. The clothing industry, originally attracted by the local clientele, always had been of importance in the city. Although to a smaller extent, also factory-made men's clothing was concentrated in Toronto. In this case about half of the workers in the province employed in this industry worked in Toronto plants. Toronto had 41 per cent of the printing and bookbinding establishments of the province with 49 per cent of the provincial total of workers in those plants. For the printing and publishing establishments the proportions were seven per cent and 35 per cent respectively of the provincial employment. The rising importance of the city as a distributing point is also revealed by the concentration of the bread and biscuit industry there. In 1911, 36.5 per cent of the workers in the bread, biscuit, and confectionery industry were employed in Toronto plants. The average bread and biscuit factory in Toronto employed 66 workers as compared with an average employment of 23 workers in the rest of the province.

The rise of modern industries

The rise of Toronto and the decline of the region in general as far as manufacturing is concerned was chiefly due to the change-over to large modern industrial establishments. The small plants declined in number, while the larger ones concentrated in Toronto and in a few other towns in South-Central Ontario. This change-over from small establishments to large modern plants did not set in until after 1890.

The development can be traced by comparing the number of manufacturing establishments and workers for the various census years. Unfortunately, changes in census definitions reduce the value of data on the number of plants.* In places from 1,500 to 5,000 inhabitants the number of establishments increased from 23,070 in 1881 to 32,150 in 1891, and the number of workers from 118,000 to 166,000 (166/279). During the next decade, the number of establishments decreased to 6,540, while the number of workers remained approximately the same. In 1911, there were 8,001 establishments in the province with 238,817 employees.

At the same time, the average number of workers per establishment increased steadily. In 1871, the province possessed 173 plants for the manufacturing of agricultural implements, with an average employment of 12 workers per establishment. Ten years later, there were 141 factories with an average employment of about 23 workers. By 1911, there were 54 plants with an average employment of 165. In 1911, the average employment in the foundries and the machine shops was 62, in sawmills 20, in factories for women's clothing 119.

---

* The 1901 census excluded plants with fewer than five workers, except cheese and butter factories, and brick and tile works. In 1911, flour and grist mills, lumber products, fish-curing plants, lime kilns and power plants with fewer than five employees were added. Many of these mills were located in the smaller places.

The rise of large modern manufacturing establishments concentrated in a relatively small number of places and the decline and disappearance of the widely scattered small establishments was due to a great variety of circumstances. The new big factories in their new location were subjected to an entirely different set of influences compared with the traditional small shop which had grown out of local needs. Labour supply, access to raw materials and markets, and contact with related industries were factors which were essential in the location of the new larger plants. For the traditional industries those factors had been much less important. They processed locally available raw materials for a small local market and their demand for labour also was small. The new industries favoured the large cities.

Decline of manufacturing in the small places

With the building of the railways it was thought that any place with railway connections had the same advantages for industrial location as any other. Gradually, however, the assets of the large town, especially Toronto, as a place for the location of large industries began to be appreciated. Toronto, which for long had concentrated the import trade for the province, offered a wider variety of raw materials than any other place. Raw materials and coal could easily be shipped in from all directions. In 1877, Toronto harbour received 174,417 tons of coal, while large quantities were also imported by rail (10/616). The city offered better marketing facilities and more capital for investment than any other centre in the province. An important pool of skilled and unskilled labour was available. From all over the province, the city drew those elements of the population which found their local framework too narrow, and were attracted by the life and the opportunities in the city. Large numbers of immigrants first arrived in the city and stayed there. These factors drew many industries from other parts of the province to Toronto, and many a small town lost a promising industry to the capital city. The extensive woollen mills at Streetsville moved to Toronto around 1880 (10/608). Toronto firms purchased factories in the smaller centres and then moved them to the city. Thus the ingrain carpet factory near Elora was removed to Toronto about 1874 (191/170). Of far-reaching significance was the move of Massey from Newcastle to Toronto in 1879. The financial demands, labour supply, and cheap transportation facilities made this move desirable (298). A few years later the firm employed more than 300 workers.

This migration of industries was destined to continue for many decades. But it was not the only factor which contributed to the decline of the industries in the smaller towns. The environment in which their industries had grown up gradually changed. The clearing of the land affected the water regime of the streams. The spring floods washed out the smaller dams, while in summer there was not a sufficient head of water to keep the mills running. This phenomenon had been mentioned as early as 1850 by Smith (129, II/17). A resident on the Humber complained that during the dry season there was scarcely enough water to turn a single run of stones. The small mills in general suffered from high costs as a result of maintenance expenditures for dams, gates, raceways, etc. Local raw materials became exhausted or disappeared. Sawmills closed down when the forests were cleared; this was most pronounced in the older counties. York County numbered 117 sawmills in 1871, but 67 in 1881, and only 16 in 1911; Northumberland, 66 in 1871, against 39 in 1881. The same development led to the decline of the tanneries, as with the clearing of the land the source for tanning bark also disappeared. In 1881, Northumberland had only two tanneries left of the nine it possessed in 1871. York County and Toronto still had, in 1871, five pot and pearl asheries, but by 1881 there were none. The gristmills declined in number because of the abandonment of wheat farming. The capital costs for the small mills became too high after the introduction of rollers (258/469). The desire for more comfort and luxury meant a decrease in the use of home-spun and woven materials. This reduced considerably the number of carding and fulling mills. Ontario numbered in 1881, 72 carding and fulling mills as against 158 in 1871. On the other hand, the number of woollen mills increased from 233 to 993 in Ontario. The finer, factory-made product was apparently preferred to the coarser home-made material. Practically all the factory-made woollen products were for the domestic market, and the industry grew with the increase of that market (10/607-610). Finally, there was the factor of improved transportation facilities. Originally, isolation had fostered the rise of many small industries. The building of the railways changed this entirely. The small local shop had now to compete with the products of plants in the larger centres. Those factories were larger, more modern, and more efficient than the small local establishment. The Massey-Harris firm, for example, absorbed several prosperous agricultural implements factories in small towns (297).

The changes in manufacturing which occurred during this period reduced the opportunities of growth for the smaller urban centre considerably. On the other hand, they stimulated the expansion of the larger towns, Toronto in particular. The towns recognized the assets of having a large and prosperous industry within their precincts. And the same as was true in connection with the railways, municipalities granted bonuses and extended other privileges in order to attract manufacturing. Oshawa granted a bonus to the Ontario Malleable Iron Company, in order to obtain a source of malleable iron for other local industries, in particular the agricultural implement factory of Hall. This undoubtedly has been a vital factor in Oshawa's growth as an industrial centre. When McLaughin's factory burned in 1899, the town of Oshawa granted a bonus of $50,000 to build another plant. Beardmore's tannery received from the municipality of Bracebridge a bonus of $2,000 and a remission of taxes for ten years (152/68).

Often the decline of the number of industrial establishments in urban centres was astonishing, even when taking into consideration the above-mentioned changes in census definition. Kingston in 1891 still had 401 industrial establishments; ten years later, this had been reduced to 42. In Toronto the decline was from 2,401 in 1891 to 847 in 1901. Bowmanville saw its number of plants reduced from 86 to 10 during this decade. Aurora from 64 to 8, Newmarket from 41 to 3, and Orangeville from 103 to 6 (37). In practically all places in South-Central Ontario with 1,500 or more inhabitants, 1891 was the census year with the smallest number of industrial establishments. In a few cases the minimum came later. In many of them also the number of industrial workers declined. It reflected the downfall and disintegration of the old industrial pattern which had contributed so much to the rise of towns and villages. Its decline meant ruin for many a centre, in particular the small and very small ones.

Manufacturing towns in 1911

However, out of this disintegrating pattern and partly dovetailed in it, grew the modern industries. They were subject to a different set of location factors, but for the most part they attached themselves to existing urban centres. These towns show characteristically a decrease in the number of establishments, but the

| | establishments | | | employees | | | |
	1891	1901	1911	1891	1901	1911	1911 1891 = 100
Collingwood	78	36	28	324	1,021	1,044	322
Guelph	159	68	78	1,886	2,206	3,072	163
Orillia	73	29	40	482	543	729	151
Oshawa	94	22	24	921	1,206	3,220	350
Peterborough	216	44	65	1,876	2,166	4,029	214
Toronto	2,401	847	1,100	26,242	42,515	65,274	247
Newmarket	41	3	7	251	372	693	276
Pene-tanguishene	35	14	19	376	519	766	204
Bracebridge	—	9	10	—	465	609	—
Midland	35	17	17	203	771	544	268

number of workers continued to rise. They were the places in which the rebirth of manufacturing was most pronounced. Outside Toronto, there was a vigorous development in Collingwood, Oshawa, Peterborough, Newmarket, and Penetanguishene during this period of industrial readjustment. Midland also belongs to this group of towns, as its number of workers in 1911 was considerably higher than in 1891, although there had been a decline since 1901. Moreover the population of the town more than doubled during those 30 years. The accompanying table gives a summary of the development of manufacturing in those places.

Three of the ten most promising industrial centres in 1911 were situated on the shores of Georgian Bay. Collingwood, Midland, and Penetanguishene were large saw-milling centres, with several new types of industry. Collingwood had one of the largest ship-building plants in Canada; the town also had a large dry-dock, steelworks, foundries, and other industries. Metal industries also became important at Midland, when the lumber industry declined. The government subsidized the erection of a blast furnace, and flour milling, ship and engine building also began to develop. Penetanguishene was less successful after the decline of the lumber industry. By 1911 it had a variety of industries such as machine building, boat building, and leather tanning. These towns were favourably located on break-of-bulk points in the rail and water route between eastern and western Canada.

Peterborough was another town which saw its declining

lumber industry replaced by a variety of new industries. The city had an attractive site for industries because of the power supply which could be obtained from the Otonabee River. In the ten miles above the city, the river has a fall of about 280 feet. Like Midland, Peterborough was greatly helped by an influx of outside capital, mainly British and American. Consequently, the city became a centre for flour-milling, manufacture of electrical appliances, locks, machinery, etc.

Oshawa, Newmarket, Guelph, Orillia, and to a smaller extent towns such as Dundas, Belleville, Lindsay, Port Hope, Aurora, and Bowmanville, did not attract new industries, but some of their original local industries weathered the changeover and gradually developed into large modern plants.

This development was most spectacular in Oshawa, where McLaughlin's carriage factory grew into a large scale modern motorcar industry. In 1907, a contract was signed between McLaughlin and Buick for the production of automobiles, using Buick engines and a McLaughlin built chassis. In 1915, the Chevrolet Motor Company affiliated with this plant and two years later, the entire McLaughlin organization became part of General Motors of Canada Ltd.

In contrast with the new industrial towns, some centres which had been prominent during the earlier periods had not recovered their former position by 1911. Some of them were sawmill centres which lost their lumber industry: Deseronto, Gravenhurst, Napanee, and Trenton. But, Cobourg, Kingston, Brampton, Whitby, and others also had by 1911 still fewer manufacturing workers than in the two previous census years.

In 1911, only five centres in South-Central Ontario had more than 2,000 workers employed in their manufacturing establishments, namely, Toronto, Peterborough, Oshawa, Guelph, and Kingston (fig. 16). The next important centres were Belleville, Collingwood, Port Hope, and Lindsay. North Toronto may be considered as part of Toronto. A concentration of small industrial towns occurred between Toronto, Guelph, and Hamilton.

During the second part of this period, modern industry came to the fore and became concentrated in a few towns. Good transportation facilities (Georgian Bay towns), outside capital, and momentum gained during the earlier period seem to have been the main factors in this development. From this period on, modern manufacturing was destined to be the primary influence in the growth of cities.

Urban Development 1881 to 1911

1911 was selected for a survey and analysis of the urban pattern in South-Central Ontario because it shows conditions just before the modern highway began to cause a new type of city development, and before the war gave a new stimulus to industry.

Central places

In order to assess the importance of the central services as a factor in urban growth, the towns and villages have been classified as service centres. The data forming the basis for this classification were mainly obtained from the Canadian Almanac for 1911 (57). The key services chosen as criteria were selected out of a total of 19 services, which had been listed for all places in the region. Thus we obtain an insight into the nature of settlements, for which census data or other statistics are not available. Six criteria were selected to serve as a basis for the classification. These are banks, weekly newspapers, high schools, barristers, physicians, and public libraries. There was no value in taking shops or stores as criteria, because many combinations occurred, especially in the small places. A store. listed as fancy goods could also sell watches and jewelry, while no store for these articles would be found in the directory. Many of these combinations were possible, such as jewelry and bicycles, wall-paper and photography, groceries and photography, etc.

A place which possessed all six key services was called a fully-fledged town. Such a place had one or more banks, a weekly paper, one or more barristers and physicians, a high school and a public library. The key services selected for a fully-fledged town are the same as in 1881 with the exception of the public library. In all, 42 places were classified as fully-fledged towns (fig. 17).

In the sub-towns, one of the six key services was absent. Of the 20 sub-towns, 15 were so classified, because they had no public high school; 4 others were without a library.

If two or three of the six services were not available, then the place has been called an urban village. Of a total of 26 urban villages in South-Central Ontario, 24 did not have a public high school, while a similar number did not offer library facilities. In 12 urban villages there was not a barrister. All together, 15 urban villages were without two key services – in general a high school and a library – and 11 without an additional third key service – a barrister. It is of importance to note that almost all urban villages – 23 out of 26 – had a newspaper. Together with the banking facilities, this serves to emphasize their function as a central place for a small district.

The smallest service centre recognized is the rural village. In almost all cases they offered banking facilities and had a physician. In total there were 43 of such rural villages in South-Central Ontario in 1911.

The number of inhabitants in each of these types of urban settlement varied widely. Six fully-fledged towns had less than 1,000 inhabitants in 1911, the smallest of them being Streetsville with a population of 543. This was also the minimum size of the sub-towns, the smallest of which had just over 500 inhabitants; the largest sub-towns had more than 2,700 inhabitants. Only one sub-town was not incorporated as a self-governing municipality. Among the service centres of lower order, the number of unincorporated places was much higher. Ten urban villages were not incorporated, and therefore it is difficult to determine their size accurately. The smallest urban village, with census population figures available, was Woodville in Eldon township which had 394 inhabitants. The largest urban village, Victoria Harbour, had 1,616 inhabitants. Practically all the rural villages were not incorporated and most of them had probably fewer than 200 inhabitants. The largest of the incorporated rural villages, Wellington in Prince Edward County, had 785 inhabitants.

This great variation in the relation between the size of settlements and their status as a service centre meant that a place of just over 500 inhabitants could be a fully-fledged town, a sub-town, urban village or rural village. This also reveals the shortcomings of making incorporation dependent upon the number of people living in a given area. A place could be a sub-town or urban village, in other words a commercial, social, and cultural capital in a small region and still be considered as rural, although its function was purely urban. The census definition of rural and urban was based on the administrative status of the population, and did not take into consideration the function of the settlements.

The distribution of the central places in 1911 reflected to the fullest extent the influence of the railway on urban development. Richmond Hill on Yonge Street, north of Toronto, was the only larger central place which was not located on a railroad.

By and large, the service centres were situated on older railways, those which had been built before 1881. This was particularly true for the area south of the Canadian Shield, where no new central places had developed by 1911 on railways constructed after 1881. Only on and near the Shield did new centres develop on railways built after that year. Several new fully-fledged towns and sub-towns developed in that area, and by 1911 there was an almost continuous row on and near the Shield. Most of them were on railways, a few on colonization roads.

During the thirty years after 1881, the number of rural villages underwent the biggest change. Fifty centres which had been classified as a rural village in 1881 are absent from the map of 1911. It should, however, be noted that to be classified as a rural village, a centre in 1881 needed to have only one of the key services. That was nearly always the presence of a physician. In 1911, a rural village had to have two of the key services; in general they had a bank and a physician. Of the 50 centres mentioned above, 28 did not have a key service at all in 1911; they had lost their medical service after 1881. The remaining 22 failed to grow and to attract one more key service, especially a bank, to be classified as a rural village in 1911. Therefore, although a different classification was used, it may be concluded that many rural villages declined or became stagnant after 1881. Stagnation meant a relative decline, as the region as a whole continued to expand.

In addition to the 50 rural villages which experienced a decline, there were 70 other central places which did not change their service status; 30 of them had already reached the status of a fully-fledged town in 1881. Several of these towns expanded as central places, but this has not been further differentiated. Only one of the central places of higher order saw its central function decline after 1881. This compares very favourably with the large decline among the rural villages.

By 1911, 21 new central places had developed since 1881, among them 14 rural villages. Thirty-five other places expanded their status as central places, so that by 1911 they found themselves in a higher category than thirty years before. Of those 35, 23 had been rural villages in 1881.

Thus the rural villages were the group which underwent the largest changes. They suffered the greatest losses, while the central places of higher order underwent practically no decline. The latter category had already been well established by 1881 and maintained itself during the succeeding period.

The railways played a major part in the birth, growth, or decline of the central places between 1881 and 1911. Of the 50 rural villages which were stagnant or had declined during those thirty years, 39 were not located on a railroad. On the other hand, 19 of the 21 new central places shown on the map of 1911 were on a railway.

Finally, many places suffered as a service centre because of the revolutionary changes in the pattern of manufacturing. This was accompanied by a decline in population which reduced the demand for their services, especially in the central place itself.

It has been pointed out that the central places were practically all located on railways. Also, the new ones sought such a location. This left wide areas outside the immediate sphere of influence of a service centre. Arbitrarily, the places have been given an umland with a radius of 4.5 miles (fig. 17). These umlands are clearly arranged in rows and cover a zone which parallels the railways on both sides. From the overlapping of the circles it is evident that often the central places were too closely spaced on the railroads. They tapped the area on both sides of the road and their real umland was not circular but elliptical, with the short axis formed by the railway and the long axis perpendicular to it.

In the interstices outside the circles, the rural villages tended to be concentrated; they already existed in 1881 and had not become "filled in" by 1911. In other words, these interstices remained dependent on peripherally located central places. Only where the interstices were traversed by railways, could a new central place develop in them. Thus Bolton sprang up as a sub-town in the centre of a large gap which existed in 1881 to the northwest of Toronto.

Such was the development of central places in South-Central Ontario between 1881 and 1911. During this period the railways were the most important factor which governed their decline and rise.

Urban growth and manufacturing

After 1881, the urban population of the province, that is the population living in incorporated places, increased considerably. The proportion rose from 31.5 per cent in that year to 38.7 per cent in 1891, 42.9 per cent in 1901, and to 52.5 per cent in 1911. During this same period the population living outside the incorporated places declined from a maximum of

1,351,074 in 1881 to a low of 1,198,803 in 1911. That was less than the rural population in 1871 (Table XIII).

TABLE XIII — Rural and urban population in Ontario, 1851-1951 (census figures)

Year	rural	urban	
1851	818,541	133,463	
1861	1,137,899	258,192	
1871	1,264,854	355,997	
1881	1,351,074	575,848	
1891	1,295,323	818,998	
1901	1,246,969	935,978	
1911	1,198,803	1,328,489	
1921	1,227,030	1,706,632	
1931	1,335,691	2,095,992	
1941	1,449,022	2,338,633	1941
1951	1,844,361	2,753,226	definition
1941	1,196,161	2,591,494	1951
1951	1,346,443	3,251,099	definition of rural and urban

Although during this period the urban population of the province as a whole continued to increase, there was nevertheless a great amount of variation as far as individual urban centres was concerned. This is also revealed by the hesitant increase of the provincial urban population between 1891 and 1901. During this decade, out of 76 places in South-Central Ontario, at least 49 experienced a decrease in population and about 25 of them had a smaller population in 1911 than in 1901. These drastic shifts in population were mainly caused by the revolutionary changes in manufacturing.

Of the 37 places in South-Central Ontario with 1,500 and more inhabitants in 1911, 19 and possibly 20 showed a continuous increase in population between 1891 and 1911. For 11 of these centres, figures are available on the manufacturing establishments and the manufacturing workers within their boundaries (37, III). In nine of them the number of manufacturing workers also continued to increase without interruption (p. 174). The two exceptions were Barrie and Campbellford. In 15 other places with 1,500 or more inhabitants in 1911, for which data are available, the fluctuations in manufacturing employment were very closely reflected by similar fluctuations in the total population of the town. In most of them, 1901 was the year with the lowest number of manufacturing workers and also the year in which their total population reached a minimum. This shows to what extent modern industries had become the decisive factor in the growth of towns. Places which did not attract them and which did not have a flourishing service function were doomed.

The decline of the smallest centres

It is not possible to obtain statistical data on the population decline of unincorporated hamlets and villages. The stagnation and decline of those which were large enough to act as small central places has been noted before. Yet, an impression of the loss of population suffered by these unincorporated places may be obtained by observing the trend of the population figures for the townships; the unincorporated nucleated settlements form part of the township population. Most of the townships near Lake Ontario reached a population maximum before 1861 (fig. 18). After that a decline set in. This decline, however, was not due to a decrease in the rural farm population, or a decrease in the acreage of cultivated land. It has been pointed out previously that the acreage of cultivated land continued to expand and that the number of farmers began to decline at a later date (p. 154). In Durham County, five of the six townships had reached their maximum population by 1861 and the sixth township, the one in the southwest, as early as 1851, after which the total rural population began to decline. But the rural farm population continued to increase till 1891. Three of the five townships in Peel County reached a population maximum in 1851; but the number of farmers and the acreage of improved land continued to increase long after. Therefore, the decline of the township population cannot have been caused by a decline in the rural farm population; a decrease in the rural non-farm population was the cause. And it was in the hamlets and small villages that the rural non-farm population was concentrated. Numerous small settlements disappeared entirely or were reduced to a few buildings. At one time about sixty villages and hamlets flourished in Peel County. At present only fourteen remain as more or less important centres, and even of those, about half are not more than fair sized hamlets. Only three had the status of a rural village in 1911; the rest had disappeared or declined to a few houses near a gas station and a small store.

Several factors contributed to the elimination and decline of the small centres. There was first of all the falling away of the traditional local industries and the rise of modern industries in the larger cities and towns.

The fact that the railway by-passed many small centres was another extremely important factor in their decline. On the other hand, improved transportation facilities made the stores in the smaller places suffer from the competition of similar but better-equipped establishments in the nearby towns. The competition from the mail-order business of the big department stores has been mentioned before.

Later, in 1908, the introduction of rural mail delivery brought the farming population less often to the village post office, and more decline of business was the result for the village stores.

Many small places were destroyed by a fire. Often the settlement was not rebuilt and the manufacturing establishments moved to larger centres. Cooksville suffered from a fearful fire in 1852 from which it apparently had not fully recovered in the late seventies (82). Bell Ewart, the booming sawmill settlement on Cook Bay lost its extensive steam mills in a disastrous fire. The mills were never rebuilt and in the early eighties only two of the four churches were still left. A fire ruined the Durham Woollen Company at Newcastle and the industry moved to Toronto.

Since the decline of manufacturing and the disintegration of trade and commerce in the villages occurred mainly through the influence of the larger cities and towns, it is understandable that the townships first to be affected would be adjacent to those cities and towns. The area in which the townships reached their maximum population by or before 1861 coincides very closely with the oldest settled part of the region (fig. 18). It was in that area that the best developed towns offering the best services were found; in 1881, it contained 13 of the 22 towns in the region with 2,000 or more inhabitants and 17 of the 29 fully-fledged towns; in 1911, the same figures were 14 out of 28, and 25 out of 44 respectively. These towns and service centres had drawn to them most of the functions of the villages and hamlets. The result was that the larger centres expanded at the cost of the smaller ones. This tendency increased as the means of transportation became better.

Population changes in other places

The urban population of the entire province increased by 137 per cent between 1881 and 1911. In South-Central Ontario there were not many cities or towns which experienced an unusual growth during those decades. Actually only the eight places listed in the following table saw their population more than double during this period.

	1881	1911	increase
Acton	848	1,720	103%
Bracebridge	1,260	2,776	120%
Campbellford	1,418	3,051	115%
Midland	1,095	4,663	325%
Orillia	2,910	6,828	134%
Penetanguishene	1,089	3,568	227%
Peterborough	6,812	18,360	169%
Toronto	86,415	376,471	335%

Most spectacular was the increase of Toronto's population. Its increase accounted for about 38 per cent of the total increase of the urban population of the province, and it explains why only a small number of other towns experienced an unusually rapid growth. The city was clearly growing at the expense of the other cities and towns of the province. It acquired more and more of their industries and services. In 1911, 1,100 of the 8,001 industrial establishments in the province were concentrated in Toronto, employing over 27 per cent of its industrial employees. This was a considerable change since 1881 when Toronto had only 10.7 per cent of the industrial employment of the province. The city had first grown as an administrative and commercial centre, now manufacturing had become the dominant element in its growth.

Six of the seven other centres which more than doubled their population during this period enjoyed an uninterrupted expansion of their manufacturing. In contrast to so many other places, their manufacturing employment did not show a relapse after 1891. Campbellford is the only exception. Its population more than doubled, but its manufacturing employment remained more or less the same between 1891 and 1911. The town had excellent water-power facilities, and manufacturing (woollen mills) played an important part in its growth. At the same time, it was the main central place between Peterborough and Belleville. This was probably the main factor in its growth.

Of 85 incorporated places, at least 27 had a smaller population in 1911 than in 1881. Some of those which lost most heavily are listed in the next table.

Seven of the centres in this list had in 1901 a population even smaller than in 1911; in 1901, Port Hope had 4,188 inhabitants, or about 26 per cent less than in 1881. In general the smaller centres lost proportionally more population than the larger ones. Of the eighteen heavy losers listed above, only five had more than 2,000 inhabitants in 1881. The larger places tended to maintain themselves better, and as has been noted earlier, they grew at the cost of the small ones.

	1881	1911	decrease %
Bath	546	347	37
Bowmanville	3,504	2,814	20
Bradford	1,176	946	20
Brighton	1,547	1,320	15
Elora	1,387	1,197	14
Fergus	1,733	1,534	12
Millbrook	1,148	793	31
Napanee	3,680	2,807	24
Newburgh	834	465	45
Newcastle	1,060	655	39
Omemee	744	505	33
Orangeville	2,847	2,340	18
Port Hope	5,585	5,092	9
Port Perry	1,800	1,148	37
Richmond Hill	867	652	25
Streetsville	755	543	29
Uxbridge	1,824	1,433	22
Whitby	3,140	2,248	29

Various factors were responsible for the decline of population in these villages and towns. All of them lost many of their traditional industries. Orangeville possessed, in 1891, 103 industrial establishments with 293 workers; ten years later only six establishments remained with 64 workers. In 1911 the town had again eleven plants with a total of 133 employees.

As a result of changes in the economic geography of the region many places lost their trade, especially in wheat and lumber. Port Perry was in the seventies and early eighties a flourishing trade centre. Large quantities of wheat were received via Lake Scugog and shipped by rail to Whitby. About 5 million feet of lumber were handled annually at this point. Around 1881, agricultural implements, machinery, steam engines, iron castings, mill gearing, etc. were manufactured in the village. Thirty years later, nearly all the grain and lumber trade had gone, and of the industrial establishments only some flour- and sawmills and an engine works had remained.

The McKinley Tariff considerably reduced the grain export trade from the lake ports, such as Port Hope, Whitby, Oakville, and others. At the same time, export of agricultural products decreased on account of the growing importance of the home market and the shift to mixed farming.

Ship-building in the small ports came to an end with the arrival of steel ships. Many shipwrights migrated to the larger centres to find employment there in the big ship-yards.

It was a combination of these factors which ruined the economic foundation of many lake ports which had been seriously weakened already by the tapping of their hinterlands by railways converging upon Toronto. Only the rise of modern industries could bring new life to these villages and towns.

TABLE XIV – Occupational structure of Toronto, Guelph, Kingston, and Peterborough in 1911

Occupation	Toronto	Guelph	Kingston	Peterborough
Building trades	12%	11%	9%	11%
Manufacturing	35%	42%	31%	48%
Trade and merchandizing	23%	16%	20%	16%
Transportation	7%	8%	9%	5%
Domestic and personal services	11%	11%	14%	10%
Civil and Municipal Government	4%	3%	8%	3%
Professional	7%	4%	7%	6%
Others	1%	5%	2%	1%

The occupational structure of four cities

For South-Central Ontario the census gives the occupational structure of only four centres (table XIV).

Two of them, Guelph and Peterborough, were among the most important manufacturing towns at that time. Only Oshawa had proportionally a higher concentration of industry. With a total population half as big as Guelph, it had more industrial workers than that city, as may be seen from the following summary for the five largest centres.

	pop. 1911	industrial workers 1911
Toronto	376,538	65,274
Guelph	15,175	3,072
Kingston	18,874	2,145
Oshawa	7,436	3,220
Peterborough	18,360	4,029

Oshawa had become the most highly industrialized centre in South-Central Ontario by 1911. Toronto and Kingston had a more diversified occupational structure. In both, trade and merchandizing was of more importance, while they also were better developed service centres, both having 7 per cent in the professional group. Kingston had a high percentage in the governmental class on account of the military establishments in that city.

Conclusion

Such was the urban development between 1881 and 1911. During this period modern manufacturing established itself as the most powerful factor in urban growth. It brought population growth to the towns and cities in which it located itself. The service function which had been the dominant factor in urban growth before 1881 had declined considerably in relative importance. The traditional industries catering to a local market disappeared, while the decline of the rural population and the improved transportation system resulted in a smaller demand for services from the villages and small towns. The large towns and cities grew at the expense of the smaller ones. In particular, Toronto surpassed by far all other centres in the province during this period. The concentration of modern industries within its boundaries and the expansion of its trade and finance made it the undisputed leader of Ontario.

6. Urban Predominance, 1911-1951

Extent of Urbanization in 1951

The urban population of the province of Ontario rose from
52.52 per cent in 1911 to 61.04 per cent in 1931 and 61.74 per
cent in 1941, and it declined to 59.88 per cent in 1951. However, those percentages do not reflect the true proportion of
urban and rural population. Urban is defined in the census as
the population of incorporated municipalities, but especially
during the last few decades, with the increased deconcentration
and decentralization of the urban population, the rural non-
farm population increased considerably. Accordingly, in 1951,
the census changed its definition of urban. It now includes the
population residing in cities, towns, and villages of 1,000 or
over, whether incorporated or not, as well as the population of
all parts of census metropolitan areas. According to this revised
definition, the urban population in 1941 amounted to 68.41
per cent, and by 1951 it was 70.71 per cent. It is pointed out
in the preliminary report of the 1951 census that the increase in
the relative size of the urban population is chiefly the result of
the inclusion of metropolitan area parts. For the country as a
whole, these parts increased the urban population, according to
the old definition, by 851,130, while the inclusion of unincorporated places with more than 1,000 inhabitants added
another 265,584. However, the omission of incorporated places
with fewer than 1,000 inhabitants constitutes a loss of 429,683
inhabitants.

In 1951 South-Central Ontario contained 46.5 per cent of
the urban population of the province; between 1941 and 1951,
46.19 per cent of the total increase in urban population occurred in that region.

In this chapter it will be attempted to trace the urbanization
process since 1911. During that period, urban development was
greatly influenced by two world wars which suddenly changed
the Dominion into a modern industrial nation, and by the
fabulous increase in automobile traffic.

Density of Population

Changes in density pattern

After 1911, the density of population changed considerably as
a result of the forces which had gained momentum in the
preceding period. First, there were the results of the decrease
of the rural population, and secondly, the effects of an increased
urbanization. In the less urbanized areas of the region the
population density continued to decline. A block of several
townships to the northwest of Toronto saw its density decrease
to fewer than 20 persons per square mile (fig. 19). Also, south
of the margin of the Shield, the zone with 10 to 20 persons per
square mile expanded. This was in particular true for the
Lindsay area where the 20 isopleth swung sharply southward,
far into Durham County. Most of those changes took place
during the two decades before 1931; after that year, the 20-
isopleth remained practically stationary, except in northern
Durham. Also, before 1931, the areas with from 40 to 60 and
with more than 60 persons per square mile were reduced,
though not as much as the zone of 20 to 40. In a few districts
the trend had already been reversed by 1931, as the zones with
the higher densities showed an increase in area. The increases
took place near the larger urban centres only – Guelph, Hamilton, Toronto, and Oshawa. This expansion of the zones with
higher population densities was accelerated after 1931. By
1951, the 40-isopleth reached Lake Simcoe, forming a broad
triangle between Newcastle and Dundas. It is the expansion of
the zone between the 40 and 60-isopleth which blocked the
migration of the 20-isopleth, especially to the northwest of
Toronto.

The actual course followed by the various isopleths is the
result of a variety of factors. On the Shield, transportation
routes and pockets of better soils are the main determinants.
Over a long distance, the 10-isopleth follows more or less the
margin of the Shield, except in Frontenac County, where it is
replaced by the 20-isopleth.

Historic influences are still noticeable in the trend of the
20-isopleth in the Peterborough and Lindsay areas. The Peterborough area, comprising the southern townships of the county,
is one of the older settled parts of the region and always has
had a denser population than the Lindsay district. Originally,
accessibility was a main factor, but gradually the town and

later the city of Peterborough began to exert a major influence upon the population density of the surrounding districts.

Several urban centres are surrounded by a zone of denser population. The nearby city offers a market for a variety of agricultural produce and makes for a more intensive occupation of the land. But more important was the increase in the rural non-farm population, as the means of transportation improved. In particular, the automobile led to this migration of the urban population and the growth of the rural-urban fringe. It is this migration which largely accounts for the increase in population density around Toronto and other large towns.

The rural-urban fringe

Early in the 19th century, the larger towns already had suburbs, which in later years were annexed by the central municipality. Kingston had four suburbs around 1840, three of which had been added to the town by 1850 and the fourth by 1880. Peterborough had annexed Ashburnham, a suburb of more than 1,600 inhabitants, by 1911. Allandale was added to Barrie in 1897. Well developed suburbs of Toronto in 1884 were Parkdale, Brockton, Seaton, Yorkville, Rosedale, and Mount Pleasant. The inhabitants of these suburbs commuted daily to their work in the central city. An author remarked in 1884: "Every morning the streetcars which run from Yorkville townhall to King Street are crowded with business men, merchants, clerks, employees of all kinds. . . . Yorkville is a healthy, as well as an economical, location; its quiet streets and well-shaded avenues afford a pleasant relief after the heat and dust of the city streets in summer" (233/260).

The city of Toronto was considerably enlarged through a series of annexations between 1881 and 1914. After 1922 no new annexations took place, and the central city became gradually encircled by a number of incorporated municipalities. Weston was incorporated in 1882, and Mimico in 1911. Leaside, New Toronto, Forest Hill, Swansea and Long Branch followed later. Some municipalities were not incorporated, but became nevertheless extremely urbanized. The "townships" of York, East York and North York had in 1951 populations of 101,582, 64,616 and 85,897 respectively. The central city and the suburbs form a continuous urban area traversed by municipal boundaries. In order to solve some of the many problems which had risen over the years, the provincial government established in 1953 the municipality of Metropolitan Toronto. The suburbs were not added to the central city, but a federation of thirteen municipalities was founded. The municipalities kept their own governments, but with a metropolitan government responsible for a number of "federal" affairs.

The growth of the large city not only resulted in the rise of a belt of suburbs, but it also affected population density far beyond this belt. In the townships close to Toronto the population increased because of a large influx of urban dwellers. Land values began to rise suddenly in Toronto Township in 1910, when inhabitants of Toronto began to establish homes in the southern part of the township. During the first decade of the century, the population of the township, which had been declining since 1851, began to increase again and rose sharply as Toronto grew in importance. Its population increased from 5,208 in 1901 to 28,528 in 1951. During the same half century Scarborough Township saw its population increase from a minimum of 3,845 in 1901 to 56,292 in 1951. At a somewhat later date the population trend in the townships to the north of the city was reversed.

In those townships long strings of homes appeared along the highways and side roads. Many subdivisions sprang up almost overnight along the main traffic routes leading into the city. This expansion had an over-all chaotic aspect, as it was quite unplanned. In January 1952 only one of the 26 municipalities in the County of York had comprehensive zoning by laws on a permanent basis. The general characteristic of the fringe area therefore is one of confusion and sharp contrasts in land use. This fringe development was in particular concentrated along both sides of Yonge Street which has become the central traffic artery for an urban zone of about three miles wide and fifteen miles long. Similar developments occur along the highways southwest of the city, and also, to a slightly smaller extent, to the east of it. It is this deconcentration of urban population which led to an increase in the density of rural population in a wide zone around the city.

Toronto became built up and its population growth began to level off. In the decade of the twenties, the population of the city had still shown an increase of 20 per cent. In the thirties, however, there was only an increase of 5.7 per cent, and in 1951 the population had almost become stationary; the increase since 1941 was one per cent. The city proper had, in 1951, a population of 675,754 inhabitants. The census metropolitan area, however, had a population of 1,117,470 in that year, an increase of 22.7 per cent since 1941. The growth of the city proper had halted, but its rate of increase had been taken over by the metropolitan area as a whole.

The Toronto metropolitan area, as established for the 1951 census, is the second largest of the Dominion, coming after Montreal. In the Province of Ontario, however, it towers high above the next largest metropolitan area, that of Ottawa, with a population of 281,908, closely followed by Hamilton with 259,685 inhabitants. None of the other cities in South-Central Ontario is considered a metropolitan area. The second city of the region is Oshawa with a population of 41,545 in 1951.

The Changing Occupational Structure

In the province as a whole manufacturing was the main source of income for a rapidly increasing number of persons during this period (table XV). However, this increase occurred entirely after 1931. The proportion of workers in manufacturing remained practically the same during the first two decades of the period. The percentage in 1931 was 16.7 compared with 17.6 in 1911. Agriculture, on the other hand, declined steadily. In 1911, according to the occupational census, about 31 per cent of the gainfully occupied population in the province was still engaged in agriculture. In the forties it declined from 18.6 per cent in 1941 to 10.8 per cent in 1951. Trade and finance has increased but slowly since 1911 as far as the number of the gainfully employed is concerned, while service increased much more.

In general, the province's occupational structure reveals about the middle of the 20th century an extremely urbanized aspect, with less than 12 per cent in the primary industries. The primary industries include agriculture, fishing and trapping, logging, mining, and quarrying. Since 1850, when about 75 per cent of the population was still engaged in agriculture and forestry, the occupational structure of the province has been greatly changed. These changes are reflected in the tremendous urban growth which resulted from the expansion in the non-rural activities.

A large part of that urban growth took place in South-Central Ontario. In 1931 the region contained about 45 per

TABLE XV – Percentage distribution of the labour force by occupation group in Ontario since 1911 (41)

	1911	1931	1941	1951
Agriculture	30.98	22.66	18.57	10.79
Fishing and trapping	0.38	0.47	0.43	0.17
Logging	1.06	0.67	0.99	0.91
Mining and quarrying	1.69	1.11	1.66	1.13
Manufacturing & Mechanical	17.64	16.67	22.11	23.19
Construction	5.43	5.69	5.34	6.38
Transportation	5.90	8.15	7.81	9.35
Trade and finance	8.54	10.02	9.69	10.57
Service	11.99	15.74	17.22	17.68
Clerical	4.54	8.07	9.60	12.55
Labourers	11.85	10.68	6.30	6.27
Not stated	—	0.07	0.28	1.01
	100.00	100.00	100.00	100.00

cent of the urban population of the province, and in 1951, 46.5 per cent on the basis of the revised definition of urban and rural population (p. 187). It is of interest to note that this proportion remained practically unchanged during the last 100 years. In 1851 also, about 45 per cent of the total urban population of the province lived in South-Central Ontario.

The urbanized occupational structure – a structure largely composed of non-rural occupations – found its geographical expression in the landscape. It not only consisted of the rise of industrial, commercial, and transportational establishments, but also in a form of rural land use which, to a great extent, has been conditioned by the presence of the large urban population. In the following sections the various industries – agriculture, manufacturing, trade, etc. – will be discussed.

Agriculture

In the province as a whole, agriculture employed in 1951, 10.8 per cent of the working population according to the occupational census. For South-Central Ontario the proportion was 6.9 per cent.

Intensity of agriculture

The density of agricultural workers, which includes farm operators and farm workers, is very low on the denuded precambrian Shield. Most of the townships in this area had two or fewer agricultural workers per square mile. There were only a few small pockets with five or six workers per square mile. The 5-isopleth follows closely the border of the Shield, except for the southeast, where it crosses the Frontenac axis. Here the topography consists of rock-knobs and clay flats, resulting in a higher proportion of arable land. Furthermore, the axis is crossed by major transportation routes, while Kingston provides a welcome market. Thus, the Kingston district forms an agricultural link between South-Central Ontario and Eastern Ontario (fig. 20).

To the south of the Shield the influence of physiography is much less evident, and agricultural intensity seems to have been much more affected by the many towns. Differences in soil do not explain the contrast between the Peterborough and Lindsay areas. The fertile township in which Lindsay is located had 8 workers per square mile, while the heavily drumlinized townships near Peterborough had from 11 to 16. The Peterborough district, being more accessible, had been settled at an earlier date, and the city itself always had attracted new settlers to the district. The Lindsay area, on the other hand, was settled at a later date, while it never had the same attraction as Peterborough.

Agriculture is most intensive around Toronto, where a large area has more than 15 workers per square mile. To the southwest of the city a fruit and vegetable belt, mainly concentrated on the Iroquois lake plain, merges with the Niagara fruit belt; eastward a fruit and canning crop belt hugs the north shore of Lake Ontario. To the east of Toronto the variations in soil and climate on the old lake plain are not as important as the presence of Toronto and other towns in creating the variations in agricultural intensity. The townships near Toronto had as many as from 30 to 46 agricultural workers per square mile. In the lakeshore townships of Durham, however, this decreased to 11 and 12 workers per square mile. Further east physiographic influences are more important. Prince Edward County enjoys a somewhat milder climate because of its almost being surrounded by Lake Ontario.

Yonge Street carried Toronto's influence to the north and

a zone of intensive farming reached the approaches to Lake Simcoe. Here the great number of truck farms on the peat soils of the Holland Marsh account for the larger number of agricultural workers.

Size of farms

Farming in South-Central Ontario about the middle of the 20th century differs very much from the agricultural forms of production during the previous century. Instead of an extensive grain farming we find now a highly intensive type of agriculture with emphasis on high quality products. The number of farm operators in most of the region, as in the whole province, continued to decline. This led to a steady increase in the size of the average farm. In 1901 the average farm size in Ontario was 105 acres, but by 1951 this had become 139 acres. This increase, however, did not occur uniformly over the entire province. It took place only in areas away from the influence of larger urban centres and in particular in areas with poor soils. This was especially true for the farm areas on and near the Shield. In Haliburton and Victoria counties the average size of the farms between 1941 and 1951 increased from 192 to 224, and from 170 to 206 acres respectively. Near the larger urban centres, however, the average size increased much less as a result of the expansion of fruit and vegetable gardening and increased pressure on the land in general. In the two southern townships of Peel County the average size increased only from 58 to 60 and from 122 to 130 acres, respectively.

These figures also illustrate the variations in the average size of farms in the different parts of the region. The counties near Toronto had the smallest farms. The average farm in York County measured 119 acres, in Peel 111, and in Halton 100 acres. Eastward of Toronto the average size increased gradually to 143 in Northumberland and 222 in Frontenac. This increase results from a decline of urban influence, but also from the fact that the eastern counties include large tracts of the Canadian Shield.

Types of farming

General farming and dairying have become the most important forms of agriculture. Dairying is dominant in the southern half of Victoria County and in the counties of York, Peel, and Halton. The large urban population in this zone has stimulated the large-scale production of fluid milk. Another dairy region is found farther east in the counties of Hastings, Lennox and Addington, and Frontenac. In this district, however, the emphasis is on cheese production. The shallow soils of the limestone plain and those on the Frontenac axis do not permit the growing of grain crops for feed, and as a result summer dairying prevails. In 1951 Peel, at one time one of the foremost wheat producers, had only 18,655 acres under wheat. On the other hand, 53,976 acres were under cultivated hay, 24,823 under oats, and 20,830 under mixed grains. The cropland of the county served almost entirely to support the large number of dairy cattle. This was true for all counties in the region in 1951. In all counties hay crops occupied the largest acreage, with oats in general coming second in acreage, followed by mixed grains and wheat.

The rest of South-Central Ontario is largely taken up by general farming. Here also the farmer obtains most of his income from livestock and livestock products. The crops are predominantly raised for feed. Simcoe, a general farming county, had, in 1951, 119,453 acres under cultivated hay, 76,207 under oats, 64,922 under mixed grains, and 50,657 under wheat.

On the pre-cambrian Shield agricultural settlement is sparse. Over most of the Shield area, farming is of a subsistence and part-time type; a more productive type is only found in a few isolated districts with favourable soil conditions. The future of this part of the Canadian Shield lies in reforestation, the tourist industry and possibly some mining.

Along the border of the Shield a very quick transition occurs. To the south of this border more than 80 per cent of the land is in farms, and more than 60 per cent of that is improved. On the Shield, however, most of the land is wooded and not in farms; over large areas the farm land amounts to less than 25 per cent of the total area, and in general less than 25 per cent of that farm land is improved. Many farmers here benefit from the demand for food and services created by the summer tourist industry.

In addition to these major types of farming, South-Central Ontario contains several small districts and areas in which fruits and vegetables are produced. To the west of Toronto the sandy soils of the narrow Iroquois Lake plain form the basis for an important production of fruits and vegetables for the nearby urban markets. The Oakville and Port Credit districts are old producers of strawberries and other small fruits. In 1951, Halton and Peel Counties still ranked among the largest fruit producers of the province, with 706 and 606 acres respectively. More than 7,000 acres in the two counties are occupied by orchards, mainly apples, pears, and cherries. In vegetable growing the emphasis is on the production of tomatoes and carrots.

Peel County has near Brampton the largest concentration of greenhouses in the Dominion: 2.2 million sq. feet is under glass – more than 24 per cent of the provincial total. This industry developed here through the initiative of a truck gardener, who in the early 1860's built a greenhouse to supply vegetables to the farmers coming to this wheat market town. Some time later, he introduced successfully the growing of flowers. The proximity of the ever expanding Toronto market and improvements in transport led to the further expansion of the industry.

The lake plain between Toronto and Kingston, and also Prince Edward County produce large quantities of fruits and canning crops. Apples, pears, and cherries are the dominant fruit trees, while tomatoes, sweet corn, and green peas are the leading canning crops. Several small centres in Prince Edward County, such as Wellington and Bloomfield, continued to prosper around canning factories when the old mills declined. As has been pointed out, the variation in intensity of agricultural production within the fruit and vegetable zone along the north shore of Lake Ontario is largely the result of urban influences.

York County is one of the foremost vegetable producers of the province. Most of the production of the county is concentrated in the Holland Marsh, where large quantities of onions, carrots, lettuce, cabbage, cauliflower, tomatoes, and celery are produced. The products are shipped to Toronto and other urban centres in eastern and western Canada, and also to American cities. The soil consists of peat formations which developed at the head of the southern arm of Lake Simcoe, and through which the Holland River winds its way to the lake. Originally the swamp was covered with sedges, cattails, and reeds near the river, while farther away from the stream a swamp forest prevailed consisting mainly of white cedars. The southern part of the marsh was reclaimed in the late twenties by diking the land and the digging of drainage ditches. The project, however, was not successful until a party of Dutch settled in the marsh in 1934. Since then many more Dutchmen have arrived as well as East Europeans, Italians, Germans, and a few Japanese (237).

Thus, farming in South-Central Ontario has been considerably influenced by the proximity of a large urban population. This affected the size of the farms, the intensity of agricultural production, and the types of farming. On the other hand, the farming population has affected the growth of manufacturing, trade, and also urban development. Large quantities of produce serve as raw material for processing plants. Meat packing became one of the leading industries in Toronto. The farmer himself has become an extremely important buyer of city-produced goods. In 1950, the farm implements and equipment bought by the Ontario farmers had a wholesale value of $51.9 million, or 23.8 per cent of the Canadian total (42). The manufacturing of farm machinery is one of the oldest and most important of Ontario's industries. The importance of the Ontario farmer as a market for consumer goods may be illustrated by the fact that in 1950 the net income from farming operations amounted to $458.5 million (42). In that same year, the sale of farm products brought in $678 million – more than 30 per cent of the Canadian total.

Other Primary Industries

As far as South-Central Ontario is concerned, the other primary industries are at present of no importance. The lumber industry, which at one time brought great wealth to the region, employed, in 1951, only 1,848 workers or 0.23 per cent of the workers employed in all industries. Forestry and logging are mainly concentrated on the Shield. Huntsville has an important sawmill.

Fishing and trapping employed only 271 persons in 1951. It occurs widely scattered on the shores of the lakes. The main concentration is in Prince Edward County where 80 persons are employed in this industry.

Mining and quarrying employed, in 1951, 1,401 persons in South-Central Ontario. Almost half of this number are concentrated in Metropolitan Toronto and are employed by local brick works or by firms operating elsewhere in Canada. Mining is of very little importance in the region. In December of 1952, the Bethlehem Steel Corporation began the removal of the overburden from recently discovered low grade iron ore deposits near Marmora. It is expected that the deposits will yield 20 million tons of ore which, after having been converted into iron pellets, will be shipped to American furnaces (355).

Mining is of some importance for such centres as Lakefield,

Havelock, Marmora and Madoc. Nephton is a small new mining community near the head of Stoney Lake; it is based upon the exploitation of nepheline syenite at Blue Mountain.

Those primary industries do not play an important part in the urban development in South-Central Ontario.

Manufacturing as a Factor in Urban Growth

In 1951 South-Central Ontario, according to the industrial census of that year, contained 37.0 per cent of the Ontario population employed in manufacturing. Within the region itself Toronto was by far the most important manufacturing centre (fig. 21). In the above mentioned year the census Metropolitan area accounted for 83 per cent of the population of the region employed in manufacturing (industrial census). The other major centres are Oshawa, Peterborough, Kingston, and Guelph. In 1951, in the region as a whole 28.5 per cent of the workers in all industries were employed in manufacturing. By the middle of the 20th century Ontario, in many aspects, has become the most important manufacturing province of Canada and within the province South-Central Ontario and more specifically the Toronto Metropolitan area plays a leading part.

The manufacturing belt of the province is located around the western end of Lake Ontario, in the form of a huge horseshoe extending from Oshawa to the Niagara River. The Toronto Metropolitan area constitutes the major part of this tremendous industrial concentration. The factors which have led to the industrial expansion in South-Central Ontario are, in the main, the same as those which account for the manufacturing development in the rest of Southern Ontario. However, South-Central Ontario had the additional advantage of having the largest conurbation within its boundaries.

The basis of manufacturing

The oldest source of wealth in the province, and basis for its industrial and urban growth has been the products of the soil. At first, this was lumber, but later rich wheat crops led to a lively trade and accumulation of capital. The fertile land attracted thousands of immigrants, and a dense rural population was the result. With the changes in agricultural production and the rise of modern manufacturing rural Ontario became a tremendous source for the cities to draw upon for the increase of their population. At the same time, rural Ontario became a large market for consumer goods, and a huge producer of a great variety of agricultural products, including both food for the urban population and raw materials for the industries.

The most important factor which contributed to the rise of manufacturing in this rich agricultural region has been the tariff policy. A notable expansion of industrial development began with the introduction of protective tariffs against the United States under the National Policy in 1878. It not only gave young Canadian industries a sheltered home market, but it also led to the establishment of American branch factories in Canada, in particular in Ontario which is so close to the main American manufacturing belt. In 1919, it was reported that over 500 branches of American manufacturing concerns had been established in Canada. This was considered to be the result of the tariff which at that time averaged slightly more than 21 per cent on dutiable goods. These 500 branches employed about 80,000 persons (357). More than 400 of the 3,400 industries in Toronto were foreign businesses in 1948, including British and American (267). The majority of the factories in Peterborough in 1947 were branches of American firms (240). A city like Oshawa depends almost entirely on industries controlled by American capital.

The American branch factories crossed the border, not only to gain access to the growing Canadian home market, but also to profit from the market possibilities in other Commonwealth countries. A typical example is the automobile industry which is largely concentrated in Southern Ontario and is considered almost fully American controlled (235). In 1947 about 34.7 per cent of Canada's total vehicle production was destined for export. About 55 per cent of the Ford products alone went to the various Commonwealth countries and the East Indies (236).

Industrial development in South-Central Ontario profits considerably from the presence of a basic iron and steel industry at Hamilton. Ontario had no iron industry in 1879, but in 1893, Hamilton attracted American iron and steel enterprises by offering a free site and financial grants (284). Also, two places in South-Central Ontario had an iron industry for a short time. A small iron industry began operating at Deseronto in 1899. It remained in operation till 1919, when a 6-ton blast furnace was blown out. The plant never resumed production. A similar fate befell the iron industry at Midland, which became idle early in 1921. The industry at Hamilton, however, flourished and became the chief centre of iron and steel industry in Canada. Its location on the lake makes it relatively easy to assemble ore and coal, while the limestone escarpment constitutes the source for the flux. Numerous plants in Southern Ontario obtain their steel and iron from that city.

Southern Ontario lacks coal, but large quantities are imported from the United States. The region has, however, an important alternative supply of power in the form of hydro-electric power. South-Central Ontario obtains its power from three major sources – the Ottawa River, the Niagara River and Welland Canal, and the St. Lawrence Canals. The generation of power has not kept pace with the expansion of manufacturing, and it was necessary to construct two steam-electric plants, one of them in Toronto. The threatening shortage of power in Southern Ontario is a major consideration in the building of the St. Lawrence Seaway, which has a waterpower potential of 2,200,000 hp., to be shared with the United States.

Finally, the industrial development of Ontario was stimulated by the two world wars, especially the last one (Table XVI). The number of employees in manufacturing establishments began to rise gradually after 1910, and after a slight relapse in the early twenties, it reached a maximum in 1929. During those nineteen years, the number of employees increased by 37.6 per cent. A serious decline occurred during the depression of the early thirties. By 1932, a recovery had set in, but, in 1939, the number of employees was still lower than in 1929. The Second World War led to a phenomenal expansion in manufacturing. A maximum employment was reached in 1943, after which some decline occurred. But, in 1947, a new period of expansion began, which still continued in 1953. In the years between 1939 and 1950, the number of manufacturing employees in the province increased by 77.6 per cent.

The Korean War was a new stimulus. In 1951 it was reported that at that time the bulk of the defense contracts had been placed in Ontario (235).

A typical example of the astounding growth of manufacturing as a result of the war is the aircraft industry. In 1930, the aircraft industry employed 672 workers in the province. By 1944, this had risen to more than 33,700, and after the war it continued to be a large-scale industry in the Toronto Metropolitan area, employing more than 16,000 employees at the end of 1953 (47).

TABLE XVI – Manufacturing in Ontario 1910-1950[1]

Year	establishments	employees
1910	8,001	238,817
1917	9,061	299,389
1920	9,113	295,674
1922	8,703	235,070
1929	9,348	328,533
1933	9,542	224,816
1937	9,796	321,743
1939	9,824	318,871
1943	10,587	570,017
1944	10,731	564,392
1945	10,869	518,056
1946	11,424	498,120
1948	12,118	551,556
1949	12,951	557,190
1950	12,809	566,513

[1] Canada Yearbooks.

Degree of industrialization

Manufacturing affects the economic structure of the cities and towns in South-Central Ontario in varied ways. The census of 1951, which gives the occupational structure for places of 1,000 inhabitants and more, makes it possible to evaluate the importance of manufacturing. In that year 17.3 per cent of the gainfully occupied urban population of Ontario listed manufacturing as their main occupation. This does not include labourers in manufacturing, which in the census have been grouped with labourers in other secondary industries. Neither are included the proprietary and managerial, and clerical categories. It is felt, however, that the proportion of the population employed in manufacturing, as given by the occupational census, is a good indicator of the degree of industrialization.

Several of the more important towns were only little or moderately industrialized; in 1951 they had 25 per cent or less of their gainfully occupied population employed in manufacturing. Those towns are, in geographical order, Midland, Orillia, Barrie, Lindsay, Kingston, Belleville, Trenton, Cobourg, Metropolitan Toronto, and Oakville (fig. 21). Nearly all towns in the Oshawa-Toronto-Guelph area had a relatively high proportion employed in manufacturing.

In 1951, manufacturing, as a fundamental factor in the economic structure of towns, was primarily concentrated in the southwestern part of the region. Its importance decreased in eastern direction and especially northward, where manufacturing was almost entirely absent on the Canadian Shield.

Growth of manufacturing 1935 to 1949

For 23 places data are available which make it possible to evaluate their increase in manufacturing and to compare this increase with their occupational structure. These centres with their employment in manufacturing in 1941 and 1951, and with the proportional increase in factory employees between 1935 and 1949 are listed in the following table.

For the province as a whole, the number of employees in manufacturing establishments increased by 105.9 per cent between 1935 and 1949. The increase in the number of employees over the same period in South-Central Ontario varied considerably, and the pattern displays a great diversity. Of the 23 places listed below, 11 more than doubled their industrial employment after 1935, while 12 others had increases smaller than 100 per cent. The biggest proportional increases did not occur in towns which were strongly industrialized in 1941; of the 11 towns with rapidly growing manufacturing, only two had more than 30 per cent of their gainfully occupied population employed in manufacturing – Peterborough and Bowmanville.

On the other hand, the towns with a relatively small increase in manufacturing employment during this period (less than 100 per cent) had, in 1941, in general an economic structure in which manufacturing was strongly represented; eight of the 12 towns in this category had more than 30 per cent of their gainfully occupied population employed in manufacturing.

It seems therefore that in South-Central Ontario the greatest proportional expansion in manufacturing did not occur in places which were already considerably industrialized, but in those towns which were more diversified in their occupational structure. This is particularly true for Kingston, Midland, Oakville, and Orillia. Highly industrialized towns such as Acton, Georgetown, Guelph, Newmarket, and Oshawa had a relatively small increase in employment in manufacturing. It should, however, be pointed out that the larger the industrial employment is within a town, the more unlikely it becomes that it will double in volume. It remains nevertheless a fact that several

| | Occupational census % employed in manufacturing | | industrial census % increase |
	1941	1951	1935-1949
Acton	45	40	81
Aurora	38*	23	52
Barrie	15	15	143
Belleville	20	19	185
Bowmanville	34	36	104
Brampton	32	28	34
Burlington	21	22	108
Cobourg	23	24	95
Collingwood	29	27	81
Dundas	41	34	167
Fergus	42	33	—
Georgetown	48	30	94
Guelph	39	35	67
Kingston	16	18	349
Lindsay	22	24	97
Midland	20	24	396
Newmarket	40	30	44
Oakville	22	21	241
Orillia	26	22	239
Oshawa	40	41	72
Peterborough	34	34	112
Port Hope	31	27	68
Toronto (Metropolitan)	26	23	96
Trenton	29	23	146

large towns which were moderately industrialized in 1941 have made important gains. Nearly all of those towns are outside the highly industrialized southwest part of the region.

Manufacturing in the Toronto area

Metropolitan Toronto steadily maintains its position as the chief manufacturing centre of the province. In 1935, Toronto and the three suburbs for which data are available employed

* Aurora and other towns have many persons employed in industrial establishments in Metropolitan Toronto.

33.5 per cent of the workers in manufacturing in Ontario. This proportion was 31.2 per cent in 1941, and 31.4 per cent in 1949. In 1951 the census metropolitan area of Toronto employed 83 per cent of the employees in manufacturing in South-Central Ontario; in 1911 the proportion was 70 per cent. In spite of the industrial expansion elsewhere in the region, Toronto increased its lead in the field of manufacturing. Of all new industrial development in Canada in 1946, 47 per cent took place in Toronto (235).

Toronto has always attracted the bulk of the new industries which came to the province. Its early industrial development was marked by the fact that it harboured a considerable number of industries which did not occur elsewhere in the province. At an early date, it became the largest market of the province, and with the changes in the transportation network, it became a focal point both for railways and roads. Goods and raw materials can easily be assembled at Toronto, while it also has an excellent location for the distribution of the finished products. It has been frequently pointed out that within a 100 mile radius of the city, there is one-third of the buying power of Canada.

In the city proper, about 24 per cent of the gainfully occupied population were employed in manufacturing in 1941, and ten years later, 22.5 per cent. It would seem that a considerable decrease had occurred since 1911, when the percentage amounted to 35 per cent, but these figures are based on different criteria and classifications and therefore are not comparable. The general trend nevertheless is toward a declining importance of manufacturing in the city and toward greater diversity.

According to the industrial census, the manufacturing establishments of the city proper employed in 1941, 36.1 per cent of the workers in all industries and in 1951, 35.3 per cent. For the census metropolitan area the percentage amounted, in 1951, to almost 36. The relative importance of the different industries is shown in Table XVII.

In the category of foods and beverages, slaughtering and meat packing, and bread and bakery products were the two largest groups. The Toronto area is important for printing and publishing; in 1951 it had more than 29 per cent of the employees in this industry in Canada. The manufacture of agricultural implements is the chief member in the category of iron and steel products; it employed 5,371 workers. Others in this group are boiler and plate works, hardware and tools, heating and cooking apparatus, household, office and store machinery,

TABLE XVII – Manufacturing in Metropolitan Toronto in 1951

Industry	total labour force	
manufacturing	189,812	100%
foods and beverages	18,760	9.9
rubber products	5,822	3.1
textile products (except clothing)	5,056	2.6
clothing (textile and fur)	20,511	10.8
wood products	6,572	3.5
paper products	7,699	4.1
printing, publishing, etc.	18,590	9.8
iron and steel products	33,610	17.7
transportation equipment	12,220	6.4
non-ferrous metal prod.	9,088	4.7
electrical apparatus and supplies	21,443	11.4
chemical products	10,761	5.7
others	19,680	10.3

and sheet metal products. In the group of transportation equipment, the aircraft industry with 5,200 employees is the largest. In the category of electrical apparatus and supplies, the plants for the production of heavy electrical machinery, refrigerators, and electrical appliances were the most important.

In Metropolitan Toronto industrialization varies greatly. Toronto proper in 1949 had about 24 employees in manufacturing for every 100 inhabitants.[1] In Leaside, New Toronto, and Weston the ratios were 55, 59, and 30 respectively. Long Branch had a ratio of 15 and Mimico of only 5. A new industrial suburb of 32,000 people is being developed on the northeast fringe of the city, on a 2,200 acre site.

To the west of the city, a number of small industrial towns link Toronto with Hamilton and Guelph. Some of them are old manufacturing centres, such as Acton and Georgetown. However, their recent industrial expansion to a great extent has been due to their proximity to Metropolitan Toronto. In many ways

[1] The population figure for 1949 was obtained by plotting the growth of population on semi-logarithmic graphs. This ratio is used, because no occupational census is available for 1949; in 1951, an industrial census was taken only for places with 10,000 inhabitants and over.

these centres offer the same advantages as Toronto. They have good transportation facilities, as they are located in the main east-west stream of traffic; they have abundant hydro-electric power which became available relatively early, just before the first world war; and they can also draw upon the labour supply of Toronto and Hamilton. In almost all these small towns there are one or more industries which are branches of Toronto firms, or plants which have moved from Toronto in search of more space. Burlington and Dundas have become suburbs of Hamilton.

Industries in these small centres are very varied. Acton continues its tradition with an important leather industry. Oakville has rapidly become a centre for the production of automobiles, since the Ford Motor Company of Canada Ltd. recently moved its assembly plant from Windsor to Oakville. In the past, Oakville grew rather independently of Toronto; at one time it was an important shipping centre. But nearly all the industries of the 19th century have disappeared and its modern industries are more closely linked with Toronto; a few industrial establishments moved from that city to Oakville. Farther to the southwest, near Burlington, the Studebaker Company is planning another plant for the production of automobiles. On the lakeshore in Peel County, extensive oil refineries have been established at Clarkson and Port Credit. Malton, slightly farther to the north, has become a centre for the manufacturing of aircraft.

This industrial growth has caused an expansion of large shopping facilities in the outlying districts of Metropolitan Toronto, Hamilton, and intervening urban areas (358). These new industrial and commercial developments have created a great amount of urban settlement on the lakeshore between Toronto and Hamilton. It is only systematic regional planning that would be able to prevent the development of a continuous urban belt between these two cities.

The Oshawa industrial area

At the time of the industrial census of 1951, 63.2 per cent of all industrial workers in Oshawa were employed in manufacturing; it is a highly industrialized city. Like Oakville, Oshawa developed independently from Toronto. Originally, better water-power facilities had given it an advantage above its old rival Whitby. Of major importance had been the arrival of

McLaughlin, the founder of the automobile industry in the city. During the last war, the port of the city was developed and ships with a draught of 22 feet can now enter.

Oshawa depends heavily on one main industry. In 1951, about 63 per cent of the workers in manufacturing was employed in the automobile industry and many more in auxiliary plants. This makes Oshawa very vulnerable in times of depressions. In February 1946, the city had 6,483 unemployed, as compared with a total population of 26,813 in 1941 and of 41,545 ten years later (238).

Other important industries with their employment are leather tanning (199), printing, publishing, etc. (449), iron castings (1,429), sheet metal products (423), glass and glass products (677). In total 11,722 persons were employed in manufacturing in Oshawa in 1951.

The industrial area centred on Oshawa extends westward beyond Whitby. Just to the west of Whitby, a new industrial centre is being developed. During the last war, plants were erected here, and houses were built for the employees in the defense industries. After the war, it was decided to develop a new town on the site, using the extensive service facilities and the vacant industrial buildings which were available. The plans for the development are based upon an assumed eventual population of 20,000 to 25,000 persons. Early in 1951, Ajax, as the project is called, had a population of about 4,000 (181). Many of its residents commute to Toronto and Oshawa.

Bowmanville may also be considered part of the Oshawa area. Among others, the town possesses an important rubber industry. Many workers from both Whitby and Bowmanville are employed in Oshawa.

Peterborough

Industrially, Peterborough resembles Oshawa, and like it developed independently of Toronto; both centres depend heavily on American capital and the two cities were always willing to promote the cause of manufacturing by granting bonuses and other privileges. Peterborough is more diversified in its economic structure and in the composition of its industries. In 1951, 54.7 per cent of the working population was employed in manufacturing (industrial census). The largest industry in the city is the manufacturing of electrical appliances, which employs 4,055 persons out of a total employment in manufacturing of 8,725 workers. Other important manufacturing industries with their employment are as follows: prepared breakfast foods (553), slaughtering and meat packing (238), cordage, rope and twine production (213), woollen and worsted yarn (213), hardware and tools (217), boat building and repairing (565), professional and scientific equipment (632).

An excellent supply of water-power has fostered the industrial expansion of the city. In the 19th century sawmills and flour mills were important, but the main period of growth came with the development of hydro-electric power shortly after 1900. This is shown by the growth of population. In 1901, Peterborough had 11,239 inhabitants, but by 1911 this figure had risen to 18,360. Part of this increase is due to the incorporation of a suburb of 1,650 inhabitants.

The city also serves as a regional capial for a wide agricultural area from which there is a steady flow of labourers. About 50 per cent of the business transacted in the city is with people in the surrounding rural area (240). This gives the city a more balanced and stable economy, aside from its varied manufacturing development. Unlike Oshawa, the city is not subjected to seasonal lay-offs.

The city government is very active in fostering the industrial development (239).

Peterborough grew very rapidly during and after the last world war. Its population increased from 25,350 in 1941 to 38,272 in 1951; this is mainly the result of its industrial expansion. The stability and diversity which characterize the city are probably two of the main reasons why Peterborough, although highly industrialized, continued to have an unusual increase in manufacturing after 1935.

Manufacturing in other centres

Outside the three main industrial agglomerations, South-Central Ontario possesses several smaller industrial centres (fig. 21). The most important are Guelph, Kingston, and Belleville.

In 1951, 48.8 per cent of the total labour force of Guelph was employed in manufacturing. This is lower than in 1941, when it amounted to almost 56 per cent. This indicates that the city now has a more varied economy. The attitude towards industrialization in Guelph is quite different from that in Peterborough or in Oshawa. The Guelph Board of Trade does not encourage the establishment of large industries employing

URBAN PREDOMINANCE, 1911-1951 209

hundreds of workers (201). It wishes to maintain a diversified structure. Between 1935 and 1949, the number of manufacturing workers increased only by 67 per cent, one of the smallest increases among the larger cities and towns of the region.

Of a total employment in manufacturing of 5,836 in 1951, 295 were employed in the production of woollen and worsted yarn, 333 in the making of hats and caps, and 229 in the women's clothing industry; 1,955 in iron and steel products (agricultural implements, hardware and tools, heating and cooking apparatus, iron castings), and 1,402 in the manufacturing of electrical apparatus and supplies (heavy electrical machinery and equipment, refrigerators and electrical appliances, etc.).

Of all manufacturing centres, Kingston is one of the most rapid growing towns in South-Central Ontario. In 1941, only about 28 per cent of the persons employed in all industries worked in manufacturing. But, since 1935 tremendous changes have taken place, largely as a result of the war. The number of employees in manufacturing rose by 349 per cent between 1935 and 1949; in the latter year the total was 5,556. Until the last war, the city possessed a variety of small industries, but then an aluminium and synthetic fibre industry were located in the city. Together they employed in 1951 more than 50 per cent of the workers in manufacturing. Other important industries are railroad and rolling stock equipment and ship-building.

Kingston is about halfway between Toronto and Montreal, and has good rail and water communications with both. Despite its recent phenomenal industrial growth the density of manufacturing workers remained relatively low. In 1949, there were only 17 factory employees for every 100 inhabitants, as compared with 24 in Toronto, 22 in Guelph, 26 in Oshawa, and 27 in Peterborough. In Kingston, manufacturing employed 26.7 per cent of the workers in 1951.

In Belleville, the density of manufactory workers was also rather low in 1949 – 17 per 100 inhabitants. Between 1935 and 1949, the number of workers in manufacturing increased by 195 per cent, while in 1951 almost 30 per cent of the total labour force was employed in manufacturing. The town produces hardware and tools, electrical apparatus and supplies, and chemical products.

In recent years several smaller centres have benefited by the trend of decentralization of industries. The spread of industries from Toronto to the smaller towns to the west of the city has been mentioned previously. But other centres in the region have also been influenced by this trend. The increased attraction of the smaller towns is apparent from the distribution of new industries which came to the province in recent years, and which was as follows (47):

	1949	1950	1951	1952
New industries	47	78	92	126
Greater Toronto area	31	26	25	37
The rest of Ontario	16	52	67	89

This decentralization is an entirely new trend. In particular, Midland, Orillia, Barrie, and Trenton experienced a considerable increase in their number of factory workers between 1935 and 1949. This increase varied from 396 per cent in Midland to 143 per cent in Barrie. Similar to Kingston and Belleville, the density of factory employees is still relatively low. In 1949, the index ranged from 7 per 100 inhabitants in Barrie to 16 in Midland and Trenton and 18 in Orillia.

As far as industrial location is concerned, the smaller centres have certain advantages (235). The labour conditions in them are considered to be more stable, as the lives of the workers are not affected by the large unions to the same extent as in the cities. Land values in a small town are lower; also the living costs for employees generally are lower, particularly since they can live close to the factory. This makes lower wages acceptable. In 1951 wages were said to be 8 to 10 per cent lower than in the cities (235). On the other hand, it was observed that the freight costs are frequently higher, particularly if the towns are far from water transportation.[1]

Such has been the industrial development in South-Central Ontario since 1911. Metropolitan Toronto is still by far the most important agglomeration for manufacturing, but a trend towards decentralization has set in. This trend may gain more momentum in the future for reasons of defense in addition to those listed above.

[1] The accelerating trend towards decentralization gained momentum in 1953, because the towns being aware of the necessity of a 50 per cent industrial assessment waged aggressive campaigns to attract industries (302).

It is particularly the more diversified centres which are attracting new industries.

If more industrial centres like Peterborough could develop away from the main manufacturing belt in the Southwest, it would benefit the entire region, as it would lead to a more balanced settlement pattern. Such a development would not necessarily weaken Toronto's position. Many firms with plants in outlying centres maintain offices in Toronto and a great deal of the marketing of the products is done from that city. The increasing diversification of the city's economy is partly attributable to this development.

Transportation

Overland transportation

After the First World War, the main addition to the transportation system occurred in roads, hydro transmission lines, canals, and pipelines. The changes in the railway network consisted of the abandonment of long stretches of track (p. 162). The railways even lagged behind and failed to keep pace with the tremendous increase in the volume of traffic. In the densely populated wider Toronto area, no system of fast passenger trains exists at present to carry commuters from the city to outlying centres. In January of 1954, eight trains a day left from Oakville for Toronto; only three left daily from Aurora. Earlier in the century, inter-urban railways ran from Toronto to Port Credit, Woodbridge, and Guelph, to Newmarket and beyond to Keswick and Sutton, and to West Hill in Scarborough Township. Another inter-urban railway ran from Hamilton to Burlington and later to Oakville. After 1925, the lines were gradually discontinued, the last one, that to Richmond Hill, ceasing operations about 1948. Private automobiles and motor-coaches have captured their business.

In the early 1920's the Hydro-Electric Power Commission had an ambitious scheme for the construction of a high-speed "radial" system from Toronto to Bowmanville, Guelph, and Hamilton, and other lines elsewhere in Southern Ontario. The project, however, fell through after a Royal Commission advised against it. It was felt that the highways and the recently organized Canadian National Railways would provide uneconomic competition (48/82).

Highway traffic increased tremendously. The present road network was developed almost entirely after the First World War. The highway between Toronto and Hamilton was one of the first asphalt motor roads in the country. It was opened late in 1917. Older roads were straightened, widened, re-surfaced, and provided with lower grades. By 1930, most of the towns and villages in Southern Ontario were connected with a paved highway (336) (fig. 23).

However, although the expansion was enormous, it did not keep abreast of the rapidly increasing volume of traffic. In the 1930's a new four-lane highway was built from Toronto to Hamilton and into the Niagara Peninsula. A similar road was built to Oshawa. After the Second World War, another four-lane highway was constructed from Toronto northward to Barrie. A new four-lane express highway will connect with Windsor. A better road network on the Shield would stimulate the growth of the tourist industry in that area.

In 1950, it was estimated that some 100,000 persons were employed in the construction and maintenance of the provincial highways (235).

A map compiled by the provincial Department of Highways shows that in 1947 the bulk of the highway traffic was concentrated in the south-western section of the region (103). The distribution of highway traffic (commercial vehicles) shows how closely Toronto is linked with the industrial belt of the province. Of the total flow of traffic (all vehicles) at the western, northern, and eastern approaches to the city, 48.2 per cent was concentrated on the three highways leaving the west end of the city, near Lake Ontario; 27.5 per cent was concentrated on Yonge Street, about two miles north of the municipal boundary; and 24.3 per cent on the two main outlets at the east end of the city. The flow to the east decreases rapidly in volume beyond Oshawa. The flow to the north falls off at a much slower rate; between Washago and Gravenhurst it is approximately of the same volume as between Newcastle and Port Hope.

The phenomenal increase in the number of motor vehicles has caused traffic congestion on the streets in the major cities, especially in Metropolitan Toronto. In March 1949, the average speed of passenger cars on the main routes in Toronto during non rush-hours and under good weather conditions was 19.0 miles per hour. Over a distance of more than three miles on Yonge Street, the average speed was 11.7 miles per hour, and on more than six miles of Bloor Street – one of the main east-west arteries in the city – it was around 17 miles per hour

(333). In order to simplify its traffic problems, the city has built a subway at present more than four miles long.

Lake shipping

All through the history of transportation in South-Central Ontario, the trade of the Canadian West has played a dominant part. Roads and railways especially were constructed between Georgian Bay and Lake Ontario to serve this trade. The grain trade of the prairies in particular was a highly coveted price. Grain elevators were erected in the Georgian Bay ports of Collingwood, Midland-Tiffin, and Port McNicholl. Collingwood had a grain elevator as early as 1871. The major concentration of grain storage facilities, however, is in the Midland-Port McNicholl area. The total capacity of the elevators there amounts to about 20 million bushels out of an aggregate of 33 million bushels for all Canadian ports on Georgian Bay and the Upper Lakes, not including Fort William-Port Arthur. Midland-Tiffin and Port McNicholl received in 1951, a total of 78.9 million bushels of grain from Fort William-Port Arthur, and Collingwood 7.9 million bushes. The total amount of Canadian grain unloaded in that year at the four other receiving ports on Georgian Bay and Lake Huron was nearly 46 million bushels (281). The handling of grain products is an important source of income for those towns.

The amount of grain shipped to the Atlantic Seaboard decreased when the opening of the Panama Canal made Vancouver a grain shipping port. In the 1930's, Churchill on Hudson Bay also began to export grain. This too affected the receiving ports in Ontario.

The Lake Ontario ports were handicapped for many years by a Welland Canal which was too small. Until the completion of the new Welland Ship Canal in 1930, 90 per cent of the traffic on the upper lakes could not enter Lake Ontario. Before 1931, tremendous quantitites of Canadian grain were received at Buffalo to be forwarded to American ports or to be transferred into smaller vessels for the Lake Ontario and St. Lawrence run. Particularly Kingston lost much of its importance as a transshipment point. In 1928-29, Buffalo received more than 168 million bushels of grain from the Canadian lake-head points.

After the opening of the new Welland Canal, the receipts of Canadian grain at Buffalo decreased considerably. In 1951, Fort William-Port Arthur shipped only 36.6 million bushels of grain to that port. A large proportion of this, however, was destined for use in the United States. In the crop year 1950-51 the United States seaboard ports exported a total of only 4.6 million bushels of Canadian grain (281).

The shipments via Georgian Bay and lower lakes ports also declined, but the handling of grain became of much more importance at Toronto, Kingston, and Prescott. In 1920, no grain was unloaded at Toronto and Prescott, and only 34,000 bushels at Kingston. However, in 1951, Kingston received 33.3 million bushels of grain from the Canadian lake-head, and Toronto and Prescott 11.4 and 7.6 million bushels respectively. Kingston had become again an important trans-shipment point in Southern Ontario, and followed in total volume unloaded after Midland, Port Colbourne, and Port McNicholl. The grain unloaded at Toronto is almost entirely for consumption in that city and in its hinterland. There is no transference of grain into smaller lake vessels at Toronto.

In the crop year 1950-51 a small amount of American grain was unloaded in Ontario ports. Toronto received 2.3 million bushels, of which 1.69 million bushels were corn. Kingston received only a very small amount of American grain. Collingwood and Midland received small shipments of corn, but Port McNicholl handled 1.1 million bushels of American wheat and 1.9 million bushels of corn.

In addition to the trans-shipment of grain, the ports in South-Central Ontario imported considerable quantities of coal, oil products, and a small quantity of other products (table XVIII). Toronto, Midland, Belleville, Oshawa, and Kingston were, in 1951, the most significant importers of coal. Oil products constituted an important commodity for Port Credit with its nearby refineries and for Toronto.

As far as foreign trade is concerned, Toronto outranks all the other ports of the region. It is the only one which carries on an export trade by water, although the volume shipped out is extremely small. In total of registered net tonnage of departed ships, Toronto is also by far the most important, followed by the grain handling ports of Kingston, Midland, and Port McNicholl. Toronto's water-borne trade, as a whole, increased rapidly with the opening of the new Welland Canal. In 1929, the year previous to the opening of the new canal, the port handled a total cargo tonnage of 959,234 tons. During the first full year of operation after the opening of the new canal, the total cargo tonnage jumped to 2,122,066 tons. An all time record was reached in 1951, when the cargo tonnage amounted to 4,596,915 tons (339).

The St. Lawrence Seaway

It is generally expected that the St. Lawrence Seaway will greatly benefit the ports of Ontario. For Toronto a doubling of the water-borne trade has been predicted (235). Several considerations make it likely that such an increase may not occur, and the seaway project may prove to be of far greater benefit to South-Central Ontario as a source of hydro-electric power than as a stimulus to water-borne trade. This increased supply of power may, however, encourage industrial expansion which in turn may increase Toronto's lake traffic.

Several ports in South-Central Ontario are important as trans-shipment points for western grain, despite the competition from Vancouver and Churchill. The new seaway, however, would take this business away from them, as the efficient and specialized lake carriers will move the grain directly from the lake-head elevators to Montreal. The Georgian Bay ports are very certain to lose.

Coal, the other important item in the trade of the ports of the region, comes almost entirely from the United States and thus will not be affected by the new seaway. It may, however, be possible for the mines of the Maritime Provinces to send their coal farther up the St. Lawrence, providing they can reduce their present operating costs. On the other hand, coal consumption will probably not expand at the same rate as the economy of the region as a whole because of the increased supply of hydro-electric power as well as the increased supply of western oil and natural gas.

The seaway will have no effect on the shipment of oil, because new pipe-lines from both Montreal and Alberta may eliminate all movement by tanker.

Thus we see that, after the building of the seaway, the three most important commodities handled in the harbours of the region will either decline in volume, as is the case with grain, or will not be affected by it at all, as is true for oil and coal. Both coal and oil shipments will decline.

At present a port like Toronto does not seem to be in pressing need for a better water communication with the Atlantic Ocean. In 1951 the total inbound cargo was 4,350,000 tons, of

TABLE XVIII – Ports in South-Central Ontario in 1951. Cargoes loaded for foreign countries. Cargoes unloaded from foreign countries. Total reg. tons, in coasting service and foreign service, vessels departed (280)

Port	Loaded (tons)		Unloaded (tons)	Reg. Net tons
Belleville	—	total	194,557	223,743
		coal	181,937	
		oil products	10,120	
		molasses	2,500	
Cobourg	—		42,014	72,463
Collingwood	—		42,076	171,304
Kingston	—	total	100,731	928,467
		corn	3,388	
		flaxseed	3,093	
		coal	89,735	
		oil products	4,495	
Midland	—	coal	194,166	801,674
Napanee	—		19,351	12,647
Oshawa	—	total	129,690	79,080
		coal	99,660	
		oil products	30,030	
Penetanguishene	1,200		—	26,407
Picton	—		10,740	21,326
Port Credit	—	oil products	765,772	432,544
Port Hope	—		19,837	17,133
Port McNicholl	—	total	56,701	578,832
		grain	40,701	
		coal	16,000	
Toronto	total 14,147	total	2,603,739	3,246,794
		soya beans	121,025	
		coal	1,926,002	
		oil prod.	438,101	
Trenton	—		39,610	16,964

which 2,603,739 came from foreign ports, nearly all from the United States. The outbound cargo in that same year was 240,000 tons of which only 14,147 went to foreign ports. Of the Canadian inbound cargo, 11.4 million bushels of grain alone came from Fort William-Port Arthur. Toronto does not seem to make the fullest use of the existing St. Lawrence canals, although they have a draught of more than 14 feet.

On the other hand, branches of trade and manufacturing may become more aware of the possibilities of water-borne transportation after the opening of the Seaway. In that case, Toronto would have the advantage of being the hub of the provincial transportation system, with large distributing and wholesaling facilities as no other Canadian lake port. The most important export items, however, are industrial products, much of which is package freight and which may tend to continue to be shipped by rail. The Toronto hinterland does not produce bulky mass goods, which would prefer transportation by water.

It will be essential for the development of the Toronto harbour to have open traffic arteries converging upon it, so that trucks may have easy and speedy access to the harbour area. The truck becomes increasingly more important as a carrier of industrial products (340).

Finally, it is doubtful whether Toronto's metropolitan status will be strengthened after the building of the seaway. Toronto grew into a metropolitan city and became independent from Montreal because of its isolated location. The barrier of the St. Lawrence – the cause of the isolation – led to an early opening of the Erie Canal, and so provided Toronto with an alternative outlet to the ocean. Toronto as a metropolitan city could gain a considerable amount of independence from the two rivals Montreal and New York by leaning upon one against the other. In a similar way, the new seaway might give other cities farther west the opportunity to deal directly with Montreal and to by-pass Toronto.

Transportation in the economic structure of towns and cities

In the 65 places in South-Central Ontario for which data are given in the occupational census,[1] the proportion of the population employed in transportation varied from 4.1 per cent to 16.6 per cent. The number of places in the different percentage groupings was as follows:

[1] Centres with 1,000 or more inhabitants.

4— 6% –	11 places
6— 8% –	15 places
8—10% –	14 places
10—12% –	11 places
12—14% –	11 places
14—17% –	3 places

Of the 65 places mentioned above, 31 had fewer than 100 persons listing transportation and communication as their employment. The importance of transportation and communication in the occupational structure of those places varied from the lowest to the highest percentage. Havelock, a small centre of 1,132 inhabitants, had 16.6 per cent of its gainfully occupied population employed in those occupations, nearly entirely with the railway. In general these 31 places had fewer than 2,000 inhabitants; only seven had a larger population. Georgetown (3,452) was the largest centre in this group, with only 4.7 per cent of its working population employed in transportation and communication.

Thirty-four places had each more than 100 persons working in transportation and communication. All those centres had more than 2,000 inhabitants but, as was true for the first group, the importance of these activities in the occupational structure of the places varied considerably. Such important towns and cities as Bowmanville (5,430), Brampton (8,389), Oakville (6,910), Whitby (7,267), Oshawa (41,545), and Peterborough (38,272) had less than 6 per cent of their gainfully occupied employed in transportation and communication. In Guelph (27,386) the proportion was 6.2 per cent, in Kingston (33,459) 6.1 per cent and in Metropolitan Toronto 6.8 per cent. On the other hand also in some of the larger centres, transportation and commnuication played a more important part in the economic structure: Collingwood (7,413) 10.3 per cent, Lindsay (9,603) 11.7 per cent, Midland (7,206) 12.5 per cent, Barrie (12,514) 12.9 per cent, Belleville (19,519) 13.4 per cent, Orillia (12,110) 8.1 per cent and Trenton (10,085) 8.9 per cent.

In the ports listed in Table XVIII, the proportion of the gainfully employed working in transportation and communication varied from 5.9 per cent (Oshawa) to just over 13 per cent (Belleville and Port Credit). Belleville, however, has this relatively high proportion not as a port, but because a large number of persons is employed by the railways.

The occupational census does not include clerical workers, labourers, etc. working in transportation. This may be obtained from the industrial census. But this supplies data only for places of 10,000 and over. Of those, there are nine in South-Central Ontario. In this group, Barrie and Belleville are the towns with the highest employment in transportation, storage, and communication; the percentages were, in 1951, 12.6 and 12.9 respectively. In both of them railways are important employers. Next came Trenton with 8.5 per cent and Metropolitan Toronto with 7.2 per cent. The proportions for Guelph, Kingston, Orillia, Oshawa, and Peterborough ranged between 3.8 and 6.5 per cent.

Trade

With the tremendous increase in agricultural and industrial production, trade expanded and stimulated urban development. In the early 19th century, trade had led to the rise of many a town, but it gained in importance as a cause for population concentration, as the production of goods and the demand for them became more diversified. Particularly the rural market for consumer goods formed a sharp contrast with the highly self-sufficient agricultural population of the early 19th century.

The commercial heart of the province lies within South-Central Ontario. In 1941, the region accounted for about 55 per cent of the 111,042 employees in the retail trade of the province.[1] The concentration of the wholesale trade was even more pronounced. In that same year, South-Central Ontario contained more than 67 per cent of the persons employed in wholesale establishments in Ontario. The results of the 1951 retail and wholesale trade census are not yet available. However, the position of trade and finance in the occupational structure of the province as a whole remained practically the same between 1941 and 1951, i.e. about 10 per cent (table XV).

[1] For the evaluation of the relative importance of the wholesale and retail trade in the various centres, the employment figures have been used, and not the total value of the sales. The latter varies with the purchasing power over the different parts of the region.

A. The retail trade

The distribution of workers employed in the retail trade in South-Central Ontario is highly irregular (fig. 22). Within the region sharp contrasts exist as a result of the juxtaposition of the almost uninhabited Canadian Shield and the Toronto metropolitan district. The northern and eastern counties have only a very small amount of retail trade, while Metropolitan Toronto in 1941 had approximately 72 per cent of those employed in the retail trade of the region. The remaining 28 per cent is mainly concentrated in seven or eight other large centres.

The Toronto trading area

The Toronto trading area (see fig. 23 and p. 226) contained more than 1,000,000 inhabitants in 1941, and about 1,250,000 by 1951. The trading area extends in a broad half circle around the city, and within it Toronto has an absolute monopoly of the retail trade. Most of the area is within a 25 to 30 mile radius from downtown Toronto. Toronto stores deliver by truck in all parts of this area.

Metropolitan Toronto had in 1941 about 49,220 persons employed in its retail establishments (table XIX). Of the gainfully employed in the metropolitan city, 15 per cent worked in trade and finance, while Metropolitan Toronto had a retail density of 6.07 retail workers for every 100 inhabitants.

The retail density in the centres around Toronto varied in general between 3.8 and 4.4 retail workers per 100 inhabitants. This was, as may be expected, much lower than the Toronto density. Port Credit was the only exception; it had 5.6 retail workers per 100 inhabitants. Retailing was of most significance in the economic structure of Oakville and Port Credit, where 15 and 14 per cent respectively of the gainfully occupied population was employed in trade and finance. In the three remaining towns – Georgetown, Brampton, and Newmarket – the proportion varied from 10 to 13 per cent. Finance was of very small importance in those places and the proportion represents largely the number of persons employed in retail trade.

The retail trade in other centres

Several of the other cities and towns in South-Central Ontario

TABLE XIX – Retail Trade in 1941 (40, X)

	number of employees retail	per 100 of total pop.	proportion of gainfully occupied persons in trade and finance in 1941 %
Barrie	626	6.43	16
Belleville	944	6.00	13
Bowmanville	120	2.91	10
Bracebridge	135	5.72	16
Brampton	246	4.08	11
Burlington	137	3.59	14
Campbellford	119	3.94	16
Cobourg	196	3.28	13
Collingwood	201	3.20	10
Dundas	151	2.86	10
Georgetown	112	4.37	10
Gravenhurst	113	5.32	12
Guelph	811	3.48	9
Huntsville	164	5.85	—
Kingston	1,593	5.28	11
Lindsay	421	5.01	14
Midland	237	3.48	13
Napanee	233	6.84	20
Newmarket	142	3.52	13
Oakville	157	3.81	15
Orangeville	116	4.26	18
Orillia	467	4.76	15
Oshawa	1,063	3.96	9
Peterborough	1,195	4.31	12
Picton	239	6.12	18
Port Credit	122	5.64	14
Port Hope	171	3.38	14
Greater Toronto	49,220	6.07	15
Toronto	44,673	6.69	14
Trenton	335	4.02	11
Whitby	104	1.76	9

lose part of their retail trade to Metropolitan Toronto, although they are outside the main trade area of Toronto. Along the north shore of Lake Ontario, Toronto influence reaches beyond Hamilton in the Southwest and past Port Hope and Cobourg in the East. Such towns as Guelph, Whitby, Oshawa, Bowman-ville, Port Hope, and Cobourg have less than 4 workers per 100 inhabitants.

Many people in Guelph purchase in stores in Toronto and Hamilton. The trading area of this latter city is relatively small and in 1941, 9 per cent of its gainfully occupied workers were employed in trade and finance.

Whitby, Port Hope, Cobourg, and Bowmanville were vigorous trade centres in the 19th century. The first three especially were powerful competitors of Toronto and pushed their own rail lines into the interior and to Georgian Bay. However, their hinterland was tapped by Toronto, or was lost for other reasons, as in the case of Cobourg, and the trade of the towns became insignificant. Oshawa, on the other hand, never was an important trade centre, but it rose mainly as an industrial town. The city overshadowed Whitby, but it captured only a small portion of Whitby's hinterland, which at one time extended as far as the shores of Lake Simcoe. Similar to Guelph, the Oshawa retail trade serves largely the local market. There are only about 4 workers in the retail trade per 100 inhabitants, and only 9 per cent of the gainfully occupied population was employed in trade and finance in 1941.

In the centres farther away from metropolitan Toronto, the retail trade becomes more important. Altogether, there are fifteen outlying towns in South-Central Ontario which have relatively big concentrations of retail trade. Of those, nine had more than five workers in retail establishments for every 100 inhabitants, while only three – Collingwood, Midland, and Campbellford – had fewer than four. The first two had close to 7,000 inhabitants in 1941 and Campbellford about 3,000. All three served relatively small areas. For Campbellford retail trade was nevertheless important, as it employed 16 per cent of the gainfully occupied.

In the other outlying centres and also in Midland, the tourist industry fostered their retail trade. Midland is one of the main supply bases for the tourist settlements on the numerous islands in Georgian Bay and along its shores. The Martyrs' Shrine attracts annually about 150,000 visitors to the town. During the summer months, the port receives regular calls by tourist cruisers from large American lake cities.

The tourist industry has a similar influence on the towns from Barrie to Huntsville. In the Barrie area about 4,500 cottages receive mail during the entire summer and about the same number are supplied with electricity (192).

Lindsay and Peterborough supply the tourists visiting the Kawartha Lakes. As early as 1832, John Langton mentioned the fancy log houses on the shore of Pigeon Lake (154). After the American Canoe Association had held its meeting in this area in 1883, the lakes became famous as a summer resort. The Trent canal system helped to open up this area.

The tourist trade also stimulated considerably the retail trade of Kingston. The historic attractions of this city and its connection with the Rideau lakes attract thousands of visitors to the city. The opening of the Thousand Islands Bridge across the St. Lawrence has noticeably increased the tourist traffic of the city. In 1952, more than 126,000 persons visited historic Fort Henry.

The retail business of Barrie and Trenton and partly also of Belleville receives an additional impetus from the nearby large-scale establishments of the armed forces. It has been estimated that one-eighth of the total annual retail sales of Barrie is contributed by personnel from Camp Borden (192).

Barrie has become a town in which the retail trade is most important. In 1941, the town had 6.43 workers in the retail trade per 100 inhabitants, a proportion similar to that of Toronto (table XIX). About 16 per cent of the gainfully occupied persons in the town listed trade and finance as their main occupation. Barrie is the only town relatively close to Metropolitan Toronto which has an important retail trade.

Picton in Prince Edward County may be taken as an example of a prosperous retail centre in a farming region with very little industrial development. In 1941, the town had 6.12 per 100 inhabitants engaged in retail trade, while 18 per cent of the gainfully employed gave trade and finance as their main profession. Only 14 per cent were engaged in manufacturing.

B. The wholesale trade

Even more than is the case with the retail trade, the wholesale trade of the region is concentrated in Toronto (fig. 22). The city proper had, in 1941, 24,664 persons employed in wholesale establishments, and the rest of South-Central Ontario had only about 2,900. Early in the 19th century the import trade had already begun to concentrate in Toronto, and from this its function as a distributor and wholesaler had evolved. The development and changes in the transportation system of the province greatly contributed to the rise of the city as the dominating wholesale centre.

TABLE XX – Wholesale trade in cities and towns of 5,000 population or over (40, X)

Places	employees	per 1,000 of population
Barrie	220	22.51
Belleville	231	11.47
Brampton	13	2.15
Cobourg	36	6.02
Collingwood	101	16.10
Dundas	21	3.98
Guelph	161	6.91
Kingston	352	11.68
Lindsay	82	9.16
Midland	49	7.20
Orillia	89	9.08
Oshawa	139	5.18
Peterborough	198	7.81
Port Hope	20	3.95
Toronto	24,664	36.95
Greater Toronto	25,000[1]	30.86
Trenton	32	3.84
Whitby	3	—

[1] Estimate based on census data.

In 1941 Toronto nearly equalled Montreal in the wholesale business. In that year it had 20.1 per cent of the workers employed in wholesale establishments in Canada as compared with 21.3 per cent for Montreal. The next largest centres were Vancouver with 7.1 and Winnipeg with 6.8 per cent of the total.

Also in total value, Toronto stood second to Montreal. Toronto had, in 1941, a wholesale trade value of $1,136 million and Montreal $1,449 million.

In Ontario, Toronto had a much greater density of wholesale trade than any other large centre. In 1941, it had 36.9 workers per 1,000 inhabitants compared with 18.9 in London,

12.7 in Hamilton, 12.3 in Ottawa, and 10.8 in Windsor. In a similar way, Toronto also ranked far above the larger centres in South-Central Ontario (table XX).

As is true for the retail trade, the centres farther away from Toronto show a tendency towards a higher wholesale density. Kingston, Belleville, Barrie, and Collingwood each had more than 10 wholesale workers per 1,000 inhabitants. But the wholesale trade was of relatively minor importance in Oakville, Guelph, Whitby, Oshawa, Port Hope, Cobourg, and Peterborough. Some of these towns had been important trade centres in the past, but they had lost their trade to Toronto.

Outside Toronto, there was no other centre in South-Central Ontario in whose economy the wholesale trade played such an important part as in Barrie. It had, in 1941, a wholesale density of 22.5. This important position in the wholesale trade supplements its similar position as a retail centre.

The nature of the Toronto wholesale trade

Toronto employed 20 per cent of the workers in the wholesale trade in Canada. In several branches of the wholesale trade, however, the Toronto proportion was much less than 20 per cent. The wholesale trade in all kinds of food products, groceries inclusive, was rather low in the city. Only from 10 to 13 per cent of the national employment in this branch worked in Toronto in 1941, as compared with 16 to 18 per cent in Montreal. The wholesale trade in farm products (raw materials) and in tobacco and tobacco products also was relatively unimportant in Toronto, with 1.7 per cent and 13 per cent respectively of the national employment. On the other hand, Toronto ranked high as a centre for the wholesale trade in chemicals, drugs and allied products (36 per cent); dry goods and apparel (29 per cent); electrical goods (29 per cent); furniture and house furnishings (33 per cent); and jewelry (40 per cent).

Finance and insurance in Toronto

Ever since Toronto usurped Kingston's banking charter in the early years of the 19th century, it has risen steadily as a financial centre. Very early it was the financial capital of the province, but by the middle of the 20th century it has become in many aspects the financial focus of the entire Dominion. In 1941, the finance and insurance establishments of the metropolitan city employed 23.8 per cent of the persons gainfully occupied in those fields in Canada, as compared with 21.9 per cent in Greater Montreal. Its importance as the financial headquarters of Ontario is borne out by the fact that Metropolitan Toronto employed 55.0 per cent of the workers in finance and insurance in the province. In the greater city itself, 5.31 per cent of the workers employed in industries worked in finance and insurance. In greater Montreal this proportion amounted to 4.15 per cent.

One of the most important establishments is the Toronto Stock Exchange. The exchange started on a very small scale in 1852, organized by a dozen Toronto citizens. In 1878, it was incorporated under an act of the Provincial Legislature. The mining boom in British Columbia created a great demand for financing in the 1890's, and in 1896, the Toronto Stock and Mining Exchange was formed. The volume of trade was so large that another exchange, the Standard Stock and Mining Exchange was formed, but in 1899 the two exchanges merged.

A period of considerable expansion followed the discovery of the cobalt silver ores in 1904 and gold at Kirkland Lake and Porcupine a few years later. The prosperous mines greatly stimulated the trade of the exchange. By 1909, the transactions in listed stocks amounted to 37 million shares with a value of about $18 million. After the First World War, new mining developments occurred, as the copper-gold field of Quebec was discovered and Noranda began to grow. Also in Northern Ontario mining expanded rapidly. In the late twenties, the exploitation of the ores in the Flin Flon area began. In 1924, important wells had begun production in the Turner Valley. All these developments added further impetus to trading at the exchange and its volume of sales increased rapidly.

Thus the Toronto Stock Exchange became the largest market of mining shares in the world. In 1951, it ranked third in dollar volume on the North American continent, after the two exchanges in New York. In that year, more than 561 million shares were sold at the Toronto exchange, with a value of $1,174 million, representing 57 per cent of all the sales in Canada. The Montreal Stock and Curb Market, the second largest exchange of the Dominion, traded, in 1951, 108 million shares with a total value of $805 million (356).

The Urban Pattern in 1951

Service centres and their umland

The towns provide the population of the surrounding area with a great variety of services and goods. This is the oldest function of the towns of the region and the reason why most of them started.

In the 20th century, however, manufacturing became the dominant factor in town growth and often the traditional service function was overshadowed by it. Yet the service function remained. A vigorous growth of manufacturing in a town tended to improve its shopping and service facilities, which in turn strengthened its position as a central place.

It is extremely difficult to obtain uniform statistical data which could be used to measure the status of a town as a service centre. In particular this is true for the smaller places.

Therefore, the urban centres were checked for the presence of about 12 services, six of which were chosen as key services. The six key services are banks, weekly, bi-weekly, tri-weekly or daily newspapers, public libraries, public secondary schools, moving picture theatres, and hospitals. Banks which were open for only a few hours a week were not included as a criterion. These key services indicate whether a place is of importance as a commercial, social, and cultural centre; they measure its degree of centrality.

A centre with all the six key services present is called a fully-fledged town. In a sub-town one of the services is missing, while a place with three or four of the key services present is called an urban village. The smallest service centres classified are the rural villages with only one or two of the key services available.

The validity of the classification is shown by the fact that in general only the fully-fledged towns command a well defined umland.

The number of phone calls, as reported by the Bell Telephone Company of Canada, was used to differentiate between the larger centres, and to determine with which towns the minor centres had the strongest links. Areas were drawn in which the population had contact predominantly with one particular town. Thus, Bronte was considered to be located on the boundary between the Toronto and Hamilton umlands. Between

Bronte and Hamilton 65 calls a day were placed and between Bronte and Toronto 63 calls.

The entire region is part of the Toronto umland. Kingston, Bancroft, Gravenhurst, Barrie, Collingwood, Orangeville, and Guelph, each places more calls with Toronto than with any other centre. However, they were surrounded by a number of points which placed their largest number of calls with them. Therefore they each are dominant in a rather well defined territory (fig. 23).

The broken lines on the map represent boundaries around umlands, which form a part of the umland of a large centre, but which have a secondary centre of their own. Toronto, Belleville, and Kingston are surrounded by a fringe of "semi-independent" umlands.

In order to evaluate their validity, the umland boundaries, based on phone call intensity, were compared with traffic counts of the Provincial Department of Highways (103). The two maps reveal a striking amount of conformity. In a few cases, when the number of phone calls was not available, the umland boundaries were based on the traffic. The umland boundaries thus established, may be assumed to be fairly accurate, although they should be considered more as transition zones of varying widths than as sharply defined lines. By and large, it is the fully-fledged towns which have a well defined umland.

A total of 25 places were classified as fully-fledged towns.[1] Nine of those offered in varying degrees more specialized services (fig. 23). They were the only centres, which, with few exceptions, supported daily newspapers and radio stations. Of the nine, Barrie was the only town without a daily paper (it had a bi-weekly). Lindsay and Port Hope did not have a radio station. Twenty-three towns had their own more or less well defined umland. The two towns for which no separate umland could be established were small industrial centres near Toronto – Oakville and Brampton.

The fully-fledged towns are the most important centres in their respective regions. The other places in their tributary areas are service centres of a lower status. The minor service centres in the umlands of Peterborough, Lindsay, Barrie, Guelph, and others are away from the fully-fledged town and located in the outer fringe of the umland.

To illustrate the nature of a fully-fledged town, Lindsay

[1] No attempt was made to classify the places which constitute part of the Toronto Metropolitan census area.

nay be taken as an example. In this town of 9,603 inhabitants
n 1951, manufacturing is relatively unimportant; in 1949, there
were about 1,000 workers in manufacturing or about 11 in-
ustrial workers per 100 inhabitants, as compared with about
7 in such manufacturing cities as Oshawa and Peterborough.
Lindsay's importance as a service centre is evident in the rela-
vely large retail section in the town (Table XIX). It has four
anks and two department stores. There are two weekly papers
n the town, with a circulation in 1950 of 3,149 and 5,287
espectively. The town differs from most of the other fully-
edged towns in that it also has a daily paper. The circulation
f this paper is 2,254 (43). Together with its umland, it had,
n 1951, a total population of about 25,000. Lindsay has good
ommunications with its umland, as it serves as the hub for five
ighways; six railways lead to other parts of the province.
Nevertheless, it has a rather isolated location, away from the
ther industrial areas. This has probably retarded the rise of
manufacturing in the town, but has strengthened its position
s a service centre. On the other hand, the 1941 census indicated
nat only 20 per cent of its gainfully occupied population re-
orted one of the service professions as their main occupation.
Partly, this is due to the lower incomes in the area. The average
nnual industrial wage in the town is $1,497 as compared with
n Ontario average of $2,188 (285). Another reason is that the
ensity of rural population in the Lindsay umland is relatively
ow.

Twenty-three places in the region, the immediate suburbs
f Toronto exclusive, were classified as sub-towns; 21 of those
ere so classified because they lacked a hospital, one did not
ossess a high school, and one was without a newspaper.

Several factors have prevented those sub-towns from be-
oming fully-fledged towns themselves. Some of them are too
lose to the fully-fledged towns and cannot compete with the
ervices provided by the larger centres. This is especially true
or the sub-towns in the southwest part of the region. In other
nstances, sub-towns developed in areas farther away from
arger central places. Sometimes they even have a more or less
ell-defined umland of their own. Thus the sub-town Beaverton
eveloped between the umlands of Toronto and Lindsay. Other
uch centres are: Uxbridge, Campbellford, Trenton, Marmora,
Madoc, Tweed, and Napanee.

The region had altogether 36 urban villages, centres which
ere so classified because they possessed 3 or 4 key services; 21
ad 3 key services and 15 had 4. The most characteristic

services of urban villages are banks, libraries, newspapers an
secondary schools. Of the 36 places in this classification, 3
offered banking facilities, 31 had a library, 27 a newspaper
and 22 a high school. The newspaper is in general a weekl
paper. Only 9 urban villages had a cinema and all were withou
a hospital. The prevalence of banking facilities, secondar
schools, libraries, and weekly papers in those centres serves t
emphasize their importance as small, well developed servic
centres. However, as far as entertainment is concerned, the
are by-passed in favour of the sub-towns and particularly th
fully-fledged towns.

There are 62 rural villages in South-Central Ontario.
bank and a public library are the services most often found i
them. A bank is present in 43 rural villages and 35 have
library; a secondary school is found in 2 of them and in 2
newspaper is published. Only 22 rural villages have two sei
vices, almost always a bank and a library; 40 have one servic
23 having a bank and 17 a library. The number of rural villag
is considerably higher than in 1911. The main reason for th
is the change in classification which put many places in th
category, although only one of the key services was presen
Of the 32 new rural villages in 1952, 13 had already one servic
in 1911. A large number of those new central places develope
in and near York County.

The different service centres varied considerably in numbe
of inhabitants. The range is so wide that it is of little value
determine an average size, especially for the fully-fledged town
Of the latter, 7 had a total population in 1951 of betwee
1,000 and 5,000, the smallest having about 1,500 inhabitant
Only one fully-fledged town, Haliburton, had less than 1,00
inhabitants; this place was not incorporated. It developed i
the sparsely populated Shield area. All the remaining full
fledged towns had more than 5,000 inhabitants. Nine of tho
had between 5,000 and 10,000 people.

The sub-towns display a far greater amount of uniformi
as far as population is concerned. Of the 23 sub-towns, 11 ha
between 1,000 and 2,000 inhabitants in 1951, and 9 betwee
2,000 and 4,000. The largest sub-towns are Penetanguishe
(4,949), Dundas (6,846), and Trenton (10,085). Those thr
sub-towns are close to large service centres.

Several of the urban villages and most of the rural villag
were not incorporated in 1951, and no accurate statistics a
available on their number of inhabitants. 27 of the 36 urba
villages were incorporated in 1951. Of those 27, 20 – more tha

half of the total – had between 700 and 1,800 inhabitants. Only two larger centres were classified as an urban village: Whitby (7,267) and Burlington (6,017). Both of them were closely dependent on a larger central place, Oshawa and Hamilton respectively.

Only 11 of the 62 rural villages were incorporated in 1951. Ten had a population between 250 and 1,000, and one, Ajax, was still an unbalanced, rapidly growing new settlement of 4,100 inhabitants. Most of the unincorporated rural villages had fewer than 500 inhabitants.

In addition to the centres which have been classified as service centres, the countryside is sprinkled with numerous small hamlets. They may contain one or more stores, a service station, one or more churches, a school, a dance hall, and occasionally a creamery or egg grading station. Others have become dependent upon the tourist industry. They also attract retired farmers. The population of these hamlets may go as high as 200 or 250. The larger ones among them may have a bank office, which is open only on certain days during the week or a small public library. There are no statistics available concerning the smallest centres. They are not incorporated and their population is considered as rural, although in many, the non-rural occupations are of greater importance.

The umlands vary considerably in shape and size. There is no relationship between the size of the service centre and the surface area of the umland. Guelph had, in 1951, a population which was more than twice the number of inhabitants of Barrie. The umland of the two towns, however, did not differ much in area.

The tributary areas of central places with an interior location, away from large transportation routes, tend to be circular in shape. But, of the towns on the main transportation routes along the north shore of Lake Ontario they are more elongated, because the service centres are more closely strung out along the main railways and highways. Lakes Scugog and Rice and the Interlobate Moraine constituted a barrier giving Peterborough and Lindsay a somewhat isolated location. The barrier prevented the lakeshore centres from dominating the interior. Such a barrier does not exist to the north of Belleville, Napanee, and Kingston. On the other hand, the sterile Shield did not provide the agricultural base for the rise of market-towns, which could have competed with the lakeshore centres. Therefore the hinterland of these towns extends much farther inland than that of other lakeshore towns to the west.

Finally, Oshawa, Whitby, Oakville, and others saw their respective umlands trimmed as a result of vital changes in the railway network. As the transportation system of the region grew, the railways and later the modern highways were more and more focussed upon Toronto. This also accounts for the semi-circular shape of the Toronto umland proper with a radius of approximately 25 to 30 miles.

The trends noticeable in the changing pattern of central places around 1911 continued also in the decades after that year. With improved means of transportation, especially through a large scale use of the automobile, the competition among the service centres became extremely severe. The centres with less specialized and less attractive service facilities were by-passed in favour of the larger centre a few miles farther away. On the other hand, the growth of modern manufacturing in a place enhanced the quality and specialization of its services and therefore it could become more attractive than a much older centre nearby. Thus Whitby was completely overshadowed by Oshawa.

This trend in the decline of the smaller centres may be seen from a comparison between the rural villages of 1911 and those of 1952. Of the 43 rural villages in 1911, 16 do not occur on the map of 1952 and 19 remained a rural village. In part, this may have been caused by the different criteria selected for the classifications. In 1911, a typical rural village had a bank and a physician, and in 1952 a bank and a public library. However all 16 places which disappeared as a service centre after 1911 lost their bank and failed to attract a library. Only seven of the rural villages in 1911 rose to a higher status as service centre. Thus the existing rural villages in 1911 underwent very little expansion after that year.

In the other categories also, the smaller service centres declined most relatively. This may be seen from the loss of newspapers. In 1911, in 23 urban villages a newspaper was published. By 1952, however, 7 of these villages had lost their paper. On the other hand only one of the sub-towns publishing a paper in 1911 had lost it by 1952, while only one fully-fledged town lost its paper after 1911.

Between 1911 and 1952, 10 of the 26 urban villages of 1911 declined as service centres and became rural villages, while an additional 12 remained stationary. Only three urban villages rose to a higher category; one became part of Toronto.

Of the 20 sub-towns in 1911, 11 lapsed to a lower category and 6 remained stationary. Only 3 sub-towns became fully-fledged towns. It should, however, be remembered that for the 1952 classification hospital services have been included as a new criterion. Of the 23 sub-towns 21 were so classified because they did not possess a hospital. This change in classification is also the reason why from the 42 fully-fledged towns 21 declined to sub-towns and 20 remained stationary (one became part of Metropolitan Toronto).

As mentioned before, the change in the pattern of service centres after 1911 is in part a result of changed criteria for the 1952 classification. But banks and newspapers, which were kept as criteria, indicate that after 1911, the smaller centres also declined relatively more than the larger ones; they lost their banks and newspapers. Those smaller centres were by-passed in favour of the more diversified and more specialized towns.

As the transportation system continues to become better and more efficient and the use of automobiles still expands, this trend will continue. The pattern of 1851, consisting of a large number of small service centres, relatively close together, has been replaced by a mesh of larger service centres, more widely spaced, while many others are declining or stagnant. The better equipped establishments for commerce and entertainment together with other social and cultural institutions have become concentrated in the fully-fledged towns and sub-towns.

The small places cannot finance public water supplies, or sewage facilities. The shopping services are inadequate. Their lack of recreational facilities has been mentioned. Their churches have seen congregations decline and often are in need of repairs. The small place cannot function properly as a centre for rural districts. The urban villages, but especially the sub-towns and the fully-fledged towns are much better equipped for this purpose. Churches and schools ought to follow the example of the commercial, social, and cultural establishments and re-locate themselves in the larger service centres. This would encourage the growth of those service centres and better public services could be offered (176). Better urban services in the central places of the rural areas should be regarded as a valuable measure to counteract the migration of the rural population to the cities.

Trends in population growth

The total urban population of the province – population of

incorporated places – grew from 1,328,489 in 1911 to 2,753,226 in 1951, an increase of 107.3 per cent. Most of the incorporated places in South-Central Ontario saw their population rise during this period. But a small number declined. These places and their number of inhabitants in 1911 and 1951 are as follows:

	1911	1951	decrease %
Cannington	948	890	6.1
Coldwater	649	583	10.2
Deseronto	2,013	1,522	24.4
Hastings	883	819	7.2
Havelock	1,436	1,132	21.2
Millbrook	793	734	7.4
Victoria Harbour	1,616	953	41.0
Woodville	394	374	5.1

They all are relatively small centres in which manufacturing is not of importance. Deseronto and Victoria Harbour were, in 1911, still important centres for the lumber trade. However, when the lumber stands became exhausted, they did not find an alternative source for further growth. The population of Victoria Harbour derives some income from the tourist industry during the summer, while some people have found employment in the grain handling at Port McNicholl. It was, however, not sufficient to support the population.

All these centres are minor service centres and were classified for 1952 as urban villages or lower. Seven of these eight centres were, in 1911, service centres of a higher order than in 1952, and therefore, they not only lacked manufacturing but they also saw their importance as service centre decline.

In contrast to this relatively small number of declining centres, a large number of towns received a considerable increase in population. A period of vigorous growth for most urban centres began in the thirties. For more than twenty places in South-Central Ontario, the curve of population growth shows a definite swing upwards after the 1931 census and for a similar number after 1941. For about a dozen other places, the upward swing had already begun in the twenties.

In the province as a whole, the urban population increased by 23.6 per cent in the decade of the thirties and by 25.4 per cent between 1941 and 1951.[1] Or, in the two decades after 1931, the provincial urban population rose by 55.1 per cent.

After 1931, a much larger proportion of the increase in urban population of the province lived in the cities and towns outside metropolitan Toronto – the thirteen municipalities in the southern portion of York County. Between 1911 and 1931, those thirteen municipalities still received over 53 per cent of the total increase of the urban population in Ontario.

During the succeeding two decades, Toronto and the other twelve municipalities received only 25.9 per cent of the total increase in urban population.

This is an entirely new trend. The Toronto area always had the greatest increase of urban population in the province. Since the thirties, however, the population of other cities and towns in the province has tended to grow faster. In the following section the urban growth in South-Central Ontario will be further analysed. We will deal mainly with the two decades after 1931, as the trends in population growth until the twenties and early thirties are largely similar to those of the period just before 1911.

The small places

It has been noted earlier in this chapter that the smaller service centres tend to decline, as they are being by-passed in favour of the larger centres nearby. This trend is also evident in the population growth of the incorporated places. Of a total of 86 incorporated places, 29 experienced population increase of less than 20 per cent after 1931; eight of those actually declined (see previous table). In general those declining or slowly growing centres were small; 23 of the 29 had fewer than 1,200 inhabitants in 1931. The remaining six were larger. Those with their population in 1931 were: Bracebridge (2,436); Campbellford (2,744); Deseronto (1,476); Huntsville (2,817); Midland (6,920); Napanee (3,497).

Besides these 29 slowly growing centres Toronto also had only a small increase (7.6 per cent), but this city and the surrounding municipalities are considered as one unit; this is true for Kingston and Portsmouth also.

The 29 centres appear to have remarkable similarities in

[1] The urban population for 1941 and 1951 is taken according to the new census definition (p. 187).

their occupational structure. In the first place, it may be stated that in the slowly growing or declining places, manufacturing as a rule was of minor importance. Only six places had, in 1935, some manufacturing (fig. 21): Campbellford, Colborne, Elora, Huntsville, Midland, and Napanee. Secondly, these centres were not very flourishing as service centres. Of the 29, only five were classified in a higher category as central place in 1952 than in 1911. Six were classified as fully-fledged towns in 1911, but only two were still in that category by 1952. Ten were, in 1952, rural villages and another ten were urban villages. Finally, none of these 29 places was close enough to a large urban centre, such as Hamilton, Guelph, Toronto, Oshawa, Peterborough or Kingston, to benefit from the expansion of that centre. All of them, except for two, were situated in areas which had a rural population of fewer than 40 persons per square mile. The two exceptions are Bloomfield and Wellington in Prince Edward County. We may conclude, therefore, that the slowly growing places in South-Central Ontario tend to be unimportant as seats for manufacturing and that their service function tends to be stagnant or declining. They are found in predominantly rural areas, away from the cities.

However, not all places with fewer than 1,200 inhabitants experienced a decrease in population between 1931 and 1951. There were 21 other centres in this category, which received an increase in population of more than 20 per cent, and of these, 15 had an increase of more than 30 per cent. These 15 will be discussed more in detail.

The more rapidly growing places among the small centres had in common with the slowly growing group that they were not seats of modern manufacturing development. Only one, Streetsville, had in 1935 a small amount of manufacturing (fig. 21). But unlike the slowly growing places, they tended to be more important as service centres; four of the 15 centres in this group were classified in a higher category as central place in 1952 than in 1911. Four were sub-towns, one was a fully-fledged town, and ten were urban villages. Unlike the slowly growing places, there were no rural villages among them.

This group also differs from the slowly growing category in that eight of the fifteen places are in areas with a rural population density of more than 40 persons per square mile, while four others are close to larger urban centres outside this density zone. This proximity to the larger urban centres, especially Toronto, has in some cases retarded their expansion as a service centre, but they participated in the growth of these larger

centres; eight of this group of fifteen are situated inside the
Toronto and Hamilton umland. It was pointed out before that
about half of the new service centres after 1911 sprang up in
this same area.

Thus the small centres are mainly dependent upon their
function as central place. Their prosperity, therefore, is closely
linked with the density of population of the surrounding
districts.

The larger centres

As was mentioned previously, only a few of the larger towns
had a population increase of less than 20 per cent. The most
important among these was Midland, with an increase of only
4.1 per cent between 1931 and 1951.

It may be stated that, in general, the larger towns – those
with a population of over 1,200 in 1931 – had a population increase of more than 20 per cent. This was true for 37 of 42
towns in this group. On the other hand, the urban population
of the entire province increased by just over 55 per cent between
1931 and 1951. About 12, or 28 per cent of the larger towns in
1931, had a similar or larger increase than the province as a
whole during the next two decades. These 12 centres with their
population figures in 1931 and 1951 were as follows:

	1931	1951	% increase
Acton	1,855	2,880	55.3
Barrie	7,776	12,514	60.9
Brampton	5,532	8,389	51.6
Burlington	3,046	6,017	97.5
Georgetown	2,288	3,452	50.9
Gravenhurst	1,864	3,005	61.2
Oakville	3,857	6,910	79.2
Oshawa	23,439	41,545	77.2
Peterborough	22,327	38,272	71.4
Port Credit	1,635	3,643	122.8
Richmond Hill	1,295	2,164	67.1
Trenton	6,276	10,085	60.7

In most of them manufacturing underwent a considerable expansion between 1935 and 1949. More than half of them were

in the Toronto-Hamilton region, and received a share in the upsurge of manufacturing during the thirties and forties in this area; several underwent a large influx of Toronto commuters.

It should, however, be noted that not all centres which underwent a big increase in their manufacturing employment also experienced an expansion of their population. Centres such as Belleville, Dundas, Kingston, Midland, and Orillia were places with considerable growth in manufacturing, but their total population rose by less than 50 per cent between 1931 and 1951.

Most striking is the position of Midland. The workers engaged in manufacturing rose between 1935 and 1949 to a total of 931 employees, but its population growth between 1931 and 1951 only amounted to 286.

In a few centres, this lag between growth of manufacturing and increase of population may be due to changes in the internal economic structure of the towns. In general, however, these towns drew their labour supply from the surrounding urban and rural settlements. Undoubtedly, a major factor in the creation of this time-lag has been the wide-spread housing shortage.

Also, several other centres reveal a remarkable difference between the increase in employment in manufacturing and their population growth. Most important among those were the following.

Place	percentage of increase in employment in manufacturing 1935-1949	percentage of incr. in population 1931-1951
Belleville	195	41
Barrie	143	61
Bowmanville	104	33
Dundas	167	36
Kingston	349	43
Midland	396	4
Oakville	241	79
Orillia	239	48
Peterborough	112	71
Trenton	146	61

The only large industrial centre in which the percentages of industrial employment and population growth did not display a big lag was Oshawa. The percentages for Oshawa were a 72 per cent increase in industrial employment and 77 per cent in total population. In the thirties, the population of Oshawa increased by only 14.4 per cent, but in the decade of the forties, there was an increase of almost 55 per cent.

Manufacturing has become the main factor which will control the future expansion and growth of cities and towns in South-Central Ontario. However, from the 1951 census, there seems to be no equilibrium between growth of manufacturing and population increase. The towns which received the largest increase in manufacturing did not react with similar large increases in their total population. It may be expected that in coming years many employees in manufacturing might wish to reside in the place where they work.

A Century and a Half of Urban Growth

Patterns of growth

In their growth and development, the cities and towns of South-Central Ontario display a great amount of variety. Some of them have grown vigorously from the first, while others after a period of growth have become stagnant.

The growth of all places for which census data were available was plotted on semi-logarithmic paper. Four different types of growth could be identified. Samples of those types are shown on fig. 24, and their geographical distribution is shown on fig. 25.

Type A consists of a group of towns and cities which always were the fastest growers. By 1881, all centres of this type, except for Toronto, had a population of between 3,000 and 15,000 inhabitants. At some point during the eighties or nineties their growth leveled off somewhat or even declined for a while. Soon, however, they recovered and continued to grow steadily, although at different rates. Their quick recovery at the end of the nineteenth century was caused by the expansion of modern industries in those places, and all of them belong to the more important centres for manufacturing in South-Central Ontario at the middle of the twentieth century. As a result of their early growth, they became at an early date fully-fledged towns.

The growth curves of type A on the composite graph have a gradual transition to those of type B. Similar to the towns of type A, the B centres at first grew steadily. At a certain moment in their history however, they stagnated and their curves become quite horizontal. In several cases there was a considerable regression. In total, 18 centres belong to type B, with about two-thirds of them being ports. In other cases, the building of a railway or the development of the lumber industry led to a sudden growth of population. The ports declined or stagnated in growth when they lost their trade. Changes in the transportation network, as in the case of Kingston with improvements of the Welland Canal, or the arrival of manufacturing, created new population growth in some of these centres. Because of their initial rapid growth, these towns in general gained early importance as central places; twelve of the eighteen places in this group were already fully-fledged towns in 1881. Several preserved this function, when their population growth stopped.

The places of type C had a population of between 500 and 1,600 by 1881. They had developed as small regional supply centres with a variety of small-scale manufacturing establishments. When the small industries declined, however, they failed to get another source for further growth. The result was that most of them went through several decades of rather stagnant or extremely slow population growth. By 1950, they had, in general, between 1,000 and 2,000 inhabitants. These small places as a rule also saw their function as central place decline. Of the 31 centres in this group, 17 found themselves in a lower category as central place in 1952 than in 1911; 12 of them were sub-towns and 16 were urban villages. In general, the centres of the C type are found in the more rural parts of South-Central Ontario, outside the areas in which manufacturing is concentrated.

The last type, type D, has to a certain extent, similar characteristics as the places of type C. They were, however, slightly larger in 1881 — in that year, their population figures ranged from 1,000 to 2,000. They also entered a period of stagnation and decline, but for a much shorter time than the C towns. This was mainly the result of the development of modern manufacturing in them or of their proximity to a large city. There are twelve towns in this group and almost all of them are located in the industrial southwest corner of the region, near Toronto, Guelph and Hamilton. By 1951, their population figures ranged between 2,500 and 7,000. Unlike the C towns, they saw their function as central places expand; 5 were fully-fledged towns and 6 were sub-towns. Newmarket and Huntsville were the only two with a more or less well defined umland in 1952.

Thus is the urban pattern after more than 150 years of urban growth. The present pattern is, however, perhaps more dynamic than ever before. Most of the urban centres have experienced an accelerated growth during the last few decades.

Present-day trends; decentralization

On the basis of this last chapter we can distinguish at present the following trends in the development of South-Central Ontario:

1. The rural population density is greatest around the large cities and towns. The townships around Toronto have a density of more than 60 persons per square mile, but the rural districts, which are outside the influence of large towns, have a population density of only between 10 and 40. Another contrast is that the population density near the larger towns is increasing, while in the predominantly rural areas it continues to decline.

2. The agricultural use of the land is most intensive near the cities. There the number of agricultural workers is highest and the average size of the farms is smallest.

3. Manufacturing has become the most important element in the growth of towns.

4. Manufacturing shows trends of decentralization. Metropolitan Toronto has still a considerable growth of manufacturing, but other centres outside the immediate umland of the city show proportionally larger expansion. Manufacturing seems to prefer places with a diversified economic structure. The towns in which manufacturing expands proportionally most rapidly are Barrie, Belleville, Dundas, Kingston, Midland, Oakville, Orillia, Peterborough, and Trenton.

5. The share of Metropolitan Toronto, both in the total increase of population and in the expansion of new industries, is becoming smaller.

6. The retail and wholesale trade are concentrated in Toronto and, although in a very small amount, in centres more than 35 or 40 miles from that city. The most important wholesale centres are Toronto, Barrie, Collingwood, Belleville, and Kingston.

7. The transportation network of the region is focussed entirely upon Toronto.

8. Toronto is surrounded by a zone of 25 to 30 miles wide in which no independent service centres occur.

9. Active planning is becoming more important as a factor in the development of the region. Toronto has already one newly-planned satellite, Ajax (181).

Most significant of these trends is the tendency towards a slower growth of Metropolitan Toronto and a decentralization of industries. These developments may suggest that Toronto is approaching its maximum size.

More and more it becomes necessary to control the growth of the metropolitan area, so that a more balanced urban pattern may be established. "Ontario would be in a much sounder position if the further growth of Toronto were to be distributed amongst the smaller cities of the province" (2/273). A programme of decentralization and controlled growth has become an even greater necessity in view of the modern defense needs. From the existing trends it may be concluded that the rise of large cities outside the immediate orbit of Toronto influence would lead to a much more intensive use of the land. Around the enlarged centres the rural population density would increase to 60 or more persons per square mile.

It is extremely urgent to institute a policy of greenbelts in order to prevent the rise of a continuous urban zone between Oshawa and Hamilton and beyond. For each urban centre in this zone the maximum population should be determined, and the town surrounded by a greenbelt.

Particularly to the southwest of Toronto, the greenbelts should be as extensive as possible, because of the importance of the area for fruit growing. Canada, being a northern country, has to deal carefully with her fruit producing districts. They should be protected against urban encroachment, even more so if the population of the country continues to increase.

With Metropolitan Toronto subjected to controlled growth, manufacturing and population may be encouraged to move to other centres in and outside the region.

The towns within a radius of from 35 to 40 miles from Toronto will remain true satellites; for many services they will remain dependent upon the city. Some of these towns may develop into industrial satellites, others into dormitory satellites, and again others into a combination of both. A large part of their population will have daily contact with the city.

The maximum population of these true satellites ought to be determined, especially to preserve a greenbelt of five to fifteen miles wide around Metropolitan Toronto.

Decentralization, however, should also be directed to centres beyond the zone with satellites. Although benefiting from a policy of decentralization, these towns and cities should not be looked upon as satellites. At present such towns as Guelph, Orangeville, Alliston, Barrie, Lindsay, and Oshawa display their independence from Toronto in that they have carved out for themselves a well-defined umland. Their population is almost entirely engaged in local industries and only a small number has a daily contact with the city. Except for Oshawa and Newmarket, it would not be necessary to determine their maximum population, because they are not in danger of merging with Metropolitan Toronto.

It is preferable to direct the decentralization to existing towns and not to entirely new sites. With the great costs of building it is extremely difficult to provide all the required services in a new town. Churches and assembly halls, establishments for amusement, sport facilities, libraries, schools, welfare centres, etc., are expensive to provide, and their absence may make the new town less attractive.

An existing town has many of these services, which often can easily be expanded to meet the demands of a larger town.

It is in particular the fully-fledged towns serving an extensive umland which possess these service establishments and institutions. Watson points out that the old regional centres, after having grown industrially, are much better balanced economically, socially, and culturally than the new towns which never had a regional service function (177). In South-Central Ontario, Ajax is a case in point; athough it had over 4,000 inhabitants in 1951, it was only a rural village.

On the other hand, an existing town may have a centre which would not be suitable for a greatly expanded town; the main shopping street may be too narrow. In that case remedial measures could be taken at an early date.

One of the towns, which would seem best suited to receive some of the decentralized industries and population of Toronto is Barrie. This town is far enough from Toronto to maintain its independence, but it is linked with that city with one of the most modern highways of the Dominion. A four-lane controlled-access highway of about 50 miles leads from Barrie to Metropolitan Toronto; railroads connect it with that city and Hamilton. It is on the main transportation routes between Southern Ontario and Western Canada. Barrie itself has a beautiful location on Lake Simcoe and, if carefully planned, would undoubtedly be able to attract people from the over-crowded Toronto area.

Barrie is one of the nine towns and cities of type A, which have grown more or less steadily in the past. In the case of Barrie this has not led to a spectacular number of inhabitants by 1951, mainly because, for a long time, its main function was that of a central place. This function is still of considerable importance as is evident from its position as wholesale and retail centre (fig. 22). The town has succeeded in maintaining itself as a regional capital with a well-defined umland relatively close to Toronto. This means that the town possesses a variety of regional service establishments, which would provide a sound basis for further expansion.

Barrie is a centre which appears to be attractive to manu-facturing as is evident from its industrial growth between 1935 and 1949.

The feasibility of a large industrial centre farther inland is evidenced by Peterborough. Also, that city was, and still is, an important regional capital which became industrialized. Peter-borough originally enjoyed the benefit of a large supply of cheap hydro-electric power, but in 1952 the cost of power in Peter-borough and Barrie was the same (285).

Peterborough provides also an example of some of the in-dustries which might be attracted by a town like Barrie. They must be industries which do not require bulky or heavy raw materials, but which produce valuable and high quality prod-ucts. The finished goods should not derive their value from the raw material used, but from the application of skills, techniques, and organizational talent. Such industries are high quality textiles, electro-technical industries, machine building, optical industries, etc.

Such would be the most desirable future development of the region.

Conclusion

During this period of slightly more than a century and a half, South-Central Ontario passed through an urban development which in Europe took many centuries to be completed. In these 150 years, we see at the beginning a highly rural and largely self-sufficient economy, and at the end an extremely urbanized way of life. Unlike in Europe, where the beginnings are shrouded in obscurity, we have for Southern Ontario many sources recording the first rise of towns and villages.

Town growth did not become of real importance until the eighteen forties, when the standard of living began to rise as a result of trade with the United States. This increase in the standard of living meant a greater demand for urban services.

The towns remained mainly service centres until the end of the former century; then manufacturing became the main factor in urban growth. Protective tariffs were the most important cause for the rise of modern industries in South-Central Ontario.

The most important aspect of the urban development in South-Central Ontario has been the phenomenal rise of Toronto. Toronto began as an administrative centre, and this function remained the most important element in its growth until the late eighteen thirties. The governing circles made the capital into the main financial and educational centre of Upper Canada. Outside Toronto there were no other banks until 1832. For political and military reasons, roads were built out from Toronto, so that in the forties it had become the main centre for roads in the region. As such, Toronto's growth is similar to that of London or Paris, which for the same reasons became focal points for roads. Later those roads greatly contributed to the economic expansion of the city.

By 1840, Toronto had become the largest town of Upper Canada and this in itself became a main factor in its further growth; it was the largest market, the luxury market which determined taste and fashion in the colony; it was the centre from which the various parts of Upper Canada could be reached most easily, in particular after 1880, when it had become the hub of the railway network. By 1880, the city had also become the main wholesale centre of the province. After that year, however, manufacturing became the main factor in the growth of the city. In the 20th century, its economic structure became more diversified, in part as a result of the increased importance of commerce and finance.

Toronto has never been subjected in its growth to great upheavals or disturbances. After a forced and rather hesitant beginning, the city had gained enough momentum by 1840 to continue its growth at an ever increasing rate.

Toronto, however, never would have reached its dominant position without a great amount of active and deliberate planning by man. Southern Ontario would never have seen the development of the present-day urban pattern if it were not for the fact that Simcoe interrupted the natural development of settlement by establishing the capital at Toronto. This in itself would not necessarily have been sufficient ground for the city to become the largest and most powerful urban agglomeration; many capitals have remained insignificant towns. But after Toronto had been decided upon as the capital of the colony, the government was determined to make it also the economic capital of Upper Canada, to a great extent for self-interested reasons. Strangely enough, this planning was largely based on the false premises of a tremendous flow of trade from the north and northwest.

Another act of man, of similar consequences, has been the use of tariffs to promote the development of manufacturing.

Finally, in order to reach a balanced urban pattern in the region, still another deliberate act of man will be needed. Only a regional plan, focused on a controlled growth of Toronto, with an accompanying development of satellite towns and a general programme of decentralization, will lead to the most desirable climax settlement of the region.*

---

* For a useful supplementary discussion of some of the themes in this chapter, see my contribution to Warkentin (ed.) *Canada, A Geographic Interpretation*, Chapter 11, "Southern Ontario"; and also the Government of Ontario's *Design for Development: The Toronto-Centred Region*.

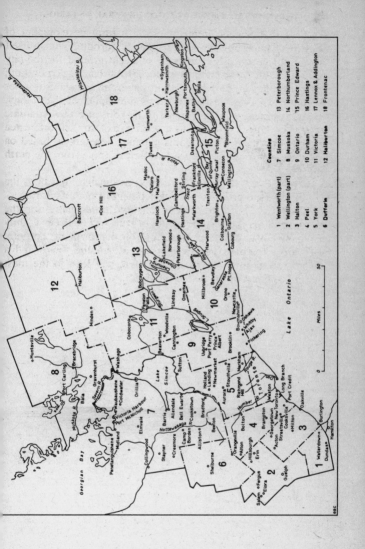

Counties

1 Wentworth (part)
2 Wellington (part)
3 Halton
4 Peel
5 York
6 Dufferin

7 Simcoe
8 Muskoka
9 Ontario
10 Durham
11 Victoria
12 Haliburton

13 Peterborough
14 Northumberland
15 Prince Edward
16 Hastings
17 Lennox & Addington
18 Frontenac

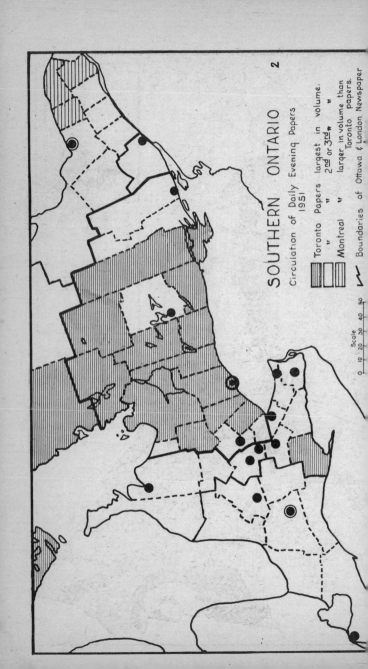

SOUTHERN ONTARIO

Circulation of Daily Evening Papers
1951

Toronto Papers largest in volume.
" " 2nd or 3rd "
Montreal " larger in volume than
Toronto papers.

Boundaries of Ottawa & London Newspaper

Scale
0 10 20 30 40 50

2

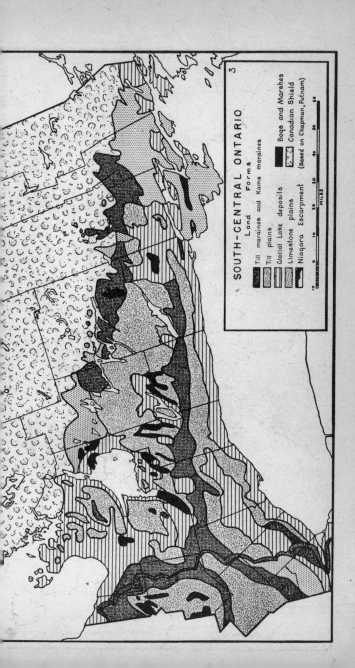

SOUTH-CENTRAL ONTARIO
Land Forms

Till moraines and Kame moraines
Till plains
Glacial Lake deposits
Limestone plains
Niagara Escarpment
Bogs and Marshes
Canadian Shield

(Based on Chapman, Putnam)

MILES
10   0   10   20   30   40   50   60

3

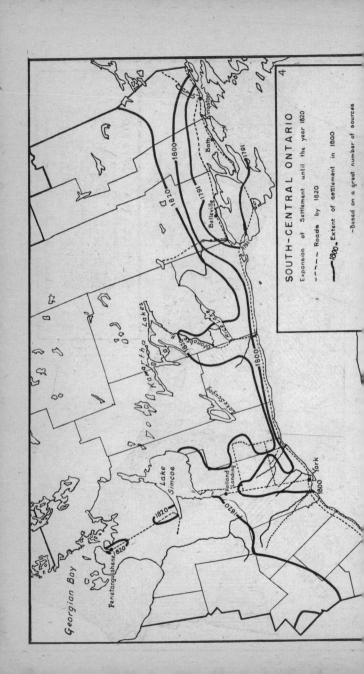

SOUTH-CENTRAL ONTARIO

Expansion of Settlement until the year 1820.

----- Roads by 1820

━━1800━ Extent of settlement in 1800

-Based on a great number of sources

Georgian Bay

Penetanguishene

Lake Simcoe

Holland Landing

Kawartha Lakes

Rice Lake

Lake Scugog

York

1800

1820

1820

1820

Cobourg

1800

1820

1820

Belleville

Bath

Kingston

1791

1800

1820

1791

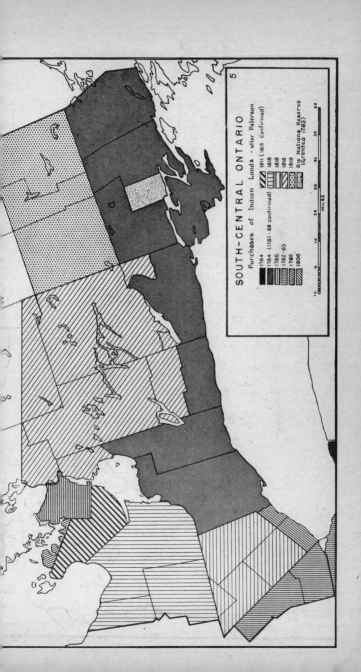

SOUTH-CENTRAL ONTARIO

Purchases of Indian Lands - after Paterson

■ 1764	▨ 1811 (1815 Confirmed)	
▥ 1784 (1787-88 Confirmed)	▤ 1816	
▦ 1785	▨ 1818	
▧ 1792-93	▨ 1819	
▨ 1795	▨ Six Nations Reserve	
▨ 1806	(Granted 1793)	

MILES

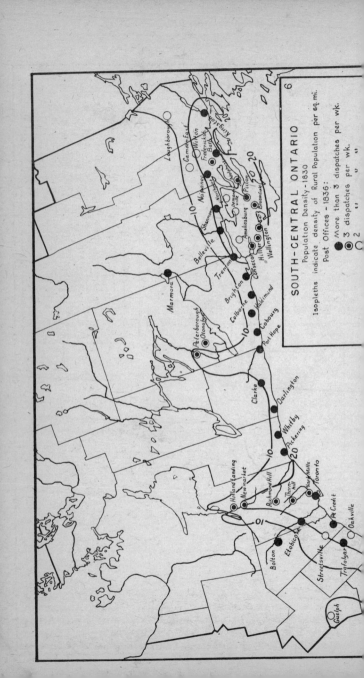

SOUTH-CENTRAL ONTARIO

Population Density - 1830

Isopleths indicate density of Rural Population per sq. mi.

Post Offices - 1836:

● More than 3 dispatches per wk.
◉ 3 dispatches per wk.
◎ 2 " "
○ 1 " "

6

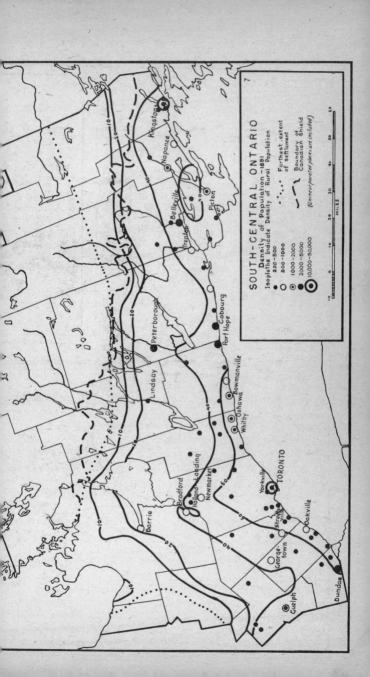

SOUTH-CENTRAL ONTARIO
Density of Population ~ 1851
Isoplaths Indicate Density of Rural Population

- 200-500
- 500-1000
- 1000-2000
- 2000-5000
- 10,000-50,000

······· Farthest extent of settlement

⌒⌒ Boundary of Canadian Shield

(Urban or parts/places are included)

MILES
0 10 20 30 40 50 60

7

Kingston
Napanee
Belleville
Picton
Trenton
Cobourg
Port Hope
Peterborough
Bowmanville
Lindsay
Oshawa
Whitby
Yorkville
TORONTO
Bradford
Holland Landing
Newmarket
Barrie
Streets-ville
Oakville
George-town
Dundas
Guelph

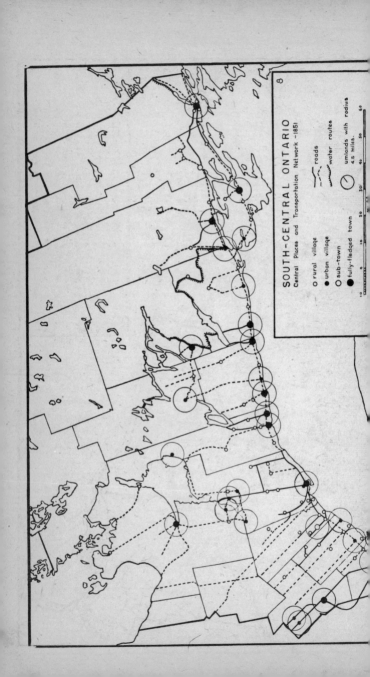

SOUTH-CENTRAL ONTARIO
Central Places and Transportation Network –1851

o rural village
● urban village
◯ sub-town
⬤ fully-fledged town

⌇⌇ roads
┄┄ water routes
◯ umlands with radius
    4.5 miles.

8

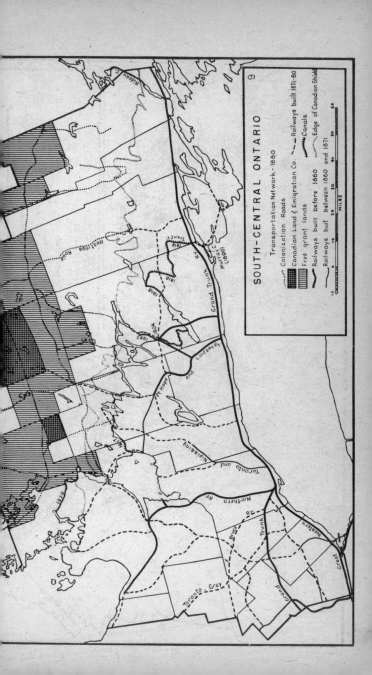

SOUTH-CENTRAL ONTARIO

Transportation Network - 1880

.... Colonization Roads
▨▨▨ Canadian Land & Emigration Co.
▨▨▨ Free grant lands
▬▬▬ Railways built before 1860
▬▬▬ Railways built between 1860 and 1871
---- Railways built 1871-80
~~~~ Canals
▬▬▬ Edge of Canadian Shield

MILES
0   10   20   30   40   50   60

9

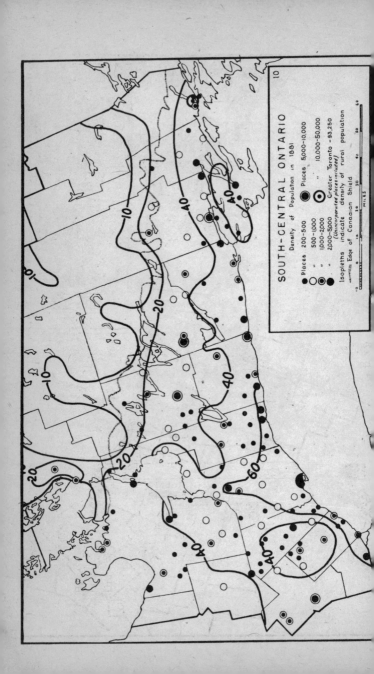

SOUTH-CENTRAL ONTARIO
Density of Population in 1951

● Places 200-500   ◉ Places 5000-10,000
○   "   500-1000   ◉   "   10,000-50,000
○   "   1000-2000   ◉ Greater Toronto - 93,250
◉   "   2000-5000   (Unincorporated places excluded)

Isopleths indicate density of rural population
⌇⌇⌇ Edge of Canadian Shield

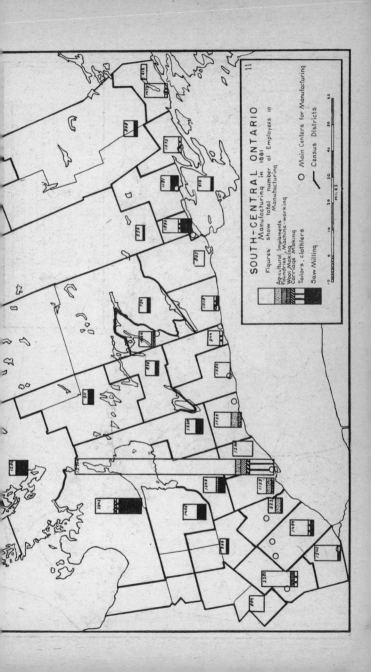

SOUTH-CENTRAL ONTARIO
Manufacturing in 1881
Figures show total number of Employees in
Manufacturing

Agricultural Implements,
Foundries, Machine-working
Wool-Making
Carriage Making
Tailors, Clothiers

Saw Milling

○ Main Centers for Manufacturing

▬ Census Districts

MILES

11

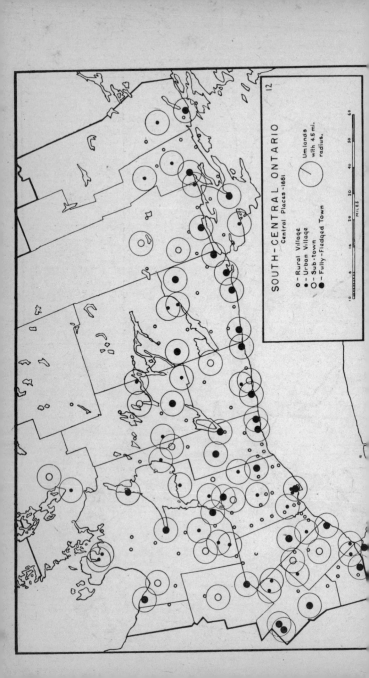

SOUTH–CENTRAL ONTARIO
Central Places – 1881

o – Rural Village
● – Urban Village
○ – Sub-town
● – Fully-Fledged Town

⬭ Umlands
with 4.5 mi.
radius.

MILES

12

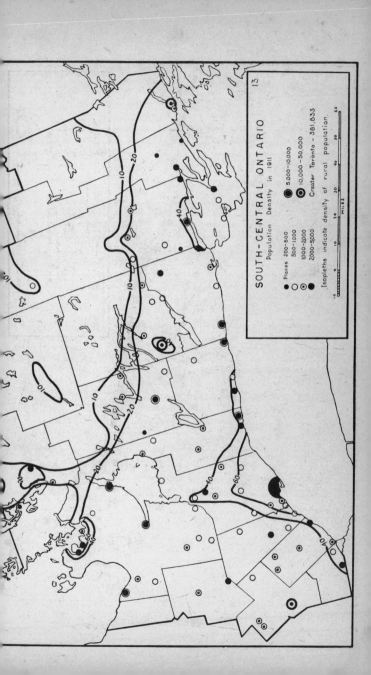

SOUTH-CENTRAL ONTARIO

Population Density in 1911

Places 200-500
500-1000
1000-2000
2000-5000

5,000-10,000
10,000-50,000
Greater Toronto - 381,633

Isopleths indicate density of rural population.

13

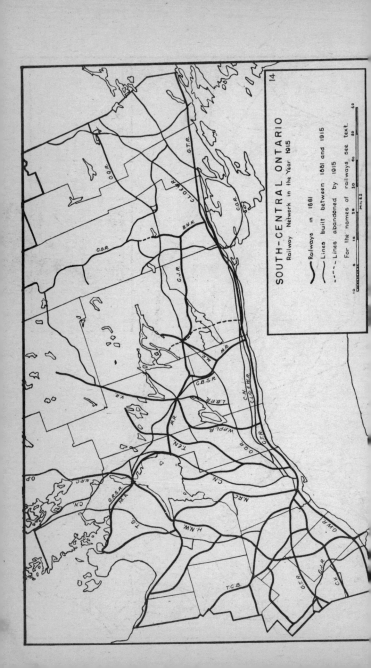

SOUTH-CENTRAL ONTARIO
Railway Network in the Year 1915

Railways in 1881
Lines built between 1881 and 1915
Lines abandoned by 1915

For the names of railways see text.

MILES
10   0   10   20   30   40   50   60

14

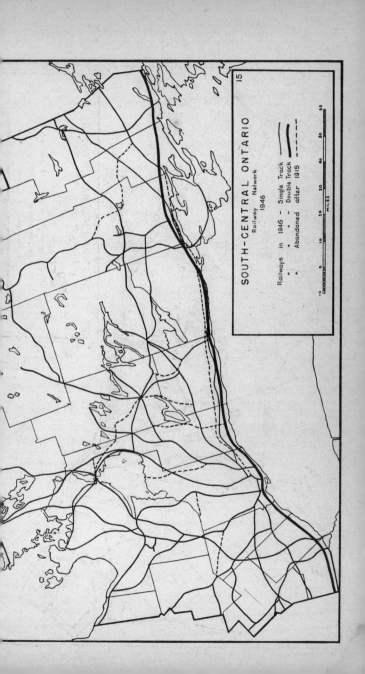

SOUTH–CENTRAL ONTARIO
Railway Network
1946

15

Railways in 1946 — Single Track
    "   "   — Double Track
    "   "   Abandoned after 1915

MILES
|10   0   10   20   30   40   50   60

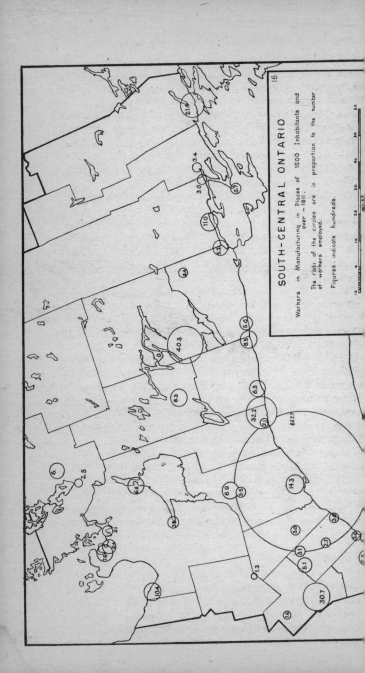

SOUTH-CENTRAL ONTARIO

Workers in Manufacturing in Places of 1500 inhabitants and over – 1911.

The radii of the circles are in proportion to the number of workers employed.

Figures indicate hundreds.

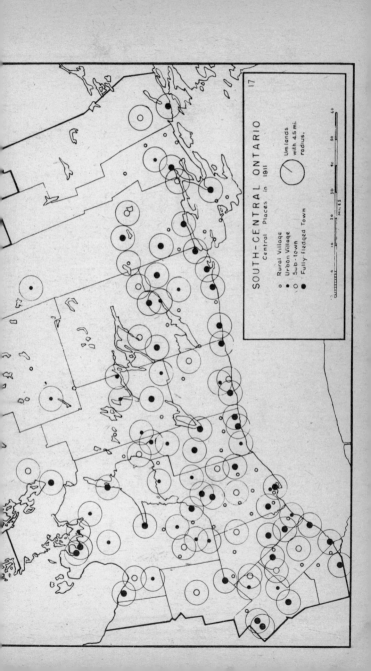

SOUTH-CENTRAL ONTARIO
Central Places in 1911

o Rural Village
• Urban Village
⊙ Sub-town
● Fully-fledged Town

◯ Umlands with 4.5 mi. radius.

MILES

17

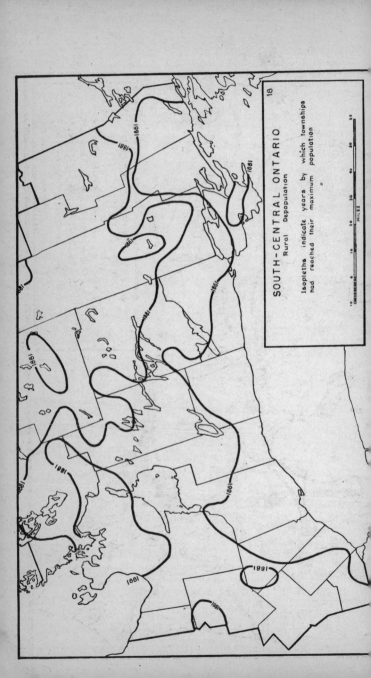

SOUTH-CENTRAL ONTARIO
Rural Depopulation

Isopleths indicate years by which townships
had reached their maximum population

18

SOUTH-CENTRAL ONTARIO
Density of Population in 1951

19

- Places 200 - 500 inhab. ● Places 2000-5000 inhab.
○ " 500 -1000 " ◉ " 5,000-10,000 "
◎ " 1,000-2,000 " ◉ " 10,000-50,000 "

Isopleths indicate density of rural population.

MILES

1,117,470

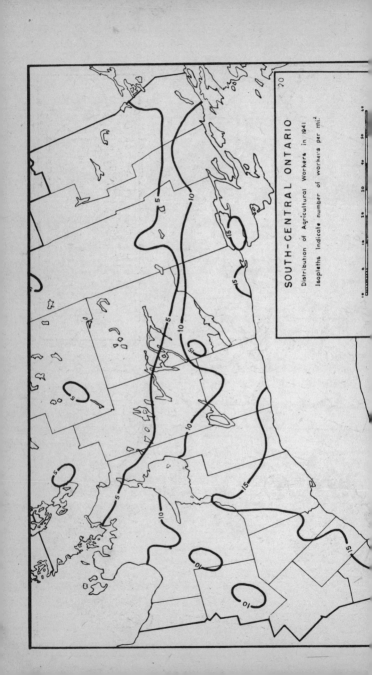

SOUTH-CENTRAL ONTARIO

Distribution of Agricultural Workers in 1941

Isopleths indicate number of workers per mi.²

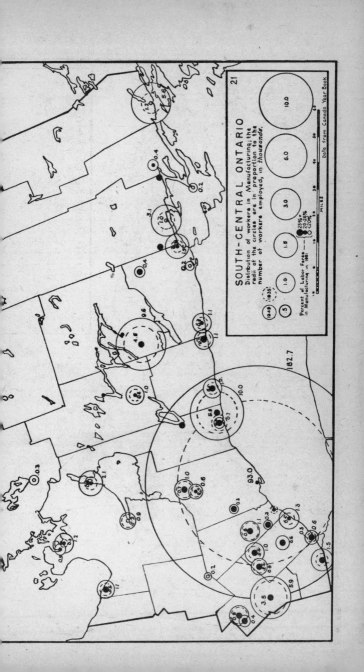

21

SOUTH-CENTRAL ONTARIO

Distribution of workers in Manufacturing; the radii of the circles are in proportion to the number of workers employed, in *thousands.*

10.0

6.0

3.0

1.5

1.0

.5

1948 1935

Percent of Labor Force in Manufacturing, 1951
25%+
20-25%
<20%

MILES
10   20   30   40

Data from Canada Year Book

182.7

93.0

10.0

5.9

3.5

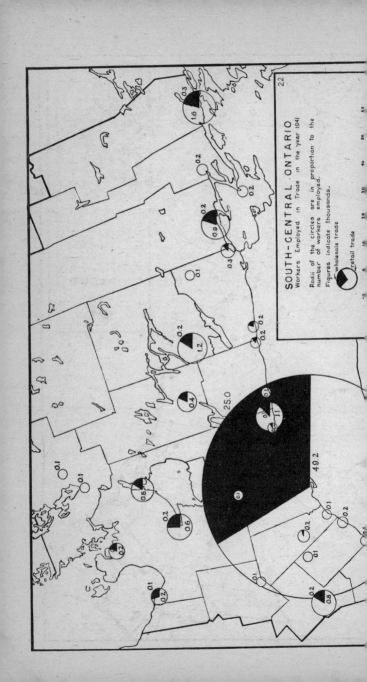

SOUTH-CENTRAL ONTARIO
Workers Employed in Trade in the year 1941

Radii of the circles are in proportion to the
number of workers employed.

Figures indicate thousands.

wholesale trade

retail trade

22

SOUTH-CENTRAL ONTARIO 23

Central Places in 1952

○ Rural Village

● Urban Village

◐ Sub-Town

● Fully-Fledged Town

◎ Service Center of Higher Order

Boundaries of Tributary Areas

Boundaries of Subsidiary Tributary Areas

Main Highways

MILES
0   10   20   30   40   50   40

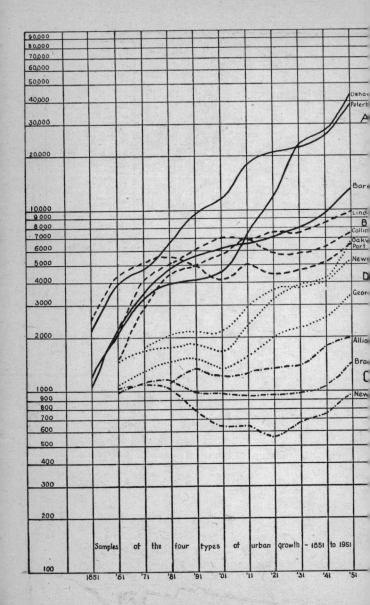

Samples of the four types of urban growth – 1851 to 1951

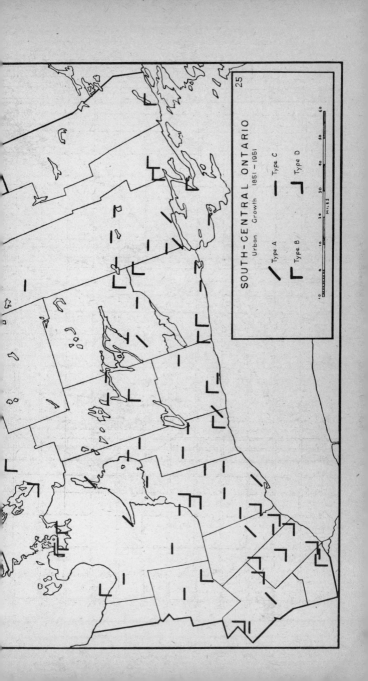

SOUTH-CENTRAL ONTARIO
Urban Growth 1851 – 1951

Type A   Type C

Type B   Type D

MILES

25

Note on the Author

Jacob Spelt was born in The Netherlands, where he received his early education. Coming to the University of Wisconsin as a Whitbeck Fellow, he earned a Master of Arts degree there in 1947. His doctorate was obtained from the University of Utrecht in 1955. He joined the Department of Geography at the University of Toronto in 1948 and is now Professor of Geography, specializing in urban geography and the geography of Europe.

His first book, *The Urban Development in South-central Ontario*, was originally published at Assen, The Netherlands, in 1955. It was followed by *The Changing Face of Toronto, A Study in Urban Geography*, written in collaboration with Donald P. Kerr, first published by the Geographic Branch, Ottawa, in 1965 and reprinted in 1967 and 1969. Dr. Spelt was also a contributor to the Centennial volume sponsored by the Canadian Association of Geographers, *Canada, A Geographical Interpretation* (Toronto, 1968).

Bibliography*

Abbreviations

C.G.J.: *Canadian Geographical Journal.*
C.J.E.P.S.: *Canadian Journal of Economics and Political
     Science.*
C.H.R.: *Canadian Historical Review.*
O.H.S.P. and R.: *Ontario Historical Society Papers and
     Records.*

General Sources – Canada

1. *The Annals of the American Academy of Political and
   Social Science.* Vol. 253, "Features of Present-Day Canada, 1947."
2. Creighton, D.G. *The Commercial Empire of the St. Lawrence 1760–1850.* Toronto, 1937.
3. *The Report of the Earl of Durham.* (London, 1902).
4. Grant, G.M. *Picturesque Canada: The Country as it was
   and is.* 2 Vol. Toronto, 1882.
5. Hedley, J. *Canada and her Commerce.* Montreal, 1894.
6. Hennepin, L. *A new discovery of a vast country in America.* ed. by R.G. Thwaites. Vol. 2. Chicago, 1903.
7. Hutchison, Bruce. *The unknown country, Canada and her
   People.* New York, Toronto, 1942.
8. Innis, H.A. "Significant factors in Canadian Economic
   Development." *C.H.R.* 18(1937): 374–384.
9. Innis, H.A. *Problems of staple production in Canada.*
   Toronto, 1937.
10. Innis, H.A. and Lower, A.R.M. *Select Documents in
    Canadian Economic History 1783–1885.* Toronto, 1933.
11. Innis, M.Q. *An Economic History of Canada.* 3rd ed.
    Toronto, 1945.
12. Knowles, L.C.A. *The Economic Development of the
    British Overseas Empire.* Vol. 2. London, 1930.
13. Lower, A.R.M. *Colony to Nation. A History of Canada.*
    Toronto, 1946.
14. Lower, A.R.M. "Geographical determinants in Canadian
    History." In *Essays in Canadian History*, ed. by R. Flenly.
    Toronto, 1939.

* The references are to be interpreted as follows: (21) from the text
  refers to number 21 in the bibliography, (21/50) to page 50 in the
  reference 21, and (23, IV/56) to reference 23, volume IV, page 56.

15. Lucas, C.P. *A Historical Geography of the British Dominions.* Vol. 5. *Canada, Part 2, the history from 1763 to 1921.* Oxford, 1923.
16. Marshall, C. *Canadian Dominion.* London, 1871.
17. Marshall, H.; Southard, F.A.; and Taylor, K.W. *Canadian-American Industry.* Newhaven, 1936.
18. Mavor, J. "A Chapter of Canadian Economic History 1791–1839." *Transactions of the Royal Society of Canada.* Series 3. 16(1922): Sect. II.
19. Patterson, W.J. *Statement relating to the home and foreign trade.* 1870.
20. Perry, G.H. *The Staple Trade of Canada.* Ottawa, 1862.
21. Putnam, D.F., ed. *Canadian Regions.* Toronto, 1952.
22. Rose, J. Holland; Newton, A.P.; and Benians, E.A. *The Cambridge History of the British Empire.* Vol. 6. Cambridge, 1930.
23. Shortt, A. and Doughty, A.G., ed. *Canada and its Provinces.* 23 Vol. Toronto, 1913.
24. Shortt, A. "Economic Effect of the War of 1812." *O.H.S.P. and R.* 10(1913).
25. Skelton, O.D. *General Economic History of the Dominion 1876–1912.* Toronto, 1913. Reprinted from Shortt and Doughty, eds. *Canada and its Provinces.*
26. Skelton, O.D. *Life and Times of Sir Alexander Tilloch Galt.* Toronto, 1929.
27. Small, H.H. *The Products and the Manufactures of the New Dominion.* Ottawa, 1872.
28. Wallace, W.S., general editor. *The Encyclopaedia of Canada.* Toronto, 1948.
29. Whitaker, J.R. "Regional Contrasts in the Growth of Canadian Cities." *Scottish Geographical Journal,* 53 (1937): 379.
30. Whitke, C. *A History of Canada.* New York, 1942.

Statistics

31. *Census of the Canadas 1851–52.* 2 vol. Quebec, 1853–55.
32. *Census of the Canadas 1860–61.* 2 vol. Quebec, 1863–64.
33. *Census of Canada 1870–71.* 5 vol. Ottawa, 1875. Vol 4 contains an account of earlier statistics of the province since the settlement started.
34. *Census of Canada 1880–81.* 4 vol. Ottawa, 1882–85.
35. *Census of Canada 1890–91.* 4 vol. Ottawa, 1893–97.
36. *Census of Canada 1901.* 4 vol. Ottawa, 1902–06.

37. *Census of Canada 1911.* 6 vol. Ottawa, 1912–15.
38. *Census of Canada 1921.* 5 vol. Ottawa, 1924–29.
39. *Census of Canada 1931.* 13 vol. Ottawa, 1933–42.
40. *Census of Canada 1941.* 11 vol. Ottawa, 1944–50.
41. *Census of Canada 1951.* Ottawa, 1953–.
42. *Canada Yearbook.* Ottawa, annually.
    1867–79 under the title *Yearbook and Almanac of British North America.*
    1886–88 under the title *Statistical Abstract and Record of Canada.*
    1889–1904 under the title *Statistical Yearbook of Canada.*
43. *Canadian Advertising.* Fourth Quarter, 1951.
44. Canada, Dominion Bureau of Statistics. "Survey of Libraries 1948–50." Ottawa, 1952.
45. Canada, Dominion Bureau of Statistics, Reference Paper. "List of public and secondary schools in Canada 1950." Ottawa, 1951.
46. Canada, Dominion Bureau of Statistics, Memorandum. "List of hospitals 1951." Ottawa, 1952.
47. Ontario, Government Statistics. "Economic Review of Ontario."
48. Ontario, Department of the Provincial Treasurer. "A conspectus of the Province of Ontario." Toronto, 1947.
49. Ontario, Statistics and Research. Bureau of the Annual Economic Survey. Toronto, 1949–.

Directories

50. Chewett, J.G. *The Upper Canadian almanac and farmers calendar.* 1831.
51. Mackay, R.W.S. *The Canada Directory.* Montreal, 1851.
52. *Lovell's Dominion Directory.* Montreal, 1871.
53. *Lovell's Gazetteer and Directory of the Province of Ontario.* Montreal, 1882.
54. *Canadian Almanac 1881.* Toronto: Copp, Clark and Co.
55. *Lovell's Gazetteer of the Dominion of Canada 1908.* Montreal.
56. *The Canadian Newspaper Directory.* Sixth Edition. Montreal-Toronto: McKim, 1909.
57. *Canadian Almanac 1911.* Toronto: Copp, Clark Co. Ltd.
58. *The Commercial Handbook of Canada 1911.* Toronto: Heaton's Annual. 7 ed.
59. Province of Ontario. *Gazetteer and Directory 1910–11.* Union Public Comp. of Ingersoll.

60. Evans, W.W., ed. *The Guelph City Directory 1885–86.* Toronto, 1884.
61. Lynch, John. *Directory of the County of Peel.* 1874.
62. Scadding, Henry. *First Gazetteer of Upper Canada with annotations.* Toronto, 1876.
63. *The City of Toronto and the Home District. Commercial Directory and Register with Almanack and Calendar for 1837.* Toronto, 1837.
64. Rowsell, Henry. *City of Toronto and County of York Directory.* Toronto, 1851.
65. *Bank Directory of Canada.* Toronto, quarterly.
66. *Film Weekly Yearbook of the Canadian Motion Picture Industry.* Annual.
67. Ontario, Dept. of Municipal Affairs. *Municipal Directory 1951.*

Atlases and Maps

68. Benson, L.R. "Historical Atlases of Ontario: a preliminary check list, 1944." (Reprint from the *Ontario Library Review,* Febr., 1944).
69. Burpee, L.J. *An historical atlas of Canada.* Toronto, 1928.
70. Canada Company. *Diagrams of the townships in Upper Canada showing the lots purchased from His Majesty's Government by the Canada Company.* 2 vol. n.p., n.d.
71. Drake, E.N. *Historical atlases of Ontario; a condensed check list.* Toronto, 1953.
72. Karpinsky, L.C. *Bibliography of the printed maps of Michigan 1804–80, with a series of over one hundred reproductions of maps constituting an historic atlas of the Great Lakes and Michigan.* Lansing, 1931.
73. *The new topographical atlas of the Province of Ontario, Canada.* Toronto, 1879.
74. *Ontario County Gazetteer and the Canadian Cyclopaedia.* Toronto, 1885.
75. *Plans of the town sites, etc. of various places in Ontario.* Circa 1850–60.
76. *Illustrated historical atlas of the counties of Frontenac, Lennox and Addington, Ontario.* Toronto, 1878.
77. *Illustrated historical atlas of the county Halton, Ontario.* Toronto, 1877.
78. *Illustrated historical atlas of the counties Hastings and Prince Edward, Ontario.* Toronto, 1878.
79. *Guide Book and Atlas of Muskoka and Parry Sound Districts.* Toronto: H.R. Page, 1879.

80. *Illustrated historical atlas of the counties of Northumberland and Durham, Ontario.* Toronto, 1878.

81. *Illustrated historical atlas of the county of Ontario, Ontario.* Toronto, 1877.

82. *Illustrated historical atlas of the county of Peel, Ontario.* Toronto, 1877. ·

83. *Illustrated historical atlas of the Dominion of Canada.* "Historical sketch of the county of Simcoe." Toronto, 1881.

84. *Illustrated historical atlas of the Dominion of Canada.* "Historical sketch of the county of Victoria." Toronto, 1881.

85. *Topographical and historical atlas of the county of Wellington, Ontario.* Toronto, 1877.

86. *Historical atlas of the county of Wellington, Ontario.* Toronto, 1906.

87. *Illustrated historical atlas of the county of Wentworth, Ontario.* Toronto, 1875.

88. *Imperial Atlas of Wentworth County, Ontario.* Hamilton, 1903.

89. *Illustrated historical atlas of the county of York and the township of West Gwillimbury and the town of Bradford in the county of Simcoe, Ontario.* Toronto, 1878.

90. Smith, W.H. *Map of Canada West.* Toronto, 1855.

91. Scobie, H. *Map of western division of Upper Canada.* Toronto, 1852.

92. Smith, D.W. *Map of the Province of Upper Canada.* Toronto, 1852.

93. *Maps of the counties of Upper and Lower Canada.* n.p., n.d. About 1840.

94. Arrowsmith, J. *Upper Canada 1838.*

75. Chewett, J.G. *A Map of the Province of Upper Canada and the adjacent territories of North America.* 1826.

86. *Upper Canada statistical survey with plans for new division into townships.* Longmans Pub. Co., 1821.

97. *Upper Canada and Lower Canada.* Photostat copy of a new map of Upper and Lower Canada by John Cary 1819. Ont. Archives.

98. Smyth, D.W. *Upper Canada, 1818.*

99. Chewitt, William. *Upper Canada, describing settlements and townships.* 1813.

100. Faden, William. *A map of the located districts in the Province of Upper Canada.* 1813.

101. Smyth, D.W. *Upper Canada, a map describing all the new*

settlements townships etc. with the counties adjacent from
Quebec to Lake Huron. 1800.
102. Simcoe, John Graves. "Map of proposed towns and military roads 1793." *O.H.S.P. and R.* Vol. 6, opp. p. 48.
103. Ontario, Dept. of Highways. "Traffic Flow Plan of the southern portion of the Province of Ontario 1947."

Physiography
104. Chapman, L.J., and Putnam, D.F. *The Physiography of Southern Ontario.* Toronto, 1951.
105. Halliday, W.E.D. *A forest classification for Canada.* Ottawa, 1937.
106. Hills, G.A. "Pedology: The Dirt Science and agricultural development in Ontario." *C.G.J.* 29(1944): 106–127.
107. Putnam, D.F. and Chapman, L.J. "The climate of Southern Ontario." *Scientific Agriculture.* 18(1938): 401–446.

Older Sources, travel and description
108. Bliss, H. *The colonial system. Statistics of the Trade, Industry, and Resources of Canada and the other plantations in British North America.* London, 1833.
109. Bonnycastle, R.H. *The Canadas in 1841.* 2 Vol. London, 1842.
110. Bouchette, J. *The British Dominions in North America or a topographical and statistical description of the Province of Lower and Upper Canada.* 2 Vol. London, 1832.
111. Bouchette, J. *A Topographical Description of the Province of Lower Canada with remarks upon Upper Canada.* London, 1815.
112. Boulton, D'Arcy. *Sketch of His Majesty's Province of Upper Canada.* London, 1805.
113. Brown, J.B. *Views of Canada and the colonists.* Edinburgh 1851.
114. Buckingham, J.S. *Canada, Nova Scotia, New Brunswick and other British Provinces in North America, with a plan of national colonization.* London, 1843.
115. Day, S.P. *English America or pictures of Canadian place. and people.* 2 Vol. London, 1864.
116. Dunlop, Dr. William. *Statistical Sketches of Upper Canada by:a backwoodsman.* London, 1832.
117. *A Gazetteer of the Province of Upper Canada.* New York 1813.
118. Gourlay, R.F. *Statistical Account of Upper Canada.* 2 Vol London, 1822.

19. Hall, B. *Travels in America in 1827 and 1828*. 3 Vol. Edinburgh, 1829.

20. Hind, H.Y.; Keefer, T.C.; and Perley, M.H. *Eighty Years Progress of British North America*. Toronto, 1868.

21. Howison, J. *Sketches of Upper Canada*. Second edition. Edinburgh, 1825.

22. Mactaggart, J. *Three years in Canada*. London, 1829.

23. Martin, R.M. *History, Statistics and Geography of Upper Canada*. London, 1838.

24. Picken, Andrew. *The Canadas*. London, 1836.

25. La Rochefoucauld-Liancourt. *Travels through the United States of America, the country of the Iroquois, and Upper Canada*. London, 1799.

26. Rolph, Dr. Thomas. *A brief account together with a statistical account of Upper Canada*. Dundas, U.C., 1836.

27. Shireff, Patrick. *A Tour through North America*. Edinburgh, 1835.

28. Smith, D.W. *A short topographical description of his Majesty's Province of Upper Canada in North America*. 1813.

29. Smith, W.H. *Canada, Past, Present and Future*. Toronto, 1851.

30. Smith, W.H. *Smith's Canadian Gazetteer*. Toronto, 1846.

31. Taylor, H. *The present condition of United Canada as regards her agriculture, trade, and commerce*. 2nd ed. Toronto, 1850.

Immigration, settlement, population

32. Brother Alfred. "The Windham or 'Oak Ridge' settlement of French Royalist refugees in York County, Upper Canada, 1798." *Can. Cath. Hist. Ass. Report* (1939–40): 11–26.

33. Burkholder, Mabel. "Palative settlements in York County." *O.H.S.P. and R.* 37(1945): 81–96.

34. Canniff, W.D. *History of the settlement of Upper Canada, with special reference to the Bay of Quinte*. Toronto, 1869.

35. Cowan, H.I. *British emigration to British North America 1783–1837*. Toronto, 1928.

36. Cruikshank, E.A. *The settlement of the U.E.L. on the Upper St. Lawrence and the Bay of Quinte in 1784; a documentary record*. Toronto, 1934.

37. Cruikshank, E.A. "Petitions for grants of land 1792–1796." *O.H.S.P. and R.* 24(1927): "1796–99." 26(1930).

138. Cruikshank, E.A. "An experiment in colonization in Upper Canada." *O.H.S.P. and R.* 25(1929).

139. Cudmore, S.A. "Rural depopulation in Southern Ontario." *Royal Can. Inst.* Vol. 9, 1910–13.

140. Davin, N.F. *The Irishman in Canada.* Toronto, 1877.

141. Fraser, Joshua. *Shanty, Forest and River Life.* Montreal 1883.

142. Geikie, J.C. *Life in the woods, a boy's narrative of the adventures of a settler's family in Canada.* Boston, 1865.

143. Guillet, E.C. *Pioneer life in the county of York.* Toronto 1946.

144. Herrington, W.S. *Pioneer Life among the Loyalists in Upper Canada.* Toronto, 1919.

145. Higgins, W.H. *The life and times of Joseph Gould* (Ontario County settlement). Toronto, 1887.

146. Hunter, A.F. "The parts borne by Fort Rouillé and Fort York in the establishment of Toronto." *O.H.S.P. and R.* 25(1929).

147. Lower, A.R.M. and Innis, H.A. *Settlement of the forest and mining frontier.* Toronto, 1936.

148. Lower, A.R.M. "The assault on the Laurentian Barrier 1850–70." *C.H.R.* 10(1929).

149. Lower, A.R.M. "Immigration and settlement in Canada 1812–20." *C.H.R.* 3(1922).

150. Jackson, D.A. "Geographical study of early settlement in Southern Ontario." M.A. Thesis, University of Toronto 1948.

151. Kirk, D.W. "Southwestern Ontario: The areal pattern of urban settlements in 1850." Ph.D. Thesis, Northwestern University, Evanston, Illinois, 1949.

152. Kirkwood, A. and Murphy, J.J. *The underdeveloped lands in Northern and Western Ontario. Information regarding resources, products and suitability for settlement.* Toronto 1878.

153. Landon, F. *Western Ontario and the American frontier.* Toronto, 1941.

154. Langton, John. *Early Days in Upper Canada, Letters of John Langton.* Toronto, 1926.

155. Lizars, R. and Lizars, K.M. *In the Days of the Canada Company.* Toronto, 1896.

156. Macdonald, A.H.G. "The clergy reserves in Canada to 1828." M.A. Thesis, University of Toronto, 1925.

157. Macdonald, Norman. *Canada 1763–1814 Immigration and Settlement.* Toronto, 1939.

158. McMurray, T. *The free grant lands of Canada, from practical experience of bush farming in the free grant districts of Muskoka and Parry Sound.* Bracebridge, 1871.

159. Morehouse, F. "Canadian migration in the forties." *C.H.R.* 9(1928).

160. Need, Thomas. *Six years in the Bush.* London, 1838.

161. Neilly, B. "The Colony of French Emigrés in York County, Ontario 1798." The Woman's Canadian Historical Soc. of Toronto. *Ann. Rep. and Trans.* 1924–25.

162. Pammett, H.T. "Assisted emigration from Ireland to Upper Canada under Peter Robinson in 1825." *O.H.S.P. and R.* 31(1936).

163. Paterson, G.C. *Land Settlement in Upper Canada 1783–1840.* 16th Rep. of Dept. of Archives for the Province of Ontario, 1920. Toronto, 1921.

164. Richardson, A.J.H. and Cowan, Helen I., eds. *William Berczy's Williamsburg documents.* Rochester Historical Soc. Publ. 20, 1942.

165. Wolfe, Roy I. "Summer Cottagers in Ontario." *Economic Geography.* 27(1951): 10–32.

166. Schott, Carl. *Landnahme und Kolonisation in Canada am Beispiel Südontarios.* Kiel, 1936.

167. Seymour, H.L. *Colonization and settlement schemes.* Eleventh annual report of the Association of Dominion Land Surveyors. Ottawa, 1918.

168. Smith, W.L. *Pioneers of Old Ontario.* Toronto, 1923.

169. Stewart, Francis. *Our Forest Home.* Montreal, 1889.

170. Stone, A.R. *Rural depopulation.* Toronto, 1924.

171. Traill, Catherine Parr. *The Backwoods of Canada.* London, 1836.

172. Strickland, Samuel. *Twenty seven years in Canada West.* 2 Vol. London, 1853.

173. Stuart, C. *The Emigrant's Guide to Upper Canada.* London, 1820.

174. Voorhis, E. *Historic Forts and Trading Posts of the French Regime and of the English fur trading companies.* National Development Bureau, Canada. Ottawa, 1930.

175. Wallace, W.S. *The United Empire Loyalists.* Toronto, 1921.

176. Watson, J.W. "Rural depopulation in South Western Ontario." *Annals of the Association of American Geographers.* 37(1947).

177. Watson, J.W. "Urban developments in the Niagara Peninsula." *C.J.E.P.S.* 9(1943).

178. Wetherell, J.E. *The Story of the Canada Company*. Toronto, 1930.
Towns and townships, counties and province, historical, economic, etc.

179. Adam, G.M. *Toronto old and new*. Toronto, 1898.

180. *Ajax, Ontario, Canada's newest industrial community*. Ajax, 1948.

181. Barker, Kent. "Ajax: Planning a new town in Ontario." *Community Planning Review*. I(1951).

182. Robinson, C. Blackett. *History of the County of Peterborough*. Toronto, 1884.

183. Boyle, D., ed. *The township of Scarborough 1796–1896*. Toronto, 1896.

184. Burrows, C.A. *The Annals of the town of Guelph 1827–1877*. Guelph, 1877.

185. Byrne, Peter. *Ontario*. (British Empire Series, Vol. 3). London, 1900.

186. Canniff, W.D. *History of the Province of Ontario*. Toronto, 1872.

187. Cartwright, C.E., ed. *Life and Letters of the late Hon. Richard Cartwright*. Toronto, 1876.

188. Clark, M.M.I. *The positive side of John Graves Simcoe*. Toronto, 1943.

189. Cobourg Chamber of Commerce. *Industrial Facts of Cobourg*. 1950.

190. Coleman, J.T. *The History of Bowmanville and vicinity*. Bowmanville, 1875.

191. Connon, J.R. *Early History of Elora, Ontario and vicinity*. Elora, 1930.

192. Copeland, R.A. "The Town of Barrie and its Umland." B.A. Thesis, University of Toronto, Dept. of Geography, 1951.

193. Craick, W.A. *Port Hope Historical Sketches*. Port Hope, 1901.

194. Cruikshank, E.A. and Hunter, A.F. *The correspondence of the Hon. Peter Russell. (During the official term of Lieut.-Governor J.G. Simcoe while on leave of absence.)* 3 Vol. Toronto, 1932–36.

195. Cruikshank, E.A. *The letters and papers of J.G. Simcoe*. 5 Vol. Toronto, 1923–31.

196. Cruikshank, E.D. and Nason, J. *History of Weston*. Weston, 1937.

197. Deacon, N.A.H. "Geographical factors and land use in Toronto." *C.J.G.* 29(1944): 80–99.

198. Dent, J.C. and Scadding, H. *Toronto memorial volume, Toronto past and present, historical and descriptive from 1834–1844.* Toronto, 1884.

199. Dix, E. "United States influence on the agriculture of Prince Edward County." *Ont. Economic Geography.* 26(1950): 179–182.

200. Edwards, F. "Peterborough." *MacLean's Magazine,* no. 16(1941).

201. Edwards, F. "The Royal City Guelph, Ontario." *MacLean's Magazine,* no. 20(1940).

202. Farewell, J.E. *County of Ontario, short notes as to early settlement and progress of the County* ... Whitby, 1907.

203. Fraser, A. *A History of Ontario. Its resources and development.* 2 Vol. Toronto, 1907.

204. Fraser, L.R. *History of Muskoka.* n.p. 1944.

205. Guillet, C.E. *Cobourg, 1798–1948.* Oshawa, 1948.

206. Guillet, C.E. *Toronto from trading post to great city.* Toronto, 1934.

207. Guillet, C.E. *Early life in Upper Canada.* Toronto, 1932.

208. "Assessment of the Township of Hallowel for the year 1808." *O.H.S.P. and R.* 6(1905): 168–170.

209. Hamilton, W.E. *Muskoka Sketch.* Dresden, Ont., 1884.

210. Harstone, J. "Early history of the County and Town of Peterborough." M.A. Thesis, University of Toronto, 1914.

211. Hathaway, E.J. "The River Credit and the Mississaugas." *O.H.S.P. and R.* 26(1930): 432–444.

212. Herrington, W.S. *History of the County of Lennox and Addington.* Toronto, 1913.

213. Hunter, A.F. *A History of Simcoe County.* 2 Vol. Barrie, 1909.

214. Hunter, A.F. *Huron village sites.* Toronto, 1907.

215. Innis, H.A. "Toronto and the Toronto Board of Trade." *The Commerce Journal Annual Review,* March 1939.

216. Innis, H.A. "The rise and decline of Toronto." *Canadian Forum.* XIII(1913).

217. Innis, H.A. "An introduction to the economic history of Ontario – from outpost to Empire." *O.H.S.P. and R.* 30(1933).

218. Kaiser, T.E. *Historic Sketches of Oshawa.* Oshawa, 1921.

219. Kirkconnel, W. *Victoria County Centennial History.* Lindsay, 1921.

220. Kling, S. "King, Markham, Vaughan and Whitechurch Townships." M.A. Thesis, University of Toronto, 1949.

221. Lizars, K.M. *The Valley of the Humber, 1615–1913*. Toronto, 1913.
222. Macdonnell, A. "Diary of Governor Simcoe's Journey from Humber Bay to Matchedash Bay, 1793." *Transactions of the Canadian Institute*, 1890.
223. McKenzie, N.H. "Economic and social development of the Muskoka area." M.A. Thesis, University of Toronto, 1943.
224. Masters, D.C. *The Rise of Toronto 1850–1890*. Toronto, 1947.
225. Masters, D.C. "Toronto versus Montreal." *C.H.R.* 22 (1941): 133–146.
226. Mathews, H.C. *Oakville and the Sixteen*. Toronto, 1953.
227. Mikel, W.C. *City of Belleville. History*. Picton, 1943.
228. Middleton, J.E. *Toronto's 100 years*. Toronto, 1923.
229. Middleton, J.E. *The Municipality of Toronto*. Toronto, 1923.
230. Middleton, J.E., and Landon, F. *The Province of Ontario, a history 1615–1927*. 4 Vol. Toronto, 1927.
231. Mills, E.R. "Early history of Elora." *Waterloo Hist. Soc. Reports.* (1935): 164–168.
232. Mulvany, C.P.; Ryan, C.M.; and Stewart, C.R. *History of the County of Peterborough, Ontario* ... Toronto, 1884.
233. Mulvany, C.P. *Toronto, Past and Present, a handbook of the City*. Toronto, 1884.
234. Norrish, J. *Nassagaweya Centennial 1850–1950.*
235. "Report on Ontario." *Monetary Times.* 119(June, 1951).
236. "Report on Ontario." *Monetary Times.* 115(December, 1947).
237. Brownell, E., and Scott, S.G. "A Study of Holland Marsh. Its Reclamation and Development." Ontario Government, Department of Planning and Development, Immigration Branch. Toronto, 1949.
238. The City of Oshawa. *Monetary Times.* 116(July, 1948).
239. Manufacturer's Committee of the Peterborough City Council. *Industrial Survey of P.* 1949.
240. The City of Peterborough. *Monetary Times.* 115(August, 1947).
241. Poole, T.W. *A Sketch of the early settlement and the subsequent progress of the Town of Peterborough and of each Township in the County of P.* Peterborough, 1867.
242. Reeds, L.G. "Agricultural Geography of the Lindsay-Peterborough Region." M.A. Thesis, University of Toronto, 1942.

243. Richardson, A.H. *A report on the Ganaraska Watershed.* Toronto, 1946.

244. Richardson, A.H. "Humber Valley Conservation Report." Ontario Department of Planning and Development, Toronto, 1948.

245. Richardson, A.H. "Don Valley Conservation Report." Ontario Dept. of Planning and Development, Toronto, 1950.

246. Richardson, A.H. "Moira Valley Conservation Report." Ontario Dept. of Planning and Development, Toronto, 1950.

247. Richardson, A.H. "Speed Valley Conservation Report." Ontario Dept. of Planning and Development, Toronto, 1953.

248. Riddel, W. *The Historical Sketch of the township of Hamilton in the County of Northumberland.* Cobourg, 1897.

249. Robertson, J.R. *Robertson's Landmarks of Toronto.* 6 Vol. Toronto, 1894–1914.

250. Robinson, C.B., publisher. *History of the County of York.* 2 Vol. Toronto, 1885.

251. Robinson, P.J. "The Toronto Carrying Place and the Toronto Purchase." *O.H.S.P. and R.* 39(1947): 41–49.

252. Robinson, P.J. "Yonge Street and the North West Cy." *C.H.R.* 24(1943): 253–265.

253. Robinson, P.J. "The Chevalier de Rocheblave and the Toronto Purchase." *Transactions of the R. Soc. of Canada.* Section 2. 3rd series. 31(1937).

254. Robinson, P.J. *Toronto during the French regime. A history of the Toronto Region from Brulé to Simcoe 1615–1793.* Toronto, 1933.

255. Roy, J.A. *Kingston. The King's Town.* Toronto, 1952.

256. Saunders, Audrey. *Algonquin Story.* Toronto, Dept. of Lands and Forests. 1947.

257. Scadding, H. *Toronto of old.* Toronto, 1873.

258. Squair, J. *The Townships of Darlington and Clarke including Bowmanville and Newcastle.* Toronto, 1927.

259. Stein, P. "A Story of the rear of Addington County." *Lennox and Addington Hist. Soc. Pap. and Rec.* 2(1910).

260. Taylor, C.C. *Toronto "called back" from 1892–1847.* Toronto, 1892.

261. Taylor, C.C. *Toronto "called back" from 1886–1850.* Toronto, 1886.

262. Taylor, T. Griffith. "Towns and townships in Southern Ontario." *Economic Geography*. 21(1945): 88–103.

263. Templin, Hugh. *A brief history of Wellington County*. Fergus, 1946.

264. Templin, Hugh. *Fergus, the story of a little town*. Fergus, 1933.

265. Thomas, G.H.O. *Bracebridge in 1884*. Bracebridge, 1934.

266. Timperlake, J. *Illustrated Toronto, Past and Present*. Toronto, 1877.

267. The City of Toronto. *Monetary Times*. 116(May, 1948).

268. Wallace, W.S. "The early history of Muskoka." *Queens University Journal*. Kingston, 1942.

269. Wallace, W.S. *History of the University of Toronto 1827–1927*. Toronto, 1927.

270. Walton, J.M. *The story of Kettleby Aurora, Ontario*. Aurora, 1939.

271. Watson, J.W. "Hamilton and its Environs." *C.G.J.* 30 (1945): 240–252.

272. Weir, G. *Scugog and its environs*. Port Perry, 1927.

273. Whitaker, J.R. "Peninsular Ontario: a primary regional division of Canada." *The Scottish Geographical Magazine*. 54(1938): 263–284.

274. Wood, W. *Past Years in Pickering*. Toronto, 1911.

275. Wonders, W.C. "Penetanguishene Peninsula." *C.G.J.* 37(1948): 118–129.

276. Young, A.H. "Toronto, How and Why it grew." *O.H.S.P. and R.* 30(1934): 189–200.

Agriculture, Manufacturing and Trade

277. Andrews, I.D. *Report on the Trade and Commerce of the British North American Colonies with the U.S.* Washington, 1851.

278. Canadian Automobile Chamber of Commerce. *Automobile facts and figures*. Toronto, annually.

279. Byrnes, T.C. "The Automotive industry in Ontario." M.A. Thesis, University of Toronto, 1951.

280. Canada, Dominion Bureau of Statistics. "Shipping Report." Ottawa, annually.

281. Canada, Dominion Bureau of Statistics, Agricultural Branch. "Report on the Grain Trade of Canada." Ottawa, annually.

282. Chapman, L.J. "Adaption of crops in Ontario." *C.G.J.* 24(1942): 213–246.

283. Cruikshank, E.A. "A Country Merchant in Upper Canada 1800–1812." *O.H.S.P. and R.* 25(1929): 145–190.

284. Donald, W.J. *The Canadian Iron and Steel Industry.* Boston, 1915.

285. *Financial Post.* "Business Year Book." annually.

286. Guillet, E.C. "Pioneer Banking in Ontario." *Canadian Banker.* (Winter, 1948).

287. Hawthorne, G.V. and Marsh, L.C. *Agriculture and the farm population: A handbook of selected statistics for Ontario and Quebec.* Toronto, 1938.

288. Innis, H.A., ed. *The Dairy Industry in Canada.* Toronto, 1937.

289. Innis, H.A. *The fur trade in Canada: An introduction to Canadian Economic History.* New Haven, 1930.

290. Innis, M.Q. "The industrial development of Ontario 1783–1820." *O.H.S.P. and R.* 32(1936).

291. James, C.C. *The development of agriculture in Ontario. Appendix to the Report of the Ontario Bureau of Industries, 1896.* Toronto, 1898.

292. Jones, R.L. *History of agriculture in Ontario 1683–1880.* Toronto, 1946.

293. Keenleyside, H.L. "American penetration of Canada." *C.H.R.* 8(1927): 31–40.

294. Landon, F. "The 1860's – A period of transition in U.C. agriculture." *Ontario Agricultural College Review.* (1937): 416–418, 451–458.

295. McDiarmid, C.J. "Some aspects of the Canadian Automobile Industry." *C.J.E.P.S.* 6(1940): 258–274.

296. MacGibbon, D.A. *The Canadian Grain Trade.* Toronto, 1932.

297. *Massey-Harris Co. Ltd.: 1847–1947.* M.H. 100th Anniversary. Toronto.

298. *Massey-Harris, an historical sketch 1847–1920.* Toronto.

299. Masters, D.C. *Reciprocity Treaty of 1854.* Toronto, 1936.

300. Morrison, N.F. *Canadian manufacturing industries: A study of the Localization of Canadian Secondary Industries.* Toronto, 1937.

301. Nasmith, C.G. *Timothy Eaton.* Toronto, 1923.

302. Ontario, Dept. of Planning and Development, Trade and Industry Branch. *Ontario Industrial Review.* Toronto, annually, 1950–.

303. Ontario, Dept. of Mines. *Annual Report.* 29(1920).

304. Ontario, Dept. of Agriculture. "Milk transportation in the Toronto Milk shed." Bulletin 417, 1941.

305. Ontario, Dept. of Agriculture. "Dairying in the Province of Ontario." Toronto, 1910.

306. Roland, J. "The Automobile Industry." *Monetary Times.* 118(1950).

307. Watson, J.W. "The changing industrial pattern of the Niagara Peninsula." *O.H.S.P. and R.* 37(1945): 49–58.

308. Whitaker, J.R. "The distribution of dairy farming in peninsular Ontario." *Economic Geography.* 16(1940): 69–78.

309. Whitaker, J.R. "Agricultural gradients in Southern Ontario." *Economic Geography.* 14(1938): 109–120.

Transportation

310. Aylworth, C.F. "A history of the Hastings Colonization Road." *Ontario Land Surveyors Association. Ann. Rep.* (1925): 180.

311. Biggar, E.D. *Hydro-Electric development in Ontario.* Toronto, 1920.

312. Bishop, D.L. "The development of land communication in the western part of Upper Canada to 1840." M.A. Thesis, University of Toronto, 1933.

313. Bladen, M.L. "Construction of Railways in Canada to 1885." *Contributions to Can. Economics.* 5(1932).

314. Bladen, M.L. *idem* "1885–1931." *Ibidem.* 7(1934).

315. Brady, A. "The Ontario Hydro-Electric Power Commission." *C.J.E.P.S.* 1(1936).

316. Breithaupt, W.H. "The railways of Ontario." *O.H.S.P. and R.* 25(1928): 12–25.

317. Breithaupt, W.H. "Dundas Street and other Early Upper Canada Roads." *O.H.S.P. and R.* 21(1924): 5–10.

318. Breithaupt, W.H. "Early roads and transportation in Upper Canada." *7th Ann. Rep. of the Waterloo Hist. Soc.* (1919): 59–66.

319. Canada, Dept. of Transport. "History of canals and related subjects." Ottawa, 1949.

320. Canada, Dept. of Transport. "A statutory History of the steam and electric railways of Canada 1836–1937." Ottawa, 1938.

321. Cousins, E.L. "The port of Toronto, the development of a major port on the lakes of Canada." *The Dock and Harbour Authority.* 20(1948): 107–113.

322. Cousins, G.V. "Early transportation in Canada." *University Magazine.* 8(1909): 607–628.

323. DeWitt, Carter. "Relative sizes and capacities of our canals reflected in trend of traffic." *O.H.S.P. and R.* 23(1926): 19–29.

324. Caby, F.A. "Some interesting aspects of the hydro system." *Bulletin of the Hydro Electric Power Commission of Ontario.* xviii(1931): 273–290.

325. Glazebrook, G.P. de T. *A History of Transportation in Canada.* Toronto, 1938.

326. Harrington, L. "Historic Rideau Canal." *C.G.J.* 35(1947): 278–291.

327. Hill, H.P. "The Construction of the Rideau Canal 1826–1832." *O.H.S.P. and R.* 22(1925): 117–124.

328. Hodder, E.M. *Harbours and Ports of Lake Ontario.* 1857.

329. Laidler, G. "The Nottawasaga Portage, Simcoe County, Ontario." *O.H.S.P. and R.* 35(1943): 39–48.

330. Lindsay, G.A. *The Great Lakes – St. Lawrence Deep Waterway.* Dept. of Transport. Ottawa, 1949–1951.

331. Lizars, K.M. "Early Roads in York." The Woman's Canadian Historical Society of Toronto. *Annual Report and Transactions.* 1912–13.

332. McCannel, Captain James. "Shipping out of Collingwood." *O.H.S.P. and R.* 28(1932): 16–23.

333. Ontario, Dept. of Highways. "Potential Traffic Volumes of the proposed Toronto City By-pass." Toronto, 1949.

334. Roberts, V.M. "Toronto Harbour." *C.G.J.* 15(1937): 89–105.

335. Shortt, A. "Railroad construction and National Prosperity: an historic parallel." *Trans. of the Royal Soc. of Canada.* 3rd series. 8(1914).

336. Smith, R.M. "Kings Highways of Ontario." *C.G.J.* 16 (1938): 159–193.

337. Talman, J.J. "Travel in Ontario before the coming of the railway." *O.H.S.P. and R.* 29(1933): 85–102.

338. Thurston, John. "The Toronto Transportation Commission." *Land Economics.* 14(1938): 10–18.

339. The Toronto Harbour Commission. *Annual Report.*

340. Turgeon, W.F.A., chairman. *Report of the Royal Commission on Transportation.* Ottawa, 1951.

Miscellaneous

341. Chabot, G. *Les Villes; aperçu de géographie humaine.* Paris, 1948.

342. Dickinson, R.E. *City Region and Regionalism.* London, 1947.

343. Gras, N.S.B. *An Introduction to Economic History.* New York, 1922.

344. Harris, C.D. *Salt Lake City. A Regional Capital.* Chicago, 1940.

345. James, P.E. *A Geography of Man.* Boston. 1951.

346. Jefferson, Mark. "The Law of the Primate City." *Geogr. Rev.* 29(1939): 226–232.

347. "Rapport Commissie van Lohuizen, Stuwende en verzorgende bedrijven." *Tijdschrift voor Economische en Sociale Geographie.* (1952): 80.

348. Lower, A.R.M. *The North American Assault on the Canadian forest.* New Haven, 1938.

349. McKenzie, R.D. *The Metropolitan Community. Recent Social trends in the United States.* Monograph. New York, 1933.

350. Park, R.E. "Urbanization as measured by newspaper circulation." *American Journal of Sociology.* 35(1929): 60–79.

351. Smailes, A.E. "The Urban hierarchy in England and Wales." *Geography.* 24(1944): 41–51.

352. Sorre, M. "Les Fondements de la Géographie Humaine." *L'Habitat,* 3. (Paris, 1952).

353. Taylor, G.T. "Environment, Village and City." *Annals of the Ass. of Am. Geogr.* 32(1942): 1–67.

354. Trewartha, G.T. "The unincorporated hamlet." *Annals of the Ass. of Am. Geogr.* 33(1943): 32–81.

355. *The Globe and Mail.* Toronto, Dec. 23, 1952.

356. *The Globe and Mail.* Toronto, Oct. 15, 1952.

357. *Industrial Canada.* April, 1919.

358. *The Telegram.* Toronto, August 21, 1953.
     Addendum.

359. Sanderson, M. "The Climates of Canada according to the new Thornthwaite Classification." *Scientific Agriculture.* 28(Nov., 1948): 501–517.

Index

ACTON, 169, 202, 205, 206
AJAX, 207, 231, 242, 243
AURORA, 175
BANCROFT, 228
BARRIE, 28, 62, 145, 180, 189, 201, 210, 218, 219, 223, 225, 228, 241, 243, 244
BATH, 147
BEAVERTON, 62
BELLE EWART, 122, 182
BELLEVILLE, 45- pop'n in 1820, 52, 66, 77, 89, 114, 115, 119, 145, 175, 201, 208, 209, 210, 218, 219, 225, 231, 241
BLOOMFIELD, 236
BOBCAYGEON, 145
BOLTON, 179
BOWMANVILLE, 67, 173, 175, 202, 207, 218, 222
BRACEBRIDGE, 105, 106, 156, 173, 235
BRADFORD, 62
BRAMPTON, 147, 148, 175, 218, 220
BRONTE, 227
BRULE, ETIENNE, 14
BUFFALO, 84, 110, 132, 157, 213
BURLINGTON, 52, 206, 231
CAMPBELLFORD, 180, 222, 229, 235, 236
CANNINGTON, 62
CHAMPLAIN, Samuel de, 14, 16
CHURCHILL, 213, 215
CLARKSON, 206
COBOURG, 60, 61, 66, 80, 83, 87, 89, 90, 111, 112, 146, 175, 201, 222, 225
COLBORNE, 236
COLLINGWOOD, 121, 134, 145, 147, 156, 163, 168, 213, 218, 222, 225, 228, 241
COOKSVILLE, 182

DESERONTO, 168, 175, 199, 234, 235
de PUISAYE, COUNT, 28
DETROIT, 18, 22, 23, 48
DUNDAS, 67, 69, 78, 89, 146, 149, 175, 206, 230, 241
DURHAM, LORD, 100

ELORA, 171, 236

FENELON FALLS, 69, 145

FLIN FLON, 226

FORT CATARAQUI (LATER FRONTENAC), 12, 18

FORT NIAGARA, 17, 18, 22, 23, 38

FORT PONTCHARTRAIN, 13

FORT ROUILLE, 13, 14, 15

FORT WILLIAM—PORT ARTHUR, 213, 217

GALT, A.T., 94

GEORGETOWN, 90, 202, 205, 218, 220

GOURLAY, ROBERT, 35, 36, 38, 39, 44, 46, 47

GRAVENHURST, 104, 105, 175, 228

GUELPH, 63, 87, 90, 92, 128, 145, 152, 163, 168, 175, 186, 188,
198, 202, 208, 209, 218, 219, 222, 225, 228, 231

HALIBURTON, 230

HAMILTON, 1, 89, 114, 117, 119, 134, 137, 146, 163, 167, 168,
188, 200, 206, 222, 225, 228, 231, 237

HAVELOCK, 198, 218

HOLLAND LANDING, 90, 92, 141

HUNTSVILLE, 106, 156, 223, 235, 236, 240

KINGSTON, 13, 17, 18, 19, 20, 23, 24, 26, 28, 29-pop'n, in 1799,
31, 36, 37, 38, 39, 40, 41, 42, 43, 44, 45—pop'n. in 1820, 46,
47, 49, 50, 51, 52, 53, 54, 59, 66, 68, 78, 79, 82, 84, 85, 90,
92, 115, 135, 137, 143, 146, 163, 164, 173, 175, 189, 193,
198, 201, 202, 208, 209, 210, 213, 214, 218, 219, 225, 228,
231, 240, 241.

KIRKLAND LAKE, 226

LINDSAY, 141, 145, 175, 188, 193, 201, 218, 223, 228, 231

LONDON, 167

MADOC, 145, 198, 229

MALTON, 206

MARMORA, 197, 198, 229

MCLAUGHLIN, George, 128, 173, 207

MICHILIMACKINAC, 15, 22, 28

MIDLAND, 121, 134, 145, 156, 163, 168, 199, 201, 202, 210, 213,
214, 218, 222, 235, 236, 237, 238, 241

MONTREAL, 18, 26, 27, 38, 39, 85, 86, 109, 139, 143, 149, 160,
162, 163, 164, 217, 224, 226

MONT ST LOUIS, 16

NAPANEE, 145, 147, 175, 229, 231, 235, 236
NEPHTON, 198
NEW YORK, 84, 85, 86, 109, 110, 142, 217, 226
NEWCASTLE, 67, 171, 182
NEWMARKET, 28, 61, 62, 90, 99, 175, 202, 226, 240
NORANDA, 226

OAKVILLE, 67, 80, 113, 115, 119, 135, 142, 153, 162, 201, 202, 206, 218, 220, 225, 232, 241
OGDENSBURG, 18, 133
ORANGEVILLE, 142, 148, 228
ORILLIA, 62, 105, 145, 148, 175, 201, 202, 210, 218, 219, 241
OSHAWA, 97, 114, 128, 130, 145, 168, 173, 175, 188, 191, 198, 202, 206, 209, 218, 219, 225, 231, 232, 239
OSWEGO, 14, 17, 18, 22, 80, 84, 132, 133
OTTAWA, 1, 89, 143, 156, 225

PENETANGUISHENE, 28, 99, 122, 145, 156, 230
PERTH, 31
PETERBOROUGH, 60, 61, 89, 92, 115, 121, 145, 163, 168, 175, 188, 189, 193, 198, 199, 202, 207, 208, 209, 218, 219, 223, 225, 228, 231, 241, 244
PICTON, 119, 145, 223
PORCUPINE, 226
PORT CREDIT, 63, 115, 135, 206, 220
PORT COLBOURNE, 214
PORT HOPE, 61, 66, 67, 83, 87, 89, 91, 111, 112, 114, 117, 175, 222, 225, 228
PORT MCNICHOLL, 213, 214, 234
PORT PERRY, 185
POWELL, CHIEF JUSTICE, 35
PRESCOTT, 214

QUEENSTON, 47

RICHMOND HILL, 177
ROBINSON, PETER, 60

SARNIA, 110
STRACHAN, JOHN, 52
STREETSVILLE, 90, 98, 146, 147, 171, 177
SIMCOE, GOVERNOR JOHN GRAVES, 13, 15, 22, 23, 24, 25, 26, 27, 28, 29, 35, 36, 42, 46, 48, 246

TORONTO CARRYING PLACE, 14, 17
TRENTON, 99, 122, 145, 157, 175, 201, 210, 218, 223, 229, 230, 241
TWEED, 145, 229

UXBRIDGE, 229

VANCOUVER, 224
VICTORIA HARBOUR, 156, 177, 234

WASHAGO, 105
WELLINGTON, 177, 236
WESTON, 146, 147
WHITBY, 67, 80, 83, 91, 113, 114, 115, 135, 175, 185, 206, 207, 218, 222, 225, 231, 232
WINDSOR, 1, 225
WINNIPEG, 224
WOODVILLE, 177

YORK, 24, 25, 26, 29, 30—pop'n. in 1799, 32, 33, 37, 38, 39, 40, 44, 45—pop'n in 1820, 46, 47, 48, 49, 50, 51, 52, 53, 54, 93
YORKVILLE, 91, 189

THE CARLETON LIBRARY

1. LORD DURHAM'S REPORT, edited and with an Introduction by Gerald M. Craig

2. THE CONFEDERATION DEBATES IN THE PROVINCE OF CANADA, 1865, edited and with an Introduction by P. B. Waite

3. LAURIER: A STUDY IN CANADIAN POLITICS by J. W. Dafoe, with an Introduction by Murray S. Donnelly

4. CHAMPLAIN: THE LIFE OF FORTITUDE by Morris Bishop, with a new Introduction by the author

5. THE ROWELL/SIROIS REPORT, *Book 1*, edited and with an Introduction by Donald V. Smiley

6. THE UNREFORMED SENATE OF CANADA by Robert A. MacKay revised and with an Introduction by the author

7. THE JESUIT RELATIONS AND ALLIED DOCUMENTS: A SELECTION, edited and with an Introduction by S. R. Mealing

8. LORD DURHAM'S MISSION TO CANADA by Chester New, edited and with an Introduction by H. W. McCready

9. THE RECIPROCITY TREATY OF 1854 by Donald C. Masters, with a new Introduction by the author

10. POLITICAL UNREST IN UPPER CANADA, 1815-1836 by Aileen Dunham, with an Introduction by A. L. Burt

11. A HISTORY OF TRANSPORTATION IN CANADA, *Volume 1*, by G. P. deT. Glazebrook, with a new Introduction by the author

12. A HISTORY OF TRANSPORTATION IN CANADA, *Volume 11*, by G. P. deT. Glazebrook.

13. THE ECONOMIC BACKGROUND OF DOMINION-PROVINCIAL RELATIONS by W. A. Mackintosh, with an Introduction by J. H. Dales

14. THE FRENCH-CANADIAN OUTLOOK by Mason Wade, with a new Introduction by the author

15. THE WESTERN INTERIOR OF CANADA: A RECORD OF GEOGRAPHICAL DISCOVERY, 1612-1917, compiled and with an Introduction by John Warkentin

16. THE COURTS AND THE CANADIAN CONSTITUTION, compiled and with an Introduction by W. R. Lederman

17. MONEY AND BANKING IN CANADA, compiled and with an Introduction by E. P. Neufeld

18. FRENCH-CANADIAN SOCIETY, *Volume 1*, compiled and with an Introduction by Marcel Rioux and Yves Martin

19. THE CANADIAN COMMERCIAL REVOLUTION, 1845-1851 by Gilbert N. Tucker, edited and with an Introduction by Hugh G. J. Aitken

20. JOSEPH HOWE: VOICE OF NOVA SCOTIA, compiled and with an Introduction by J. Murray Beck

21. LIFE AND LETTERS OF SIR WILFRID LAURIER *Volume 1*, by O. D. Skelton, edited and with an Introduction by David M. L. Farr

22. LIFE AND LETTERS OF SIR WILFRID LAURIER, *Volume 11*, by O. D. Skelton, edited by David M. L. Farr

23. LEADING CONSTITUTIONAL DECISIONS, compiled and with an Introduction by Peter H. Russell

24. FRONTENAC: THE COURTIER GOVERNOR by W. J. Eccles

25. INDIANS OF THE NORTH PACIFIC COAST, compiled and with an Introduction by Tom McFeat

26. LIFE AND TIMES OF SIR ALEXANDER TILLOCH GALT by O. D. Skelton, edited and with an Introduction by Guy MacLean

27. A HISTORY OF CANADIAN EXTERNAL RELATIONS, *Volume I*, by G. P. deT. Glazebrook, revised by the author

28. A HISTORY OF CANADIAN EXTERNAL RELATIONS, *Volume II*, by G. P. deT. Glazebrook, revised and with a Bibliographical Essay by the author

29. THE RACE QUESTION IN CANADA by André Siegfried, edited and with an Introduction by F. H. Underhill

30. NORTH ATLANTIC TRIANGLE by J. B. Brebner, with an Introduction by D. G. Creighton

31. APPROACHES TO CANADIAN ECONOMIC HISTORY, compiled and with an Introduction by W. T. Easterbrook and M. H. Watkins

32. CANADIAN SOCIAL STRUCTURE: A STATISTICAL PROFILE, compiled and with an Introduction and Commentary by John Porter

33. CHURCH AND STATE IN CANADA, 1627-1867: BASIC DOCUMENTS, compiled and with an Introduction by John S. Moir

34. WESTERN ONTARIO AND THE AMERICAN FRONTIER by Fred Landon, with a new Introduction by the author

35. HISTORICAL ESSAYS ON THE ATLANTIC PROVINCES, compiled and with an Introduction by G. A. Rawlyk

36. A HISTORY OF JOURNALISM IN CANADA *(an original publication)* by W. H. Kesterton, with an Introduction by Wilfrid Eggleston

37. THE OLD PROVINCE OF QUEBEC, *Volume I*, by A. L. Burt, with an Introduction by Hilda Neatby

38. THE OLD PROVINCE OF QUEBEC, *Volume II*, by A. L. Burt

39. GROWTH AND THE CANADIAN ECONOMY, edited and with an Introduction by T. N. Brewis

40. DOCUMENTS ON THE CONFEDERATION OF BRITISH NORTH AMERICA, edited and with an Introduction by G. P. Browne

41. ESKIMO OF THE CANADIAN ARCTIC, edited and with an Introduction by Victor F. Valentine and Frank G. Vallee

42. THE COLONIAL REFORMERS AND CANADA, 1830-1849, edited and with an Introduction by Peter Burroughs

43. A NARRATIVE, by Sir Francis Bond Head edited and with an Introduction by S. F. Wise

44. JOHN STRACHAN: DOCUMENTS AND OPINIONS, edited and with an Introduction by J. L. H. Henderson

45. THE NEUTRAL YANKEES OF NOVA SCOTIA by J. B. Brebner, with an Introduction by W. S. MacNutt

46. ROBERT LAIRD BORDEN: HIS MEMOIRS, *Volume I*, edited and with an Introduction by Heath Macquarrie

47. ROBERT LAIRD BORDEN: HIS MEMOIRS, *Volume II*, edited by Heath Macquarrie

48. THE CANADIAN MUNICIPAL SYSTEM: ESSAYS ON THE IMPROVEMENT OF LOCAL GOVERNMENT by D. C. Rowat

49. THE BETTER PART OF VALOUR: ESSAYS ON CANADIAN DIPLOMACY by John W. Holmes

50. LAMENT FOR A NATION: THE DEFEAT OF CANADIAN NATIONALISM by George Grant, with a new Introduction by the author

51. CANADIAN FOREIGN POLICY, 1945-1954 by R. A. MacKay, edited and with an Introduction by the author

52. MONCK: LETTERS AND JOURNALS, edited and with an Introduction by W. L. Morton

53. HISTORICAL ESSAYS ON THE PRAIRIE PROVINCES, edited and with an Introduction by Donald Swainson

54. THE CANADIAN ECONOMY IN THE GREAT DEPRESSION by A. E. Safarian

55. CANADA'S CHANGING NORTH, edited and with an Introduction by William C. Wonders

56. THE DEVELOPMENT OF CANADA'S STAPLES, 1867-1939, edited and with an Introductory comment by Kevin Burley

57. URBAN DEVELOPMENT OF SOUTH-CENTRAL ONTARIO by Jacob Spelt

58. CULTURE AND NATIONALITY: ESSAYS BY A. G. BAILEY; by Alfred Goldsworthy Bailey

59. COMMUNITY IN CRISIS: FRENCH-CANADIAN NATIONALISM IN PERSPECTIVE, by Richard Jones, with a new Introduction by the author

60. PERSPECTIVES ON THE NORTH AMERICAN INDIANS, edited and with an Introduction by Mark Nagler

61. LANGUAGES IN CONFLICT, by Richard J. Joy, with a Preface by Frank G. Vallee

62. THE LAST FORTY YEARS: THE UNION OF 1841 TO CONFEDERATION, by J. C. Dent, abridged and with an Introduction by Donald Swainson

63. LAURIER AND A LIBERAL QUEBEC: A STUDY IN POLITICAL MANAGEMENT, by H. Blair Neatby, edited and with an Introduction by Richard T. Clippingdale

64. THE TREMBLAY REPORT, edited and with an Introduction by David Kwavnick

65. CULTURAL ECOLOGY: READINGS ON THE CANADIAN INDIANS AND ESKIMOS, edited and with an Introduction by Bruce Cox

66. RECOLLECTIONS OF THE ON TO OTTAWA TREK, by Ronald Liversedge, with Documents Relating to the Vancouver Strike and the On to Ottawa Trek, edited and with an Introduction by Victor Hoar

67. THE OMBUDSMAN PLAN: ESSAYS ON THE WORLDWIDE SPREAD OF AN IDEA, by Donald C. Rowat

68. NATURAL RESOURCES: THE ECONOMICS OF CONSERVATION, by Anthony Scott

69. DOMINION LANDS POLICY, by Chester Martin, edited and with an Introduction by Lewis H. Thomas

70. RENEGADE IN POWER, by Peter C. Newman, with an Introduction by Denis Smith

71. CUTHBERT GRANT OF GRANTOWN, by Margaret A. MacLeod with an Introduction by W. L. Morton

72. THE NATIVE PEOPLES OF ATLANTIC CANADA: A READER IN REGIONAL ETHNIC RELATIONS, by H. F. McGee

73. FREEDOM AND ORDER/COLLECTED ESSAYS, by Eugene Forsey, with an Introduction by Donald Creighton

74. CRISIS IN QUEBEC, 1917, by Elizabeth Armstrong, with an Introduction by Joseph Levitt

75. Gourlay's STATISTICAL ACCOUNT OF UPPER CANADA, Abridged, and with an Introduction by S. R. Mealing

76. THE ADVENTURES AND SUFFERINGS OF JOHN JEWITT AMONG THE NOOTKA, with an Introduction by Derek G. Smith

77. CAPITAL FORMATION IN CANADA, 1896-1930, by Kenneth Buckley, with an Introduction by M. Urquart

78. BEYOND THE ATLANTIC ROAR: A STUDY OF THE NOVA SCOTIA SCOTS, by D. Campbell and R. A. MacLean

79. CONSOCIATIONAL DEMOCRACY, by K. D. McRae

80. VAUDREUIL, GOVERNOR OF NEW FRANCE, by Yves Zoltvany

81. CANADIAN-AMERICAN SUMMIT DIPLOMACY, 1923-1973, by Roger Frank Swanson

82. HISTORICAL ESSAYS ON UPPER CANADA, by J. K. Johnson

83. THE CANADIAN BILL OF RIGHTS, by Walter Surma Tarnopolsky

84. SOCIALIZATION AND VALUES IN CONTEMPORARY CANADA, *Volume I, Political Socialization,* by Robert M. Pike and Elia Zureik

85. SOCIALIZATION AND VALUES IN CONTEMPORARY CANADA, *Volume II, Socialization, Social Stratification and Ethnicity,* by Robert M. Pike and Elia Zureik

86. CANADA'S BALANCE OF INTERNATIONAL INDEBTEDNESS, 1900-1913, by Jacob Viner

87. CANADIAN INDIANS AND THE LAW: SELECTED DOCUMENTS, 1663-1972, edited by Derek G. Smith

88. LIVING AND LEARNING IN THE FREE SCHOOL, by Mark Novak

89. THE CANADIAN CORPORATE ELITE: AN ANALYSIS OF ECONOMIC POWER, Wallace Clement

90. SOME ESSAYS ON MAN'S IMPACT ON THE WESTERN CANADIAN LANDSCAPE, edited by J. G. Nelson

91. PERSPECTIVES ON LANDSCAPE AND SETTLEMENT IN NINETEENTH CENTURY ONTARIO, edited by J. David Wood

92. MINORITY MEN IN A MAJORITY SETTING, by Christopher Beattie